Cultural
Critique

31

Special Issue
The Politics of Systems and Environments, Part II
Edited by
William Rasch and Cary Wolfe

Print and cover design: Nora Pauwels

Cultural
Critique

Cultural Critique (ISSN 0882-4371) is published three times a year by Oxford University Press, 2001 Evans Road, Cary, NC 27513, in association with the Society for Cultural Critique, a nonprofit, educational organization.

Manuscript submissions. Contributors should submit three copies of their manuscripts to Abdul R. JanMohamed, *Cultural Critique*, c/o African American Studies Program, 305 HTC, University of California, Irvine, Irvine, CA 92717–6850. Manuscripts should conform to the recommendations of *The MLA Style Manual;* authors should use parenthetical documentation with a list of works cited. Contact the editorial office at the address above for further instructions on style. Manuscripts will be returned if accompanied by a stamped, self-addressed envelope. Please allow a minimum of four months for editorial consideration.

Subscriptions. Annual subscription rates are $28 for individuals and $52 for institutions. Outside the United States please add $11 for normal delivery and an additional $5 for air-expedited delivery. Subscription requests and checks (payable in U.S. funds) should be sent to Journals Customer Service, Oxford University Press, 2001 Evans Road, Cary, NC 27513.

Back issues. Single copies of back issues are $9.95 for individuals and $21 for institutions. Outside the United States the price is $15.50 for individuals and $25 for institutions. Copies may be obtained from the Journals Fulfillment Department, Oxford University Press, 2001 Evans Road, Cary NC 27513.

Advertising and permissions. Advertising inquiries and requests to reprint material from the journal should be directed to the Journals Department, Oxford University Press, 2001 Evans Road, Cary, NC 27513 (fax: 919 677–1714).

Indexing/abstracting. *Cultural Critique* is indexed/abstracted in *The Left Index, Alternative Press Index, Sociological Abstracts (SA), Social Welfare, Social Planning/Policy and Social Development (SOPODA), International Political Science Abstracts, MLA Directory of Periodicals, MLA International Bibliography,* and *Periodica Islamica.*

Postmaster. Send address changes to Journals Customer Service, Oxford University Press, 2001 Evans Road, Cary, NC 27513. Postage paid at Cary, NC, and additional post offices.

Photocopies. The journal is registered with the Copyright Clearance Center, 222 Rosewood Drive, Danvers, MA 01923 (fax: 508 750–4744). Permission to photocopy items for the internal or personal use of specific clients is granted by Oxford University Press provided that the copier pay to the Center the $5.00 per copy fee stated in the code on the first page of each article. Special rates for classroom use are available through the CCC or by contacting the Journals Department, Oxford University Press, 2001 Evans Road, Cary, NC 27513. Requests for permission to photocopy for other purposes, such as for general distribution, resale, advertising, and promotional purposes or for creating new works, should also be directed to Oxford University Press at the same address.

⊚ The journal is printed on acid-free paper that meets the minimum requirements of ANSI Standard Z39.48-1984 (Permanence of Paper), beginning with Number 1.

Introduction

William Rasch and Cary Wolfe

Cultural Critique 31 presents the second and final part of "The Politics of Systems and Environments," a project begun in *Cultural Critique* 30, in which we and our co-contributors—Paisley Livingston, Adam Muller, N. Katherine Hayles, Jonathan Elmer, Dietrich Schwanitz, Niklas Luhmann, Peter Hohendahl, and Drucilla Cornell—attempted to map some relatively new and, we think, promising developments in what has come to be known (for better or worse) as postmodern theory. In this issue, we continue to examine the epistemological contours and political implications of moving away from theoretical paradigms and philosophical orientations based upon the subject/object dualism, and toward a new type of thinking which it would be overly restrictive, but not wrong, to call systems theory. Throughout this project, our aim has been to explore the possibility that systems theory might offer a more productive way of thinking through the philosophical, ethical, and political challenges of postmodernity, and therefore might resist the temptation to retreat into comfortable rehabilitations of objectivity, identity, or mythologized versions of history. As early as the pioneering work of Gregory Bateson in mid-century, systems

© 1995 by *Cultural Critique*. Fall 1995. 0882-4371/95/$5.00.

theory began to offer an especially powerful means for thinking across disciplinary and discursive lines. During the course of the past few decades in the work of Maturana, Varela, Luhmann, and others, with their emphasis on the operational or procedural construction of cognitive and social reality, systems theory has sought to break with the fundamentally representationalist view of knowledge and its relation to praxis that grounds the philosophical positions of both realism and idealism—positions that, regardless of their possible political appeal, have in our view been convincingly critiqued by both pragmatism and poststructuralism.

Just what systems theory might contribute to the contemporary constructivism/realism debate is the subject of the round-table discussion, "Theory of A Different Order," that opens this volume. Here, Niklas Luhmann and N. Katherine Hayles, two scholars who have written extensively on systems theory and constructivist epistemology, discuss with us and our colleague Eva Knodt the essential features, promises, and problems of this "second-order" sort of theory. Luhmann's "The Paradoxy of Observing Systems," which offers an overview of the centrality of paradox in modern thought, exemplifies his use of systems-theoretical distinctions to engage some of the fundamental problems that have bedeviled philosophical and sociological *ortho*doxy since Kant. Timothy Luke's essay, a critique of the overdetermined logic of panopticism and the productionist ethos of much environmentalist discourse, brings the system/environment paradigm back down to political *terra firma*, while Brian Massumi's contribution explores the political implications for postmodernity of "The Autonomy of Affect," i.e., the radical disjuncture of meaning and gesture. Finally, Marjorie Levinson's concluding commentary surveys some of the theoretical challenges of theorizing praxis in a world that has called into radical question the very terms which undergird historical materialism.

Theory of a Different Order: A Conversation with Katherine Hayles and Niklas Luhmann

This discussion was conducted on September 21, 1994, at the Institute for Advanced Study at Indiana University, Bloomington, where Niklas Luhmann was a guest Fellow for two weeks during the month of September. Both Luhmann and Katherine Hayles were participating in a conference at the university later that week, organized by William Rasch and Eva Knodt, entitled "Systems Theory and the Postmodern Condition." As a basis for discussion and exchange, Hayles reviewed in advance Luhmann's essay "The Cognitive Program of Constructivism and a Reality That Remains Unknown," and Luhmann likewise reviewed Hayles' "Constrained Constructivism: Locating Scientific Inquiry in the Theater of Representation." The conversation was organized and moderated by William Rasch, Eva Knodt, and Cary Wolfe.

Cary Wolfe: I'd like to begin with a general question. In your different ways you have both explored a second-order cybernetics approach to the current impasse faced by many varieties of cri-

© 1995 by *Cultural Critique*. Fall 1995. 0882-4371/95/$5.00.

tique. And that impasse, to schematically represent it, seems to be the problem of theorizing the contingency and constructedness of knowledge without falling into the morass of relativism (as the charge is usually made) or, to give it a somewhat more challenging valence, without falling into philosophical idealism. You both have worked on this, and I'm wondering if each of you could explain, in whatever order you'd like, what makes second-order theory distinctive, and how it might help move the current critical debates beyond the sort of realism versus idealism deadlock that I've just described.

Katherine Hayles: Would you care to go first?

Niklas Luhmann: OK. Well, I reduce the general term "second-order" to second-order observing, or describing, what others observe or describe. One of the distinguishing marks of this approach is that we need a theory of observation which is not tied to, say, the concept of intelligence, the mind of human beings, but a more general theory of observation that we can use to describe relations of social systems to each other, or minds to social systems, or minds to minds, or maybe bodies to neurophysiological systems, or whatever. So, it needs to be a general theory of observing—and I take some of these things out of *The Laws of Form* of George Spencer Brown—to think of observing as an operation that makes a distinction and is then bound to use one side of the distinction, and not the other side, to continue its observations. So we have a very formal concept of observation. And the problem is then, if you link different observing systems, what can be a cause of stability, how can—in the language of Heinz von Foerster and others—*eigenvalues*, or stable points or identities, emerge that both sides of a communication can remember? And I think this is the idea which goes beyond the assumption that relativism is simply arbitrary: every observation has to be made by an observing system, by one and not the other, but if systems are in communication then something emerges which is not arbitrary anymore but depends on its own history, on its own memory.

KH: For me, second-order theory would be distinct from first-order theory because it necessarily involves a component of reflexivity. If you look at first-order cybernetics, it's clear that it has no really powerful way to deal with the idea of reflexivity. In the Macy conference transcripts, reflexivity surfaced most distinctly in terms of psychoanalysis, which was threatening to the physical scientists who participated in the Macy conferences because it seemed to reduce scientific debate to a morass of language. When they would object to Lawrence Kubie's ideas, who was the psychoanalyst there, he would answer with things like "Oh, you're showing a lot of hostility, aren't you?" To them, that was almost a debasement of scientific debate because it kept involving them as people in what the conference was trying to do. As Steve Heims's book makes clear, there were strong voices speaking at that conference in favor of reflexivity—people like Gregory Bateson and Margaret Mead—from an anthropological perspective. But because reflexivity was tied up with psychoanalysis and the complexities of human emotion, it seemed to most people at the Macy conferences simply to lead to a dead end. When Maturana and Varela reconceptualize reflexivity in *Autopoiesis and Cognition,* they sanitize reflexivity by isolating the observer in what they call a "domain of description" that remains separate from the autopoietic processes that constitute the system as a system. I think Prof. Luhmann's work is an important refinement of Maturana's approach, because he has a way to make the observer appear in a non–ad hoc way; the observer enters at an originary moment, in the fundamental act of making a distinction. Nevertheless, I think that the history I've just been relating is consequential—the point that you can get to is always partly determined by where you've been. The history of second-order cybernetics is a series of successive innovations in which the taint that reflexivity acquired through its connection with psychoanalysis has never completely left the theorizing of the observer as it appears in that tradition. This is quite distinct from how reflexivity appears in, say, the "strong program" of the Edinburgh School of Social Studies of Science, where they acknowledge that the act of observation is grounded in a particular person's positionality.

Reflexivity has been, of course, an ongoing problem in both science and the history of science. When reflexivity enters relativity theory, for example, it has nothing to do with a particular person's personality, cultural history, or language; it has only to do with the observer's physical location in space and time. Relativity theory is not reflexive; it is only relative. To try to arrive at a theory of reflexivity which would take into account the full force of the position of the observer, including personal history, language, a culture, and so forth, has been, I think, a very important and extremely difficult problem to solve. To me, it's essential to talk about the observer in terms that would take account of these positional and locative factors as well as the theoretical question of how it is that we can know the world.

CW: To what extent do you think that, in their recent work, Maturana and Varela have tried to move in this direction? I'm thinking now of the collaboration of Varela, Thompson, and Rosch in *The Embodied Mind,* but more broadly of the whole concept of embodiment in second-order cybernetics, which has certain affinities with Donna Haraway's work on this problem, which is very much in the register that you were emphasizing. I'm thinking, too, of the explicit derivation of an ethics at the end of *The Tree of Knowledge* from second-order cybernetics. To what extent, then, do you see much of this work moving in that direction? And is it moving in the way that you would like?

KH: You know, it's difficult to try to coordinate all these works, because they seem to me all significantly different, maybe because I'm geared to thinking about texts, and therefore about the specific embodiment of these ideas in the language they use. But to compare just for a moment *Autopoiesis and Cognition* with *The Tree of Knowledge:* In the latter the authors write for a popular audience, and in the process the work changes form. It goes from an analytical form into a circular narrative. And with that shift come all kinds of changes in their rhetorical construction of who the observer of that work is, as well as of themselves as observers of the phenomena that they report. In this sense, *The Tree of Knowledge* is more positioned. But it does not solve a problem also present in *Autopoiesis and Cognition*—that is, using scientific knowledge to validate a theory which then calls scientific knowledge into question. I'm thinking here specifically of "Studies in Perception: Reviews to Ground a Theory of Autopoiesis." Autopoiesis leads to a theory of the observer in which there is no route back from the act of observing to the data that was used to generate the theory in the first place. The problem is exacerbated in *The Tree of Knowledge*. Even as they move from a "domain of description" to a more capacious idea of a linguistic realm in which two observers are able to relate to each other, there arise other problems having to do with the work's narrative form.

William Rasch: What is your reaction to this?

NL: Well, there are several reactions. One is that I have difficulties, regarding the later work, comparing Maturana and Varela. Maturana advanced in the direction of a distinction between the immediate observer and the observer who observes another observer. The "objective reality" is that there are things, or niches, which are not reflected in the immediate observer's boundaries. But on the other hand, if you observe that observer, then you see how he or she sees the world by making this distinction. But the limit of this type of thought is the term "autopoiesis" itself as a system term. Autopoiesis was another term for circularity; that was its beginning. Maturana talked about cells in terms of circular reproduction and then, after some contact with philosophers, used "autopoiesis," finding the Greek term more distinctive. But there remains in Maturana the idea that circularity is an objective fact, and so the problem of self-reference is not really confronted in the theory—not in the sense of, for example, the cyberneticians who would say that a system uses its output as input and then becomes a mathematical cosmos with immense amounts of possibilities which cannot be calculated anymore, as in Heinz von Foerster or Spencer Brown's discussion of a "re-entry" of the distinction into the distinguished. And there are, within these more mathematical theories, possibilities which are not visible, I think, in the writings of Maturana and Varela. They are too empirically tied to biology. And then of course we have always this discussion of whether one can use biological analogies in sociology or in psychology or not, which doesn't lead anywhere.

WR: I have a question. Prof. Luhmann, you said that you wanted to find a definition of observation that is on a very formal basis, that does not only apply to consciousness, but to systems of all sorts. When you, Prof. Hayles, talked about observation, the sense of an individual came out more because you were talking about the person's locality, the observer's situation. Do you have a sense that observation is tied strictly to consciousness? Or is observation also for you a more formal definition that can be applied to systems other than consciousness?

KH: For me, observation is definitely tied to consciousness. In Prof. Luhmann's article "The Cognitive Program of Constructivism and a Reality That Remains Unknown," you have a paragraph where you're talking about the observer, and you list a series of things like a cell, a person, and so forth. On my own copy of that article I put a big question mark in the margin: can a cell observe? Of course, I realize that it's partly a matter of definition, and you're free to define the act of observation however you want. But, for me, a cell could not observe in the way I use the term.

Eva Knodt: Could you maybe clarify . . .

WR: Let's let Prof. Luhmann clarify how a cell can observe.

NL: Well, it makes distinctions. It makes a distinction with input/output, what it takes in or what it refuses to take in, or a distinction about its own internal reproduction, to do it in a certain way and not in another way. I'm not sure whether making distinctions implies the simultaneity of seeing both sides, or whether it is just discrimination. The immune system discriminates, of course, but does it know against what it is discriminating? And if you require for a concept of observing that you see both sides simultaneously, and the option becomes an option *against* something, then I would not say that cells are observing or immune systems are observing. They just discriminate. But for me this is not very important. It would be very important for Maxwell's Demon, for example, that he can distinguish—or it, whatever it is, can distinguish—what belongs on which side. But it is hardly thinkable for us, because we are always using meaning in constructing reality. So the problem is to think of distinction, of observation, without the idea of seeing out of the eyes, out of the corner of the eyes, the other thing which we reject or give a negative value. So we, psychologically and socially, use the idea of meaning, so that "observing" becomes a distinct characteristic. And there is a question, of course, of whether we should extend it. But this is I think a terminological . . .

EK: I have a follow-up here, because I also was puzzled in the beginning when I started reading your work about this use of observation, and how it is different from this metaphorical idea that one thinks one sees with the eyes. It's very hard to separate oneself from it. Where exactly do you see the advantage of widening this concept of observation to an extent that it is no longer located in consciousness?

NL: For me, the advantage is to make possible a kind of interdisciplinary commerce, a kind of transference of what we know in cybernetics or biology into sociology or into psychology. Saying that there are very general patterns which can just be described as making a distinction and crossing the boundary of the distinction enables us to ask questions about society as a self-observing system. What happens in a self-observing, self-describing system? This is not only a question for conscious systems. I mean, there are five or more billion conscious systems, and you cannot make any theory of society out of adding one to another or dissolving them all into a general notion like the transcendental subject. But you can make some headway, perhaps, by using the formal idea of observing, and of making distinctions, to understand a system that has a recursive practice of making distinctions and guiding its next distinctions by previous distinctions, using memory functions, and all this. There are formal similarities between psychic systems and social systems, and this is for me important in trying to write a theory, a social theory, of self-describing systems, in particular of society.

WR: Shall we move on to a topic that is perhaps broached more directly in the two articles, and that is the topic of reality? Based on your reading of each other, how would each of you distinguish your notions of reality from the other? Both of you use the term "reality," and yet strict realists would not recognize the term as each of you use it. But how do you observe each other using the term "reality"? Either one of you start.

KH: I'll be glad to start. In Prof. Luhmann's article I alluded to before, the sentence that I found riveting was this: "Reality is what one does not perceive when one perceives it." It was when I got to that sentence that I thought I was beginning to grasp his argument, because I fully agree with that, with one important reservation. I, too, agree that whatever it is that we perceive is different, dramatically different, than whatever is out there before it is perceived. If you want to call what is out there before it is perceived "reality," then we do not perceive it, because the act of perception transforms it. Where I would differ is with the distinction between reality and nonreality, the binary distinction which he uses so powerfully in a theoretical way. I am concerned about a fundamental error that has permeated scientific philosophy for over three hundred years: the idea that we know the world because we are separated from it. I'm interested in exploring the opposite possibility, that we know the world because we are connected to it. That's where I would distinguish the approach I take. It is not really even a disagreement; it's more a matter of where you choose to put the emphasis. Do you choose to emphasize the interfaces that connect us to the world, or do you choose to emphasize the disjunctions that happen as distinctions are drawn?

CW: Prof. Luhmann, I imagine you would like to respond . . .

NL: This formulation has a kind of ancestry, and in former times was associated with the idea of existence, with the idea, to put it another way, that I see trees, but I don't see the reality of trees. And if reality refers to *res,* and *res* is the thing, then you have visible and invisible things—and that's the world. In this philosophical tradition, the problem simply was not possible to formulate. But the formulation that reality is what you don't see if you see something can be phrased in different ways. And one of these other possibilities is to say that reality emerges if you have inconsistency in your operations; language opposes language, somebody says "yes," another says "no," or I think something which is uncomfortable given my memory, and then you have to find the pattern of resolution. Reality is then just the acceptance of solutions for inconsistency problems, somewhat as, in a neurophysiological sense, space is just produced by different lines of looking at it, by internal confusion and then a solution to the internal confusion, which is in turn produced by memory that could not remember if it could not make differences in time. I am here now, but before I was in the hotel, and before that I was in the restaurant, and were this everything at the same moment, then I could not have any kind of memory. So time is real because it tries to create consistency and solve inconsistency problems. And this explains why reality is not an additional attribute to what you see, but is just a sign of successful solutions. This also helps us to see the historical semantics of reality. For example, "culture" at the end of the 18th century is a term which is able to organize comparisons—regional ones (French, German, and so on, or Chinese or European) and historical ones—so that there is a new pattern, some striking insight that is possible because the compared things are different. And "reality," as a result of functional comparisons, is just this kind of insight. You needn't have a more abstract notion of culture or identity or society, or whatever, to be able to handle contradictions which otherwise would obstruct your cognition.

CW: Let me just ask, for clarification, is this reality to which you are referring here different from the reality which is a kind of a creation or accumulation of what you elsewhere call *eigenvalues,* or is that in fact what you are describing?

NL: No, I think that is just another formulation.

CW: OK, all right. I'd like to come back to something you said, Prof. Hayles, and ask you about this issue of connection versus separation that you're interested in. One of the things that's distinctive to me about second-order cybernetics—its central innovation, I think—is that it theorizes systems that are both closed *and* open: in Maturana and Varela, the attempt to theorize closure on the level of operations or organization, but openness to the environment on the level of structure. So, in a sense, isn't that a theory of self-referential systems which are nevertheless connected to the reality in which they find themselves?

KH: Well, for Maturana and Varela, systems are connected by structural coupling. What that gets you in explanatory power is a way to explain the plasticity of systems and changes in structure. Where I have a fundamental difference with Maturana and Varela is in their assumption that there is no meaningful correlation between stimuli that interact with receptors and information that the receptors generate. This may finally come down to religious dogma: I am of one faith, and they are of another. I have studied the articles on perception which Maturana and his co-authors published on color vision in humans and on the visual system of the frog. I do not believe the data support his hypothesis that there is no correlation between inside and outside. It was a bold and courageous move to make that assumption, because it allowed them to break with representation and to avoid all of the problems that representation carries with it. It did get them a lot of leverage. But it's one thing to say there is no correlation, and another to say that the transformations that take place between the perceptual response and outside stimulus are transformational and nonlinear. The latter, I believe, is more correct than the former. I think it's important to preserve a sense of correlation and interactivity. This is primarily where I differ from them.

WR: I will follow up, and then maybe both of you could comment. You mentioned before that where you had differences with Prof. Luhmann's work was with the assumption that knowledge of the world is attainable because of separation from the world. If now you're saying that there is some way of thinking of a correlation between an outside and an inside, doesn't that ontologize separation from the world, and doesn't that get you back into what you were trying to get out of—that is, the idea that we can only know the world because it is outside of us and it has causal effects on us through sensory perception? Doesn't that solidify the inside/outside distinction? Why not talk instead about closure and knowledge coming from the inside, where the inside/outside distinction is made in the inside, and there is thus a more fluid relationship between the two, where you know the world because you are the world?

KH: Well, if you allow the distinction to fall into an inside/outside, as it certainly can, then you're back essentially to realism in some form and also representation. What I was trying to do in my article on constrained constructivism was to move the focus from inside/ outside into the area of interaction, where inside and outside meet. That precedes conscious awareness, but it is in my view an area of interaction in which, precisely, a correlation is going on between stimuli and response. So . . .

EK: Could you elaborate a bit? I have a problem here because you said a little earlier that whether or not you accept the idea of closure comes down to dogma or faith, and now you're referring to some observations that seem to confirm the model that you're proposing. Could you say a little bit more about what kind of evidence leads you to your particular choice?

KH: If we start from the frog article of Letvin and Maturana, which was the beginning for Maturana, what the article concludes (this is a near quotation) is that the frog's eyes speak to the frog's brain in a language already highly processed. It does not, however, show that there is no correlation between the stimuli and the response.

EK: Yes, but what is the status of this correlation? I mean, that's what the observer constructs as the frog's reality.

KH: Yes, that's right—that is, what is constructed is the frog's reality.

EK: From the human point of view.

KH: Yes. From the experimental point of view, to be more precise.

NL: But then you have the question: Who is the observer? If it is a scientist, he or she can make theories and can see correlations, but if it's a frog itself, then things are different. Maturana talks about structural couplings and so on, but the frog as such constructs his reality as if it were outside, to solve internal conflicts. So, in this sense, the question is, why does a closed system like a brain need a distinction inside/outside to cope with its own problems, and why does it construct something outside that externalizes the internal problems of the workings of the brain, just to order his world, in which he himself is, of course, given?

WR: Can I follow up on that? This brings us to the notion of consistency, which Prof. Hayles talks about in her article. And if I understand that correctly, the fact is that each one of us in this room would probably open that door to try to walk out of this room. We're all constructing the world based on internal contradictions, but it all happens to be the same world with reference to this room and these five people. How is that possible?

NL: Well, I think it would be—to take an example from the article of Prof. Hayles—that if we jump out of the window we would contradict our own memory. We have never seen someone stop before they hit the ground, so we simply sort out our contradictions, as long as it is not necessary to change it, within the old pattern. So we go through the door and take the elevator, and this is reality as a solution of formal contradictions. Maybe we try once to jump from too high a place, but we never see apples or something stopping in the middle of the fall.

WR: So it's strictly experiential?

NL: It is just the solution of an internal conflict of new ideas or of variations within your memory.

WR: So, in a sense, you both believe in constraints. If I understand you correctly now, Prof. Luhmann, you would phrase constraints in terms of internal operations, especially memory, in this case. How do you, Prof. Hayles, see the constraints that would prevent us from walking out of this window or trying to walk through that door? If you don't want to be a realist, and say because it's a door, or because of gravity, how do you define what the constraints are?

KH: Well, the way I think about it is that "reality" already carries the connotation of something constructed, so I prefer to use the term "unmediated flux." The unmediated flux is inherently unknowable, since by definition it exists in a state prior to perception.

Nevertheless, it has the quality of allowing some perceptions and not others. There is a spectrum of possibilities that can be realized in a wide range of different ways, depending on the perceptual system that's encountering them, but not every perception is possible. Therefore, there are constraints on what can happen. We can all walk out the door together because we share more or less the same perceptual system—more importantly because we share language, which has helped to form our perceptual systems in very specific ways.

WR: How does that differ from memory as Prof. Luhmann described it? In other words, I'm being very devious here in trying to coax the word "physical" out of you. How can you describe what you're describing without using the term "physical constraints"? Or are the constraints strictly in the way the brain is structured?

KH: I believe there are constraints imposed by our physical structure; I have no doubt of that. I think there are also constraints imposed by the nature of the unmediated flux itself.

WR: What one would conventionally call the actual physical structure of the unmediated flux?

KH: Yes, that's right.

NL: Then, if you use for a moment the idea that reality is tested by resistance—that's Kant—how can you have external resistance if you cannot cross the boundary of the system with your own operations? You cannot touch the environment with your brain, and even if you touch it you feel something here [points to his head] and not there, and you make an external reality just to explain that you feel something here [points again] and not in other places on your body. So, finally, it's always an internal calculation; otherwise, you should simply refuse the term "operational closure." But if we have operational closure, we have to construct every resistance to the operations of a system against the operations of the same system. And reality then is just a form—or, to say it in other terms, things or objects outside are simply a form in which you take into account the resolution of internal conflicts.

EK: If that model holds, can you account for the historical emergence of this idea that there is, and ought to be, a difference between the reality as unmediated flux—what we do not perceive when we perceive—and the world of objects that we encounter in everyday life. I mean, does this idea itself have a similar function?

NL: I'm not sure . . .

EK: Starting with Kant, we find the distinction between the unknowable noumena and phenomena, where you locate some sort of reality outside and then you talk about constructed phenomenological reality. Could one apply this idea that you just mentioned—that reality has the function of neutralizing contradictions—to account for the emergence of this historical distinction?

NL: The emergence of this kind of internal distinction between inside and outside is even earlier. A system makes a distinction because it couples its own operations to its environment over time and has to select fitting operations, or it simply decays. Then, if it makes such a distinction, it has no way to handle the environment except by reconstructing or copying the difference between system and environment into the system itself, and then it has to use an oscillator function to explain to itself something either as an outcome of internal operations or as the "outside world." In Husserl, it's clearer than in Kant that you have noesis and noema, and you have intentions, and you can change between the two and put the blame on your own thinking or be disappointed with the environment. And to explain how our system copes with this kind of distinction, instead of just checking out how it is out there, we need an evolutionary explanation of how systems survive to the extent that they can learn to handle the inside/outside difference within the system, within the context of their own operation. They can never operate outside of the system.

WR: Do you have a response?

KH: This is not really so much a response to the thought that Prof. Luhmann was just developing as a more or less independent comment. For me the idea of closure as reproduction of the organization of the system is perfectly acceptable. It seems like a wonderful insight. But I don't share the feeling Maturana and Varela have that organization is a discrete state. According to them, if a system's organization changes, the system is no longer the same system—it is a different system if its organization changes. It seems to me that organization exists, on the contrary, on a continuum and not as a discrete state. Consider for example evolution, in which all kinds of small innovations and mutational possibilities are tried out in different environments. It's problematic when these mutational possibilities constitute a new species. Drawing distinctions between species is to some extent arbitrary, especially when there is an extensive fossil record. There are many instances in contemporary ecologies where it is impossible to say if an organism falls within the same species or constitutes a different species. Clearly the organizational pattern of that system has changed in a substantive way, enough to allow one to make a distinction, but the change falls along a spectrum. It is not black and white—either no change, or a completely different system. While it's an important insight to see that the living is intimately bound up with the reproduction of a system's organization, I don't see that it's necessary to insist there is a definitive closure in what constitutes an organization.

CW: The way I read Maturana and Varela's point is in a more cognitive or epistemological register, which is to say that if you observe something, you either call it X or not-X, X or Y, and that to cognize *at all* is to engage in the making of that distinction. Your description, it seems to me, is talking as if all these things are going on out there in nature, and then the question is, do our representations match up with them or not? That seems to me to be the pretty strongly realist and representationalist premise of the scenario you just described.

KH: Yes, but in this I don't differ in the least from Maturana and Varela, who are constantly using arguments based on exactly the kind of natural history case studies that I just mentioned in order to demonstrate the closure of the organism. I grant your point, that I'm assuming there is some way to gain reliable knowledge about these things. And of course it's always possible to open up scientific "facts"—or, as Bruno Latour calls them, "black boxes"—

and bring them into question again. But one has to argue from some basis.

WR: Can I ask you, Prof. Luhmann, about your black box? In a sense, your black box is operational closure, beyond which you will not go. You do not want to dispense with it; it's the fundamental element of your system or your theory. As we discussed before, if we are talking about leaps of faith, that's your leap of faith. What is at stake in retaining operational closure? Why is it so important for your theory?

NL: Certainly, in sociological theory, or in social theory in general, you have the problem of how to distinguish objects or areas of, say, law, the economy, and so on. You can say that the economy is essentially coping with scarcity, or something like this. And to avoid these kinds of essentialist assumptions, I try to say that the law is what the law says it is, and the economy is just what the economy in its own operation produces out of itself. This is, I think, the alternative, in which I try to opt for a tautological definition. And then I'm obliged to characterize how the operations of the system—say, communication as the characteristic operation of society—follow a certain binary code, like legal versus illegal, to be able to reproduce, say, the legal system. Recursive decision-making reproduces an organization. But then I have this problem: I do not share the opinion of Maturana and Varela that outside relations *are* cognition, that you have already a cognitive theory if you say "operational closure." Maturana and Varela present structural coupling, structural drift, and these terms as cognitive terms. But I would rather think that a system is always, in its operation, beyond any possible cognition, and it has to follow up its own activity, to look at it in retrospect, to make sense out of what has already happened, to make sense out of what *was* already produced as a difference between system and environment. So first the system produces a difference of system and environment, and then it learns to control its own body and not the environment to make a difference in the system. So cognition then becomes a secondary achievement in a sense, tied to a specific operation which, I think, is that of making a distinction and indicating one side and not the other. It's an explosion of possibilities, if you always have the whole world present in your distinctions.

WR: OK, maybe we should move on to the topic of negation. Could you summarize for us, Prof. Hayles, your use of the semiotic square in your notion of double negation in your article on constrained constructivism?

KH: I don't know how to give a short answer to this, so I'll have to give the long answer.

WR: Good.

KH: As I understand Greimas's work, he developed the semiotic square in order to make simple binaries reveal complexities that are always encoded in them but that are repressed through the action of the binary dualism. The idea is to start with the binary dualism and then, by working out certain formal relationships, to make it reveal implications that the operation of the binary suppresses. To give you an example, consider Nancy Leys Stepan's article about the relation between race and gender in physiognomic studies in the late 19th and early 20th centuries; Stepan notes the circulation within the culture of expressions like "women are the blacks of Europe." To analyze this expression, consider a semiotic square that begins with the duality "men and women." What implications are present in that duality which aren't fully explicit? Some of those implications can be revealed by putting it in conjunction with another duality, white/black. By using the semiotic square and expanding the men/women duality, it is possible to demonstrate, as Ronald Schleifer and his co-authors have done, that "men" really means "(white) men" and "white" really means "white (men)." By developing formal relationships of the semiotic square, one can make the duality yield up its implications. It is important to remember that there is no unique solution to a semiotic square. Any duality will have many implications encoded into it, connotations which are enfolded into that duality but which are not formally acknowledged in it. So there are many sets of other dualities that can be put in conjunction with the primary one. If they're doing the work they should do in a semiotic square, each second pair would reveal different sets of implications. This is a preface to explain what I think the semiotic square is designed to do. Beyond this, the semiotic square is formally precise. It is Greimas's hypothesis that there are certain formal relationships that dictate how dualities develop. So it's not arbitrary how the relationships within the square are developed.

In the semiotic square I used, I wanted a binary which is associated with scientific realism: true and false. If a hypothesis is congruent with the world it's true. Popper argued that science cannot prove truth, only falsity. According to him, a hypothesis must be falsifiable to be considered scientific. The true/false binary is rooted in scientific realism. In order to have the "true" category occupied, you have to be in some objective, transcendent position from which you can look at reality as it is. Then you can match your hypotheses up with the world and see if the two are congruent. Thus the true/false binary comes directly out of realist assumptions. The binary I proposed to complicate and unravel the true/false dichotomy with was "not-false" and "not-true." I claim that the "true" position cannot be occupied because there is no transcendent position from which to say a hypothesis is congruent with reality. The "false" position *can* be occupied, because hypotheses can be falsified, as Popper argued. More ambiguous is the "not-false" position. This position implies that within the realm of representations we construct a hypothesis is not inconsistent with the unmediated flux. Notice it is not true, only consistent with our interactions with the flux. Even more ambiguous is the "not-true" position; it represents the realm of possibilities which have not been tested, which have not even perhaps been formulated, and which may never be formulated because they may lie outside the spectrum of realizable experiences for that species. It is this position on the lower left of the square, the negative of a negative, that is more fecund, for it is the least specified and hence the most productive of new insights. Hence Shoshana Felman's phrase for it, "elusive negativity."

CW: It's very important to you, it seems to me, to insist that those other possibilities that are opened up are not solely possibilities dependent upon the context of inquiry. This goes back to what you were talking about earlier with the unmediated flux containing or acting as a constraint, a finite set of possibilities—that's what these constraints finally are. So it's important to you to insist, versus say Maturana, that these unfolding possibilities do not tell us only about the *context* of inquiry, but about the *object* of inquiry. Would that be fair to say?

KH: Yes. That would be true to say.

WR: What is your reaction to the schema?

NL: Well, again, a long one. The first is that I would distinguish between making a distinction and positive/negative coding, so that negation comes into my theory only by the creation of language, and with the special purpose of avoiding the teleological structure of communication, its tendency to go by itself to a fixed position, to a fixed point, to a consensus point. So, if we have a situation in which every communication can be answered by "yes" or by "no"— I accept or I reject your proposal—then every selection opens again into either conformity or conflict. So, negation in this sense comes into my theory of society only by coding language, or doubling language so to speak, in a "yes" version and a "no" version. And of course it is important that you have the identity of the reference, the possibility to say "yes" or "no" to the same thing, and not to something else. I say "this is a banana," and you can say "yes" or "no," but if you think that maybe it is an apple, then you have to make a distinction to talk about this. So this concerns negation. But I have also, independently of this, thought about an open question concerning distinction: distinction from what? And there are in principle, I think, two possibilities: distinction of an object from an unmarked space, from everything else (again, this is not a glass of wine, and not a tree, and so on). So, one type of distinction is that you create an unmarked space by picking out something. But then there is another type of distinction where you can cross the boundaries—male/female, for example, or in this example, true/false. And then you can oscillate between the two, and say, well, this is a job for a man or a job for a woman, this is good or this is bad, this is expensive, given our budget, and so on. But if you *can* indicate both sides by this distinction, then you also create by this very distinction an unmarked space, because then you can change from the distinction true/false to the distinction good/ bad. Or to the distinction male/female. And then you can make a kind of correlation or coupling between different distinctions. But this always creates the world, creates an unmarked space, a kind of thing which you cannot indicate. Or if you indicate the un-marked space, then you have two marks, marked and unmarked.

WR: Then you'll have another unmarked space . . .

NL: Yeah, yeah, then you create another unmarked space beyond this distinction. And if I look at this four-fold scheme of Greimas's, I think that first it is quite clear that false/true is a specifiable dis-tinction, specifiable on both sides. You can give arguments for true and you can give arguments for false, and you can have true argu-ments that something is false and false arguments that something is true. In this sense, it is complete. But then, when you make this distinction you also specify the unity of this distinction—which is, I would say, the code of science—and then you do not use, say, a political code (powerful or less powerful), or the gender code, or the moral code, or the legal code, or the economic code, or what-ever. And when I look at this enlargement, I wonder whether it would be possible to say that indeed the false/true distinction is *not* a complete description of the world, that it leaves out the un-marked space, or it leaves out what you do not imagine, what you do not see, what you do not indicate, if you operate within this kind of framework. And this is important for my theory of func-tional differentiation, because if I identify codes and systems, then of course I need always a third value or third position: the rejec-tion of all other codes. So, if I am in the legal code, then I am not in the economic code; the judge doesn't make his decision ac-cording to what he is paid for his decision . . .

CW: Sometimes! [general laughter]

NL: Well, yes, but then that's a problem of functional differentia-tion. And if I look at Greimas's table with its four positions, I think first that the lower line, the "not-true" and "not-false" line, is sim-ply representing the unmarked space. Then I would change the positions; in other words, I would make the distinction between "false" and "not-false." "False" is something which is verified as "false"; "not-false" is everything else. Or "true" and "not-true." I don't know whether this makes any sense, but the essential point is that for my theory, especially for the theory of functional differentiation, we need something which Gotthard Günther would call "transjunctional operation"—that means, going from a positive/negative distinction to a meta-distinction, rejecting or accepting this kind of distinction. And you can, of course, have a meta-distinction, then a meta-meta-distinction, and that would always mean "marked/unmarked." And at that point, of course, you are in the middle of the question of how systems evolve by marking, by making marks in an unmarked space, and then you can have a history of possible correlations between structural developments and semantic developments in the history of society.

EK: Now your reinterpretation of this scheme, Prof. Hayles, makes it look like it can no longer fulfill the function that, as I understand you, it's supposed to fill: namely, as far as I understand it, it's supposed to somehow assure us that we can somehow reach out of language and get language into contact with some sort of physical constraint. And when you interpreted the scheme . . .

WR: Negation is simply part of . . .

EK: . . . part of the inside. Then you don't need a constraint anymore. I mean . . .

NL: . . . self-imposed constraint . . .

EK: . . . in your reinterpretation of the scheme you get rid of the external constraints, and I think I have trouble really understanding how we can reach, with the square, the idea of an external constraint.

WR: I guess the question is, how? What evidence does double negativity give? What evidence not only of the outside world, but in a sense what evidence does double negativity give that it does deal with . . .

KH: It does not give any evidence, I think. I did not intend to say that it gave evidence. But Prof. Luhmann was, I think, exactly right in identifying something in that second line with what he calls the unmarked, that which lies outside distinction, and that's exactly the category that I meant to designate by "not-true." "Not-true" is absence of truth, which is not to say that it's untrue; it's to say that it is beyond the realm in which one can make judgments of truth and falsity. It's an undistinguished area in which that distinction does not operate. So his idea of distinctions is very applicable to what I was trying to do there. What I was trying to ask was, is there a place in language that points toward our ability to connect with the unmediated flux? This does not prove that the unmediated flux exists; it does not prove that the unmediated flux is consistent; it does not prove that the unmediated flux operates itself through constraints. It's simply asking the question, if we posit the unmediated flux, then where is the place in language that points toward that connection? That place is "not-true" or "elusive negativity," because that's the area in language itself which points toward the possibility I'm trying to articulate as "unmediated flux." It's no accident, I think, that in Greimas's article on the semiotic square he talks about this position emerging through the constraints that are present in the structure of language itself. In other words, his idea is that the structure of the semiotic square is not arbitrary; it's embedded in the deep structure of language. That, of course, is a debatable proposition. But just say for a moment that we accept the proposition. Then my argument is that the structural possibilities offered to us by language contain logically and semantically a category which points toward something we cannot grasp but is already encoded into our language.

CW: Can I jump in here at this specific point? What I hear you saying is that language as such does not presuppose any particular referent, but it does presuppose reference as such, right? Would that be fair?

KH: Well, I don't know that I was saying that. I thought I was saying that language has a logical structure, and part of that logical structure is to provide for a space for the unknowable and the unspeakable, even though paradoxically that space has to be provided within the linguistic domain.

CW: Right, but it's presupposed that it could be knowable and could be speakable, and moreover that that knowable and speakable is finite, right?

KH: The knowable and the speakable . . .

CW: . . . or contains a finite set of applications in language.

KH: What is in the category "absence of truth" could always be brought into the category of either "not-false" or "false." It would be possible to have a scientific theory which brings something which was previously unthought and unrecognized into an area of falsifiability. But no matter how much is brought into the area of falsifiability, it does not exhaust and cannot exhaust the repertoire of those possibilities. So, this goes back to Prof. Luhmann's idea that there is a complexity outside systems which is always richer than any distinction can possibly articulate.

CW: I guess the difference that I'm trying to locate here is that, in Prof. Luhmann's scheme, this outer space is automatically produced by the deployment of distinctions—marking produces an unmarked space—but the difference is, in principle it seems to me, your claim about constraint, as we talked about it earlier: that it depends upon this set being finite. For you, it's not possible in principle to just go on and on and on deploying yet another distinction.

KH: Right.

CW: Because otherwise the claims about reality and the constraints that it imposes seem to me to fall apart at that point.

KH: Well, here maybe I can invoke some ideas about mathematics and say that I'm not sure the range of things that can be brought in to the realm of "not-false" and "false" is finite. It may be infinite, but if it is infinite, then it is a smaller infinity than the infinity of the unmediated flux, and as you know, Cantor proved the idea that one infinity can be smaller than another. So, if it's an infinity, it is a smaller infinity than the set of all possibilities of all possible constructions.

NL: In my terms, you would then have the question, what do you exclude as unmarked if you make the distinction between infinite and finite? [laughter] But that's a book of Phillip Herbst from the Tavistock Institute entitled *Alternatives to Hierarchies,* where he refers to Spencer Brown and raises somewhere the question, what is the primary distinction? You could have the distinction finite/infinite, you could have the distinction inside/outside, you could have the distinction being/not-being to start with, and then you can develop all kinds of distinctions in a more or less ontological framework. And I find this fascinating, that there is no exclusive, one right beginning for making a distinction. The classics would of course say "being" and "not-being," and then the romantics would say infinite/finite, and systems theory would say inside/outside. But how are these related? If you engage in one primary distinction, then how do the others come again into your theory or not? This is part of the postmodern idea that there is no right beginning, no beginning in the sense that you *have* to make one certain distinction and you can fully describe the start of your operations. And that's the background against which I always ask, "what is the unity of a distinction?" or "what do you exclude if you use this distinction and not another one?"

CW: For me at least, the interest of your work, both of you, is that it is trying to take that next step beyond the mere staging or positing of incommensurable discourses. It seems to me that both of you—in finally somewhat opposed ways—are trying to move beyond this paradigmatic type of postmodern thought and move on—in your case, Prof. Luhmann—to what you call a universally applicable or valid description of social systems. And in your case, Prof. Hayles, that effort is revealed in your attempt to work out this problem of constraints—in a way, to try to rescue some sort of representationalist framework—to say that in fact there is a reality out there that does pose constraints and, moreover, can be known in different and specifiable ways by these discourses. It's possible, in other words, to see beyond that incommensurability . . .

KH: Yes, though I would not say—this sounds like a nit-picking correction, but to me it's the essence of what I'm trying to say—I wouldn't say that what is out there can be known; I would say our interaction with what is out there can be known.

CW: Then I think the question has to be, for me at least, in what sense are you using the term "objectivity" at the end of the "Constrained Constructivism" essay? A point that Maturana makes in one of his essays is that to use the subjective/objective distinction is to automatically presuppose or fall back on representationalist notions, which immediately recasts the problem in terms of realism and idealism.

KH: I don't use the word "objectivity."

CW: I have the *New Orleans Review* version . . .

KH: I don't think I use it in that essay . . .

CW: "In the process,"—this is about three paragraphs from the end . . .

KH: . . . oh, OK . . .

CW: ". . . in the process, objectivity of any kind has gotten a bad name. I think this is a mistake, for the possibility of distinguishing a theory consistent with reality, and one that is not, can also be liberating"—and you go on to talk about how this might be enabling politically, which is, I think, interesting because it does accept the challenge of moving beyond just saying, "well it's all incommensurable."

KH: Here, I accept the kinds of arguments that have been made by Donna Haraway and Sandra Harding about "strong objectivity," that to pretend one does not have a position is in fact not being "objective," in the privileged sense of "objective," because it ignores all those factors that are determining what one sees. And to acknowledge one's positionality, and explore the relationship between the components that go into making up that position and what one sees, in fact begins to allow one to see how those two are interrelated, and therefore to envision other possibilities. Sandra Harding's formulation of "strong objectivity" takes positionality into account, and is therefore a stronger version of objectivity than an objectivity that is based on some kind of transcendent non-position.

CW: Let me follow up here. I guess the problem I have, and this is the case with Harding's work, is that what you're describing is inclusion. I see how that means more democratic representation of different points of view, but I don't see how it adds up to "objectivity" in the sense that it's usually used. Unless the sense of objectivity here is procedural, that we all agree to follow certain rules of a given discourse.

KH: As a philosopher, Harding doesn't want to relinquish the term "objectivity."

CW: Yes, that's quite clear.

KH: I don't have any vested interest in keeping the word "objectivity," but I think the idea of what she's pointing to, whether one calls it "objectivity" or not, is no matter how many positions you have, they will not add up to a transcendent nonlocation.

CW: Right. The God's-eye view.

KH: P_1 plus P_2 plus . . . P_n is not God.

CW: Right.

WR: So actually what you're talking about is what you mentioned in the very beginning, the word "objectivity" basically means "reflexivity"—the reflexivity that you were missing in the early cybernetic tradition?

KH: Yes. I don't know if anybody's used the word "strong reflexivity," but I would like to. Strong reflexivity shows how one can use one's position to extend one's knowledge. That's part of what is implied in the idea that we know the world because we are connected to it. Our connection to it is precisely our position. Acknowledging that position and exploring precisely what the connections are between the particularities of that position and the formations of knowledge that we generate is a way to extend knowledge. There is a version of reflexivity that, in the early period of science studies, was like an admission of guilt: "Well, I'm a white male, and so therefore I think this." There was a period when you couldn't write an article without including a brief autobiography on who you were. But that really missed the point, because the idea is to explore in a systematic way what these correlations are and precisely why they lead to certain knowledge formations, and therefore to begin to get a sense of what is not seen.

NL: Then my opponent should be not so much for the term "objectivity," but for the term "interaction," and who sees the interaction.

WR: Interaction between us and an environment . . .

NL: Yeah, yeah. I have no trouble in posing external observers, a sociologist who sees an interaction between the capitalistic economy and the political system, or between underdeveloped countries—center/periphery, and so on—but how could we think that the system that interacts with its environment is itself observing the interaction as something which gives a more or less representational view of what is outside? How can we see this without seeing that this is a system which does the observing? How could we avoid involving the system—which means a radically constructivist point of view—when we ask the question, "who is the observer?" We say "the outside observer, of course." He sees interactions of any kind, causal or whatever, as objective reality in *his* environment, because *he* sees it. But if the system *in* interaction tries to *see* the interaction, how could we conceive this?

KH: There may be many ways to use the word "interaction," and I'm not sure I'm using it in the sense you mean. For me, when I say the word "interaction," it already presupposes a place prior to observation, whether self-observation or observation by someone else. It's the ultimate point that we can push to in imagination, it's the boundary between the perceptual apparatus and the unmediated flux, and as such it is anterior to and prior to any possible observation. So, I would say that the interaction is not observable.

NL: Then you can drop the concept.

KH: You could drop the concept, except then you have a completely different system. What interaction preserves that I think is important is the sense of regularities in the world and the guiding role that the world plays in our perception of it. If representation and naive realism, with their focus on external reality, only played one side of the street, Maturana's theory of autopoiesis, with its focus on the interior organization of systems, only plays the other side. I am interested in what happens at the dividing line, where one side meets the other side. Maturana's theory is important for me because it shows, forcefully and lucidly, how important perception and systemic organization are in accounting for our view of the world. It also opens the door to a much deeper use of reflexivity than had been possible before—an insight significantly extended by your positioning of the observer as he (or she) who makes the distinctions that bring systems into existence as such. But for me, this is not the whole picture. If it is true that "reality is what we do not see when we see," then it is also true that "our interaction with reality is what we see when we see." That interaction has two, not one, components—what we bring to it, and what the unmediated flux brings to it. The regularities that comprise scientific "laws" do not originate solely in our perception; they also have a basis in our interactions with reality. Omitting the zone of interaction cuts out the very connectedness to the world that for me is at the center of understanding scientific epistemology.

WR: Well, I think that we've hit that outer limit right here, where we are redefining boundaries. Do we have any other general questions? Maybe the system in question ought to be dinner . . .

CW: Let me just ask one more very general question, since we're on this point, and it's something we've touched on. At the end of the "Constrained Constructivism" article, Prof. Hayles, you make it clear that this rethinking you're engaged in has pretty direct ethical imperatives. Objectivity, for you and for Sandra Harding and for Donna Haraway, is an ethical imperative as well as an epistemological or theoretical one, and you go on to specify what those imperatives are. I take it for you, Prof. Luhmann, that you want to be very careful to separate ethics as just one of many social systems from other types of social systems, all of which can be described by systems theory. So what I'm wondering is, could you all talk a little bit about what you see as the ethical and political imperatives, if there are any, of second-order theory, to reach back to where we started?

KH: I don't know that I really have anything to add beyond what you just said, but it is clear for me that there are ethical implications of strong reflexivity and strong objectivity. I'm not really versed in ethics as a kind of formal system, so I'll defer that to Prof. Luhmann.

NL: Well, for me ethics or morality is a special type of distinction, and a particularly dangerous one, because you engage in making judgments about others—they are good or bad. And then if you don't have consensus, you have to look for better means to convince them or to force them to agree. There is a very old European tradition of this: the relation between standards and discrimination. If somebody is not on your side, then he is on the wrong side. And I think my work is a sociologist's way to simply reflect on what we engage in if we use ethical terms as a primary distinction in justifying our cognitive results: if you accept this you are good, and if you don't you have to justify yourself.

Works Cited

Greimas, A. J. "The Interaction of Semiotic Constraints." *On Meaning: Selected Writings in Semiotic Theory.* Trans. Paul J. Perron and Frank H. Collins. Minneapolis: U of Minnesota P, 1987. 48–62.

Günther, Gotthard. "Life as Poly-Contexturality." *Beiträge zur Grundlegung einer operationsfähigen Dialektik*. Vol. 2. Hamburg: Meiner, 1979. 283–306.

Haraway, Donna J. "Situated Knowledges: The Science Question in Feminism as a Site of Discourse on the Privilege of Partial Perspective." *Feminist Studies* 14 (1988): 575–99.

Harding, Sandra. "Introduction: Eurocentric Scientific Illiteracy—A Challenge for the World Community." *The "Racial" Economy of Science*. Bloomington: Indiana UP, 1994. 1–22.

Hayles, N. Katherine. "Constrained Constructivism: Locating Scientific Inquiry in the Theater of Representation." *New Orleans Review* 18:1 (Spring 1991): 76–85.

Heims, Steve Joshua. *Constructing a Social Science for Postwar America: The Cybernetics Group, 1946–1953*. Cambridge: MIT P, 1993.

Herbst, Phillip. *Alternatives to Hierarchies*. Leiden: Nijhoff, 1976.

Letvin, J. Y., et al. "What the Frog's Eye Tells the Frog's Brain." *Proceedings of the Institute for Radio Engineers* 47 (1959): 1940–51.

Luhmann, Niklas. "The Cognitive Program of Constructivism and a Reality That Remains Unknown." *Selforganization: Portrait of a Scientific Revolution*. Ed. Wolfgang Krohn, Gunter Kuppers, and Helga Nowotny. Dordrecht: Kluwer Academic, 1990. 64–85.

Maturana, Humberto. "Science and Daily Life: The Ontology of Scientific Explanation." *Research and Reflexivity*. Ed. Frederick Steier. London: Sage, 1991. 30–52.

Maturana, Humberto, and Francisco Varela. *Autopoiesis and Cognition: The Realization of the Living*. Dordrecht: D. Reidel, 1985.

———. *The Tree of Knowledge: The Biological Roots of Human Understanding*. Rev. ed. Trans. Robert Paolucci. Foreword J. Z. Young. Boston: Shambhala, 1992.

Popper, Karl L. *Conjectures and Refutations: The Growth of Scientific Knowledge*. 2nd ed. New York: Basic, 1965.

Schleifer, Ronald, Robert Con Davis, and Nancy Mergler. *Culture and Cognition: The Boundaries of Literary and Scientific Inquiry*. Ithaca: Cornell, UP, 1992.

Spencer Brown, George. *Laws of Form*. 2nd ed., rpt. New York: Dutton, 1979.

Stepan, Nancy Leys. "Race and Gender: The Role of Analogy in Science." *Isis* 77 (1986): 261–77.

Varela, Francisco, Evan Thompson, and Eleanor Rosch. *The Embodied Mind: Cognitive Science and Human Understanding*. Cambridge: MIT P, 1993.

von Foerster, Heinz. *Observing Systems*. Seaside: Intersystems, 1981.

The Paradoxy of Observing Systems

Niklas Luhmann

I

In spite of several attempts, it is still difficult to submit formal sciences such as logic or mathematics to a sociological analysis. Such an analysis would entail discovering empirical correlations between specific social conditions and specific formal structures. Both the conditions and the structures would then have to be treated as variables whose "values" would appear as contingent, despite their claims to be "natural" (as society) or necessary (as the principles, axioms, and rules of logic). One would have to assert that the natural is artificial because it is produced by society and that the necessary is contingent because under different conditions it may have to accept different forms. These are paradoxical statements, but we need them when we have to distinguish different observers from each other or when we have to distinguish self-observations from external observation, because for the self-observer things may appear as natural and necessary, whereas when seen from the outside they may appear artificial and contingent (see Löfgren, "Towards System"). The world thus variously

© 1995 by *Cultural Critique*. Fall 1995. 0882-4371/95/$5.00.

observed remains, nevertheless, the same world, and therefore we have a paradox. An observer, then, is supposed to decide whether something is natural or artificial, necessary or contingent. But who can observe the observer (as necessary for this decision) and the decision (as contingent for the observer)? The observer may refuse to make this decision, but can the observer observe without making this decision or would the observer have to withdraw, when refusing this decision, to the position of a non-observing observer?

All this does not affect the self-claimed validity of logic or mathematics; and we may find comfort with Dr. Johnson: "When speculation has done its worst, two and two still make four" (114). We may, however, pursue a less trivial, a less commonsensical interest and continue to ask: Who says it? Who is the observer?

II

Paradox was invented—that is, discovered—more than two thousand years ago, at the beginning of serious experiments with second-order observing.[1] Since that time we find two different, even contradictory uses, the one logical, the other rhetorical. The logical tradition tries to suppress the paradox. It exploits the ontological distinction of being and non-being to say that only being exists according to its own distinctions, above all: *hypokeimenon/symbebekos*. The observer can make true and false statements and can correct him- or herself (or be corrected by others) because being is what it is (not *as* it is, as we probably would say). Being is framed by such secondary distinctions (or categories) *and not by its distinction from non-being*. Being does not need to be distinguished from, or to exclude, non-being to be itself. It simply *is*, by itself (nature) or by way of creation. Disregarding this structure of ontological metaphysics, it has been claimed, would lead cognition the wrong way. It would end with paradoxes and destroy the telos of thinking. The appearance of unacceptable self-contradictions at the other side of the ontological scheme is then said to prove ontology as metaphysics. Thinking has to stay on the right path and avoid paradoxes.

The rhetorical tradition that invented the term[2] introduced paradoxical statements to enlarge the frames of received opinions—therefore "para-doxa"—to prepare the ground for innovation and/or for the acceptance of suggested decisions. At first sight, this seems to be a completely different notion, and the collection of examples of rhetorical paradoxes hardly ever demonstrate logical contradictions (see, for instance, Lando, *Paradossi*). After the introduction of the printing press such collections were in fact recommended and sold as amusing jokes. "They are only but exercise of wit," Anthony Munday excuses himself, sending his book on paradoxes to the King,[3] and Ortensio Lando adds to his book on paradoxes a second publication trying to extinguish the fire (Lando, *Confutatione*). But why do we communicate paradoxes in the first place if we are not supposed to take them seriously?

The conventional answer seems to be—exercise of wit.[4] This may be good advertisement for selling books, but it is not the whole truth. When we go back to the traditional definition of paradoxes as going beyond the limits of common sense,[5] the immediate intention seems to be to deframe and reframe the frame of normal thinking, the frame of common sense. The communication of paradoxes fixes attention on the frames of common sense, frames that normally go unattended. If this is the function, then it will not surprise us that deframing again needs its own frames. Therefore, we find comments on paradoxes in prefaces, in letters of dedications, in other books, or at the end of the text (as in Erasmus's *Praise of Folly*), and it seems to require other texts to frame the deframing, to look at it from the outside and to lead back to common sense—it is only an exercise of wit.

But cancellation can hardly be the whole meaning of the operation, for it could not explain Shakespeare's theater with its elaborate use of paradoxes and frames within frames, or Plato's cave as a stage for the shadows of ideas to appear, that is, as a frame for these shadows. And the cave is also itself framed by Plato's theory of ideas and of the ways we are able to remember them, which explains that in daily life we only use the cave-frame and need not, indeed cannot, reflect the double closure of the frames.

The interest in paradoxes emerging in the 16th century directs attention to the frames of common sense. It seems, when we are allowed to appeal to a further frame, to indicate the appearance, the coming on the stage, of a new historical interest, the interest in frames as frames or in limits as parts of a form that are neither inside nor outside but in a certain sense nowhere or "nothing" (Da Vinci 73). If paradoxes are teleological operations aiming at a perfect state, then this state could be described as enriched common sense. However, it may be more rewarding to ask whether the assumption of a natural end is adequate or whether we are not observing a discovery that, like Kant's final cause without finality, is inherently paradoxical.[6] The rhetorical paradox, then, may be an autological operation, infecting itself with whatever is a paradox.

During the 18th century rhetoric lost its traditional reputation, partly because of the spread of literacy, partly because the hierarchical structure of the estates of society was replaced by a class structure. The rhetorical figure of the paradox that was still in use was definitely seen as frivolous play and as insolence (see Bernard, Morellet, and Schkommodau). And finally, during the 19th and 20th centuries, with the increasing development of formalism in mathematics and logic, and with the increasing interrelation of logic and mathematics (e.g., Cantor, Frege, Russell), paradox was treated as something to be avoided by all means, be it by simple interdiction or by constructing "hierarchies" of types or levels and presenting them as logical or linguistic necessity. However, if we maintain an interest in frames, we may well describe such hierarchical distinctions as frames, this time not of commonsensical opinions but of logical operations, and revive the curiosity of the 16th century to see what would happen if we deframe these frames. In such a revival of 16th-century curiosity, we will receive the support of systems therapists who say that everyday communication cannot but confuse these levels and reproduce paradoxical communication,[7] and we will receive the support of Gödel who would say that one cannot cleanly separate (and I would like to add: in communication) the statement about numbers from the statement about statements about numbers.

If at the end of this history, observing frames is a serious consideration, does it then make any sense to maintain the traditional distinction between the logical interdiction and the rhetorical recommendation of paradoxes? Or is this double tradition but another sign for the inherent paradoxicality of the paradox?

III

We began our investigation by asking how a sociology of knowledge can include among its objects formal sciences such as logic and mathematics. We now have to answer the question: How is it possible to observe frames? Whatever difficulties may emerge during this investigation, we will certainly need a medium that is the same on both sides of the frame, on its inside and on its outside. I propose to call this medium *meaning*, and thereby exclude two other possibilities—the world and truth. The world, as an unqualifiable entity, an entity without information, seems to be too large. Truth, on the other hand, is too narrow because it itself serves as a frame, as the inner side of a form whose outside would be everything that is not true. But what then is meaning?

If we want to observe paradoxical communications as deframing and reframing, deconstructing and reconstructing operations,[8] we need a concept of meaning that does not prevent or restrict the range of such operations. "Meaning" cannot be understood as the result of obedience to the methodological instructions of the Viennese school of "logical empiricism" which would exclude metaphysics and much more as "meaningless,"[9] nor can it be understood in relation to the subjective aspiration of individuals and what seems meaningful to them and for them (see Hahn). Such definitions of meaning exclude unmarked possibilities and are valid only within their methodological or subjective frames. They are, that is, deframable (deconstructable) meanings and do not fulfill the requirements of a medium that gives access to *both* sides of *any* frame.

To avoid such limitations we need a concept of meaning that is (for systems that can use meaning as a medium) coextensive with the world. Meaning in this sense will have no outside, no antonym, no negative form. It knows, of course, negative meanings, even artificially constructed non-sense meanings (non-sense poems for example), but every possible use of this medium called "meaning" will itself reproduce meaning, and even an attempt to cross the boundary of meaning into an unmarked space will be a meaningful operation. (The unmarked space has, for this purpose, the name "unmarked space.")

With reference to Husserl's transcendental phenomenology

we can conceive of meaning as the simultaneous presentation (in Husserl's terms, intention) of actuality and possibility (Luhmann, *Soziale Systeme* 92ff). The actual is given within a "horizon" of further possibilities. Since operationally closed systems consist of operations only and have to renew them from moment to moment, they can maintain their self-reproduction only by continuously actualizing new meaning. This requires selection from many possibilities and, therefore, will appear as information. The internal dynamics of communication (in the case of social systems) and living experience ("Erleben" in the case of psychic systems) is only possible because, strangely enough, actual operations are also possible operations. The distinction actual/possible is a form that "re-enters" itself (see Spencer Brown and Kauffman). On one side of the distinction, the actual, the distinction actual/possible reappears; it is copied into itself so that the system may have the sense of being able to continue actual operations in spite of an increasing change of themes, impressions, intentions.

If we observe such a re-entry, we see a paradox. The re-entering distinction is the same, and it is not the same. But the paradox does not prevent the operations of the system. On the contrary, it is the condition of their possibility because their autopoiesis requires *continuing* actuality with *different* operations, *actualizing different possibilities*.

That psychic and social systems are *based* on a re-entry has dramatic consequences. From a purely mathematical point of view (following Spencer Brown), it means (1) creating an imaginary space that includes unmarked states and makes it possible to introduce expressions of ignorance, and (2) producing a system with unresolvable indeterminacy—the system becomes incalculable and therefore intransparent to itself. Furthermore, (3) the system nevertheless has to start every operation from a historical state that is its own product (the input of its own output) and needs a memory function to distinguish forgetting from remembering, and (4) it has to face its future as a succession of marked and unmarked states or self-referential and hetero-referential indications. It needs, in other words, to be prepared for oscillating between the two sides of its distinctions. An oscillating system can preserve the undecidability of whether something is inside or outside a form. It can preserve and reproduce itself as a form, that is, as an entity with a boundary, with an inside and an outside, and it can prevent both sides from collapsing into the other. A self-referential system that continually regenerates its re-entry will be, in Heinz von Foerster's terms, a non-trivial machine, structurally determined by its own output and therefore *unreliable* ("Principles" 8 ff.).

A system that is bound to use the meaning as a medium constitutes an endless but complete world in which everything has meaning, in which everything gives many cues for subsequent operations and thereby sustains autopoiesis, the self-reproduction of the system out of its own products. To see (and we will say: to observe) possibilities and to use meaning as a medium, the system will use the distinction of medium and form.[10] Medium within this distinction means a loose coupling of possibilities without regard to actual happenings, and form means tight couplings that construct the form, for example a thing, with an outside. Again, the medium is inside and outside, but the attention of the system has limitations and observes only forms. Forms are actualized in time, just for a moment, but since the system has memory it can reactualize well-tried forms and direct its operations from form to form, thereby reproducing the medium. The distinction medium/form serves as a frame without outside, as an internal frame that includes, via re-entry, its own outside.

IV

Now we are sufficiently prepared to observe the observer, to enter the circle of "observing systems" (in the double sense of von Foerster's *Observing Systems*). As with so many other terms, the expression observing/observer has to be adapted to this theoretical context. It does not only mean attentive sensual perception, though it does not exclude this particular definition. In more recent literature, initiated by George Spencer Brown, Humberto Maturana, and Heinz von Foerster, the term corresponds to the autopoietic self-reproduction of systems, to the operation of re-entry, and to the oscillation between marked and unmarked states, to the inside and the outside of forms and self-referential and hetero-referential indications (see Luhmann et al.). Observing means making a distinction and indicating one side (and not the other side) of the distinction.

The other side can be left completely unmarked—say, Bloomington and nothing else. But normally our indications will frame our observations with the effect that the other side implicitly will receive a corresponding specification—say, Bloomington and no other city, the university in Bloomington and no other university. In this case the indication implies a double boundary, the inner boundary of the frame "cities," "universities," and the boundary of this frame that excludes animals, numbers, fine wines, and everything else, i.e., the unmarked space. Our next operation may cross the boundary that separates Bloomington from its unmarked state and may select another frame. For example, we may ask whether it would be possible to find fine wines in Bloomington, and this would lead us to look for a further frame—say, restaurants or shops. One will thereby be led to places where one can find fine wines. Proceeding in this way from frame to frame or from form to form will, by necessity, reproduce the unmarked space (see Meyer). It will maintain the world as severed by distinctions, frames, and forms *and maintained by its severance.* "We may take it," to quote Spencer Brown, "that the world undoubtedly is itself (i.e. is indistinct from itself), but, in any attempt to see itself as an object, it must, equally undoubtedly, act so as to make itself distinct from, and therefore false to, itself. In this condition it will always partially elude itself" (105). This partiality precludes any possibility of representation or mimesis and any "holistic" theory. It is not sufficient to say that a part is able to express or to symbolize the whole. The miracle of symbolization, the marvelous, that which has been most admired by our tradition, has to be replaced by a difference that, when observed, always regenerates the unobservable.

The operation of observing, therefore, includes the exclusion of the unobservable, including, moreover, the unobservable par excellence, observation itself, the observer-in-operation. The place of the observer is the unmarked state out of which it crosses a boundary to draw a distinction and in which it finds itself indistinguishable from anything else. As such, the observer as a system can be indicated, but only by way of a further distinction, another form, a frame, for example, that makes it possible to distinguish one observer from others or psychic observing systems from social observing systems. We arrive, then, at the autological conclusion that the observing of observers and even the operation of self-observation is itself simply observation in the usual sense—that is, making a distinction to indicate one side and not the others.[11] And this again can only happen in the world and by severing the unmarked space, crossing the boundary that thereby comes into existence as a boundary separating a marked from what now can be marked as "unmarked" space. We resist the temptation to call this creation.

V

It is by no means necessary to conceptualize this situation of meaning-producing operations. To clarify the world or to indicate the unmarked space as unmarked is neither a requirement of daily life nor of autopoietic reproduction. To elaborate on its self-description remains one of the possibilities an observer sees and can, if required, actualize. But even then, it will just change its frame, cross the boundary between self-reference and hetero-reference; it will mark itself as a thing among others or as an observer among others. Switching frames, proceeding from form to form is the normal way of observing operations, and the "self" of the system can appear and disappear as suggested by circumstances. Language may make the speaker more visible if it is required to say "I love" and not simply "amo." For social systems the emergence of organizations that can communicate in their own name makes all the difference. No other social system can do that, no society, no societal subsystem, no interaction. If the "estates" of the old European society wanted to have a voice, they formed a corporation ("Standschaft" in Germany), and if the economy wants to have a voice in political affairs, it sends representatives of its organizations. Nations have names, but to be able to participate in communication they form "states." Names, addresses, persons (in the traditional sense)[12] are taken for granted. Their use has to adapt to the speed of perception, thinking, or communication, to the speed required by the necessity of replacing vanishing events by other events. There is simply no time to include the world or the complete reality of the observing systems (as "subjects" and as "objects") in the operation.

But if an observer—again, a psychic or a social system—

wants to observe and describe the continuous deframing and reframing of frames, the autopoietic operation of observing systems
(including himself), it will end up with paradoxical formulations.
It would have to say that the different is the same, that the distinction of marked and unmarked is *one* distinction among others, that
any distinction is a unity, a frame that separates two sides and can
be used to connect operations only at one side (at the positive side,
at the inner side of the form) and not at the other side. The other
side remains included, but as excluded. The excluded third, or the
"interpretant" in the sense of Peirce, or the operation of observing
in our theory, or the "parasite" in the sense of Michel Serres, or
the "supplement" or "parergon" in Derrida's sense, is the active
factor indeed, without which the world could not observe itself.
Observation has to operate unobserved to be able to cut up the
world.

When observers (we, at the moment) continue to look for an
ultimate reality, a concluding formula, a final identity, they will
find the paradox. Such a paradox is not simply a logical contradiction (A is non-A) but a foundational statement: The world is observable *because* it is unobservable. Nothing can be observed (not
even the "nothing") without drawing a distinction, but this operation remains indistinguishable. It can be distinguished, but only by
another operation. It crosses the boundary between the unmarked
and the marked space, a boundary that does not exist before and
comes into being (if being is the right word) only by crossing it.
Or to say it in Derrida's style, the condition of its possibility is its
impossibility.

Obviously, this makes no sense. It makes meaning. It makes
no common sense; it uses the meaning of "para-doxon" to trans-
gress the boundaries of common sense to reflect what it means
to use meaning as a medium. However, even paradox cannot be
observed without a distinction, but one that is involved in two different ways. On the one hand, paradox is always the unity of a
distinction (for example, in the case of the Liar's Paradox, the
unity of the distinction true/false); and on the other hand, one may
find ways to deparadoxify or to "unfold" (Löfgren, "Some Foundational Views") paradox (again, in the above case, by making a rule
to separate types or levels and to forbid "strange loops" [Hof-
stadter]). It seems, then, that any distinction can be paradoxified

and deparadoxified, depending on conditions of plausibility. The distinction used to make the paradox visible and invisible has to be presupposed to apply a second distinction, the distinction between the paradox and its unfolding, its visibility and its invisibility. Only the paradox itself provides for unconditioned knowledge; the distinction used for unfolding the paradox depends on conditions of acceptability. Paradox, then, is, as unconditioned knowledge, a transcendental necessity, the successor of what was supposed to be a performance of the transcendental subject. But all usable, connectable knowledge will be contingent.

The paradox, then, would be the *parergon,* a supplement to the work that remains to be done and that has already been done (see Derrida again, and also Dünkelsbühler). It has a double identity, a logical identity by oscillating in itself between positive and negative versions of the same, and an empirical identity due to the recursive network of operations of a system that paradoxifies and deparadoxifies its distinctions.

VI

And now, we are on our way back to a sociology of knowledge within the framework of a theory of society. Neither ontology nor cosmology, neither nature (with its substances, its essential and accidental forms) nor knowledge of God (theology) will help. We will have to distinguish observers, and the most important of them will be society, i.e., the encompassing social system.

Society produces culture—memory—and its culture will decide whether distinctions and indications may be communicated as natural (not artificial), as normal (not pathological), and as necessary or impossible (not contingent). In periods of semantic uncertainty and structural transitions, paradoxes will become fashionable, as in the 16th century after the introduction of the printing press and after the Protestant reformation and during its civil wars (see Colie, Malloch, McCanles, and Schulz-Buschhaus). We may find society, now world society, at the end of the 20th century in a similar situation of uncertainty, for very different reasons, of course. And again, paradox has become fashionable, if not *the* predicament of the century (see Lawson).

There are at least two interconnected reasons for this renewed interest in paradox. One is the establishment of a world
society with a plurality of cultural traditions. The invention of "culture" at the end of the 18th century was still a European affair,
opening European perspectives for historical and regional comparisons (Luhmann, "Kultur" and Williams). With the two world
wars of this century and with the dissolution of the colonial empires, Europe lost its centrality in both structural and in semantical
terms. We may now imagine shifting centers of modernity (Tiryakian), but no one center can assume to be the center of society as
a whole.

Secondly, that we have to live with a society without top and
without center is due to the fact that the structure of modern society is determined by functional differentiation and no longer by a
coherent hierarchical stratification nor by a one-center/periphery
differentiation. Functional differentiation requires polycontextural, hypercomplex complexity-descriptions without unifying
perspective.[13] Society remains the same but appears as different
depending upon the functional subsystem (politics, economy, science, mass media, education, religion, art, and so on) that describes it. The same is different. The integration of the system can
no longer be thought of as a process of applying principles, but
rather as a reciprocal reduction of the degrees of freedom of its
subsystems. Reason and consensus are replaced by evolutionary
tests, i.e., by uncertainty, and motivating orientations shift from
symbols of identity, principles, and norms to boundaries and differences, to ecological problems, to individuals as distinct from society, or to more or less fundamentalistic oppositions. This very
condition implies that there is no need to adapt to it, but theories
of society that refuse adaptation will increasingly be described as
counterfactual, as purely normative, as having a conservative bias
toward ideas, even of being ideological.

VII

A final consideration returns us to forms in which our Greek,
Roman, and European tradition treated, nourished, and killed
paradox (Luhmann, "Observing"). We examine here two distinc

tions which were probably the most important ones, the distinction between being and non-being, elaborated as ontology, and the distinction between good and bad, elaborated as ethics.

Ontological metaphysics presents itself, hiding its paradox, as the science of substances and essences, of individual beings (substances) and generic entities (essences) that may exist and be visible (for angels only) as ideas. There is no non-being in this world, this *universitas rerum*, but there are perfect and corrupt natural forms and, in cognition, true and false opinions. Cognition, too, is a natural process of being impressed by substances and essences. On this view, cognition exists, either with true or with false results. Its distinguishing capacity (*dihaíresis*) is its very essence, but it relates only, via mimesis, to the substances and generic forms of being. Reflection (including the reflection of reflection) is nothing but a particular way to be, a special capacity among others of the human psyche, and the category of the "infinite" serves as the asylum for all questions that cannot be solved with this approach (Günther, "Logistischer" 8). "Something is or it is not; that is all there is to it in ontology" (Günther, "Life" 286).

But why are we supposed to observe the world with this primary distinction of being and non-being, and why are we to treat the distinction finite/infinite as a supplement to this primary distinction? Why don't we, operating as observers, that is, as systems, start from the distinction between inside and outside (Herbst 88)? Apparently, being is the strong side, the powerful side of this distinction. It is the "inner side" of the ontological form. You can operate on the side of beings but not on the side of non-beings. Only beings have connecting value. The exclusion of non-beings from beings is a natural and (logically) necessary aspect of their being. But what would happen if we set out to observe the natural as artificial and the necessary as contingent? That is, what would happen if we permit the question of what kind of society lends plausibility to these ontological assumptions?

The same series of questions emerges when we look at "ethics" in its classical, premodern form. Here, the guiding distinction is good and bad or, taking the human origin of action into account, virtue and vice. Perfect action is good, corrupt action is bad; human perfection is virtue, human corruption is vice. In human society, only good actions have connecting capacities, whereas bad action or vice is seen as an isolated event or an isolating habit. This leads to the conclusion that being is good (*ens et verum et bonum convertuntur*) and that the world and society can be accepted. The good is the form that is taught in ethics and the form itself is good, which means that it is good to distinguish the good from the bad and that ethics itself is morally good. The good represents both the positive side of the distinction *and the distinction itself.* In our logical and linguistic frames, its unity is due to a confusion of levels. In social communication this presupposes authority—for example, of the old over the young, of men over women, of noblemen over commoners, of clerics over laymen. In structural terms, this form of unfolding the paradox presupposes a society with hierarchical and/or center/periphery differentiation.

What we label "modern" society, then, reacts to the dissolution of these premises. The printing press and technological advances may mean that the young have access to better knowledge than the old (Thomas) and that the reading public may have the better judgment compared to the local magnates or the clerics bound by orthodoxy (James). First the aristocracy and its political apparatus and then finally everybody needs money, so money becomes the medium, at least for this transitional period, organizing the differentiation of social status (Stone). As a result, recruitment patterns of organizations (state bureaucracies, enterprises, universities) become more and more independent of family origin, i.e., nobility. Having to digest these social changes the social and political semantics has to change its conceptual frames.[14] But it also, and this is our point, has to provide new patterns for the unfolding of the paradoxes inherent in all distinctions that are used for framing observations and descriptions.

During the second half of the 18th century new problems were invented, not to describe this social change, but to cope with increasing uncertainty. The traditional ontology became superseded by the Kantian quest for the condition of possibility of experience, and in order to provide a solution, the *hypokeímenon/subiectum* became the subject, the observer himself. Moreover, good behavior now no longer needed good manners but good reasons, and ethics became an academic discipline branching out in transcendental and utilitarian theories. So, in the subject it is now easy to recognize the observer, and in good reasons for good behavior it is easy to recognize the ambivalent duplification of the good, i.e., the veiling of the paradox. The social—treated in the tradition either as naturally domestic (economic) or political (civil) society—became thereby pulverized as the culture (*Bildung*), language, economy, or the state of individuals. The social, then, could only be reconstructed by an inherently paradoxical term—intersubjectivity.

The old-European tradition resolved its paradox by fetishism and disavowal, to use (or misuse) these Freudian terms. It used a re-entry of the distinction between being and non-being into being and a re-entry of the distinction between good and bad into the good. The substantial being and the reasonable good take the place of the paradox. This solution could efface the original differences and reconstruct them in terms of internal distinctions so successfully that medieval theology accepted it as cosmology and saw no need to reflect on paradoxes or even to retain the word. Only with Nicholas of Cusa and the early modern mystics did the problem come back and paradoxical formulations re-emerge as a form to rationally communicate ineffable experiences.[15] But the so-called "modern" solution could never achieve a similar stability. Its "present time" became "pregnant with future," that is, with the unknown and with the prospect of oscillating within the framework of its distinctions—now described as "ideologies." There were many competing distinctions, such as society and state, society and community, individual and collectivity, freedom and institution, progressive and conservative politics, and, above all, capitalism and socialism, but in none of these cases did the unity of these distinctions, the sameness of the opposites, become a problem (Luhmann, "Tautology"). The paradox now becomes resolved as oscillation, that is, as the still undetermined future. Supported by a universally accepted "open future" these distinctions (and others as well) stand in for the paradox of any frame used by an observer.

If "modernity" relies on its future for its deparadoxification, it is, and will always remain, an "incomplete project" (Habermas). The future never becomes present; it never begins but always moves away when we seem to approach it. But how long are we supposed to live with or wait for this future if we run into troubles with our present society? The more pressing need might well be to describe the present condition, but then we might have to ac-

knowledge that there are many possible descriptions, so that we
will have to move from first-order to second-order descriptions.[16]
This will require a transclassic logic in Gotthard Günther's sense
and will certainly go beyond the suggestions we find in Spencer
Brown's Laws of Form (see Esposito). I have no idea how this can
be worked out in sociological terms, but if we could develop theoretical frames of sufficient logical and structural complexity to dissolve our paradoxes, we may find that there still is one paradox
left—the paradox of observing systems.

   This theory of paradox is in no way a theory that founds itself
explicitly or implicitly on systems theory, i.e., on the distinction
between system and environment or inside and outside. All distinctions—this one too—can be paradoxified. We only need to ask the
question "of what is the unity of this distinction?" to see the paradox. And what prevents us from doing precisely that?

   We would have to use the distinction of paradoxification and
deparadoxification of distinctions. We would have to admit that all
distinctions, including this one, can be reduced to a paradox. In
this sense, paradox is an invariant possibility, and all distinctions
are of only temporary and contingent validity. We can always ask:
who is the observer? And then, why do we distinguish him or her?
If there are sufficient plausible reasons in present-day disciplinary
and interdisciplinary research, systems theory may offer itself as a
way out of the paradox—for the time being.

Notes

   1. On this, see Lloyd, in particular pp. 72 ff., about the emergence of paradoxes (Zeno) as the byproduct of the elaboration of the right way to describe the
world. Lloyd's "sociological" explanation points to the Greek culture of public
debates and the political need of consensus—and not so much to the phonetic
writing that also existed in other countries without leading to science based on
observing how observers observe.
   2. For references, see Probst.
   3. Munday, A. 3, and he adds: "Let no manne thinke then, that I or any other
would be so sencelesse, as to hold directly any of these vaine reasons."
   4. Even for officers, as recommended by La Noue 355 ff.
   5. As, for instance, "sentences ou propositions qui repugnent aux opinion (sic)
communes" (La Noue 355), or "inopiniatam atque alienam à communis sensu,
vulgataque consuedine sententiam" (Lemnius 416).
   6. This may remind the reader of Derrida's analysis of the "parergon" in

Kant's *Kritik der Urteilskraft*. And in fact, there are close similarities between parerga and paradoxa, both being forms that dissolve the distinction of inside and outside by indicating that a form (be it an aesthetic form or a cognitive or conceptual form) has to include the exclusion of the outside. See Derrida, *La vérité*, for example: "Il y a du cadre mais le cadre *n'existe pas*" (93).

7. See Ruesch and Bateson for an early statement of what now seems to be the common sense of the therapeutic profession. The therapeutic profession will then distinguish between normal and pathological confusion of levels and see a *need* for therapeutic intervention only in pathological cases. But this again is a frame that makes sense as long as there are limits to what people or insurances are willing to pay for.

8. We may also think of Derrida's *différance*. See Luhmann, "Deconstruction."

9. See among others the contributions to the section on "Meaningfulness and Confirmation" in Feigl and Sellars, eds.

10. This is a generalization and formalization of Fritz Heider's distinction of medium and thing restricted to the field of perception. A very similar distinction, used by cyberneticians and information theorists, would be variety and redundancy.

11. So, at the end of his text, Spencer Brown comes to the conclusion that was implied (but not explicable) at the beginning: "An observer, since he distinguishes the space he occupies, is also a mark" (78). And "is also a mark" means "can be observed."

12. In the sense that Hobbes explained in his *Leviathan* Ch. XVI: "So that a *Person*, is the same that an *Actor* is, both on the Stage and in common Conversation; and to *Personate*, is to *Act*, or *Represent* himselfe, or an other" (217).

13. "Polycontextural" in the sense used by Gotthard Günther ("Life"). The term "contexture" corresponds to a transclassical logic that admits transjunctional operations that can surpass "tertium non datur."

14. This is the organizing idea of the lexicon *Geschichtliche Grundbegriffe* (Brunner et al.).

15. For the very different Jewish tradition, see Atlan.

16. Or a second-order semantics in the sense of MacCannel and MacCannel.

Works Cited

Atlan, Henri. *Enlightenment to Enlightenment: Intercritique of Science and Myth*. Albany: SUNY Press, 1993.

Bernard, Jean-Fréderic. *Eloge d'Enfer: Ouvrage critique, historique et moral*. 2 vols. The Hague: Gosse, 1759.

Brunner, Otto, Werner Conze, and Reinhart Koselleck, eds. *Geschichtliche Grundbegriffe: historisches Lexikon zur politisch-sozialen Sprache in Deutschland*. 7 vols. Stuttgart: Klett, 1972–92.

Colie, Rosalie L. *Paradoxia Epidemica: The Renaissance Tradition of Paradox*. Princeton: Princeton UP, 1966.

Da Vinci, Leonardo. *The Notebooks of Leonardo da Vinci*. Trans. Edward MacCurdy. New York: Braziller, 1954.

Derrida, Jacques. *La vérité en peinture*. Paris: Flammarion, 1978.

Dünkelsbühler, Ulrike. "Rahmen-Gesetze und Parergon-Paradox: Eine Übersetzungsaufgabe." Gumbrecht and Pfeiffer 207–23.

Esposito, Elena. "Ein zweiwertiger, nicht-selbständiger Kalkül." Ed. Dirk Baecker. *Kalkül der Form*. Frankfurt: Suhrkamp, 1993. 96–111.

———. *L'operazione di osservazione: Costruttivismo e teoria dei sistemi sociali*. Milan: Franco Angeli, 1992.

Feigl, Herbert, and Wilfried Sellars, eds. *Readings in Philosophical Analysis*. New York: Appleton, Century, Crofts, 1949.

Gumbrecht, Hans Ulrich, and K. Ludwig Pfeiffer, eds. *Paradoxien, Dissonanzen, Zusammenbrüche: Situation offener Epistemologie*. Frankfurt: Suhrkamp, 1991.

Günther, Gotthard. *Beiträge zur Grundlegung einer operationsfähigen Dialektik*. 3 vols. Hamburg: Meiner, 1976–80. Vol. 2.

———. "Life as Poly-Contexturality." Günther, *Beiträge* 283–306.

———. "Logistischer Grundriß und Intro-Semantik." Günther, *Beiträge* 1–115.

Habermas, Jürgen. "Die Moderne—ein unvollendetes Project." *Kleine politische Schriften*. Frankfurt: Suhrkamp, 1981. 444–64.

Hahn, Alois. "Sinn und Sinnlosigkeit." *Sinn, Kommunikation und soziale Differenzierung: Beiträge zu Luhmanns Theorie sozialer Systeme*. Ed. Hans Haferkamp and Michael Schmid. Frankfurt: Suhrkamp, 1987. 155–64.

Heider, Fritz. "Thing and Medium." *Psychological Issues* 1.3 (1959): 1–34.

Herbst, Phillip G. *Alternatives to Hierarchies*. Leiden: Nijhoff, 1976.

Hobbes, Thomas. *Leviathan*. Ed. C. B. MacPherson. Harmondsworth: Penguin, 1968.

Hofstadter, Douglas R. *Gödel, Escher, Bach: An Eternal Golden Braid*. New York: Basic, 1979.

James, Mervyn. *Family, Lineage, and Civil Society: A Study of Society, Politics, and Mentality in the Durham Region 1500–1640*. Oxford: Clarendon, 1974.

Johnson, Samuel. *The Idler and the Adventurer*. Ed. W. J. Bate, J. M. Bullit, and L. F. Powel. New Haven: Yale UP, 1963.

Kauffman, Louis H. "Self-Reference and Recursive Forms." *Journal of Social and Biological Structures* 10 (1987): 53–72.

Lando, Ortensio. *Confutatione del libro de paradossi nuovamente composta in tre orationi distinta*. n.p., n.d.

———. *Paradossi, cioe sententie fuori del commun parere*. n.p.: Venegia, 1545.

La Noue, François. *Discours politiques et militaires*. 1587. Geneva: Droz, 1967.

Lawson, Hilary. *Reflexivity: The Postmodern Predicament*. London: Hutchinson, 1985.

Lemnius, Levinus. *De miraculis occultis naturae libri IIII*. Antwerp: Platin, 1574.

Lloyd, G. E. R. *Magic, Reason and Experience: Studies in the Origin and Development of Greek Science*. Cambridge: Cambridge UP, 1979.

Löfgren, Lars. "Some Foundational Views on General Systems and the Hempel Paradox." *International Journal of General Systems*. 4 (1978): 243–53.

———. "Towards System: From Computation to the Phenomenon of Language." *Nature. Cognition and System I: Current Systems-Scientific Research on Natural and Cognitive Systems*. Ed. Marc Cavallo. Dordrecht: Kluwer, 1988. 129–55.

Luhmann, Niklas. "Deconstruction as Second-Order Observing." *New Literary History* 24 (1993): 763–82.

———. "Kultur als historischer Begriff." *Gesellschaftsstruktur und Semantik*. 4 vols. Frankfurt: Suhrkamp, 1995. Vol. 4. 31–54.

———. *Soziale Systeme: Grundriß einer allgemeinen Theorie*. Frankfurt: Suhrkamp, 1984.

———. "Tautology and Paradox in the Self-Descriptions of Modern Society." *Essays on Self-Reference*. New York: Columbia UP, 1990. 123–43.

Luhmann, Niklas, et al. *Beobachter: Konvergenz der Erkenntnistheorien?* Munich: Fink, 1990.

MacCannel, Dean, and Juliet F. MacCannel. *The Time of the Sign: A Semiotic Interpretation of Modern Culture.* Bloomington: Indiana UP, 1982.

Malloch, A. E. "The Techniques and Function of the Renaissance Paradox." *Studies in Philology* 53 (1956): 191–203.

McCanles, Michael. "Paradox in Donne." *Studies in the Renaissance* 13 (1966): 266–87.

Meyer, Eva. "Der Unterschied, der eine Umgebung schafft." *Im Netz der Systeme.* Ed. ARS ELECTRONICA. Berlin: Merve, 1990. 110–22.

Morellet, André. *Theorie des Paradoxen.* Leipzig: Dyk, 1778. German translation of *Theorie du paradoxe.* 1775.

Munday, Anthony. *The Defence of Contraries.* 1593. Amsterdam/New York: Theatrum Orbis Terrarum/DaCapo, 1969.

Probst, P. "Paradox." *Historisches Wörterbuch der Philosophie.* Ed. Joachim Ritter and Karlfried Gründer. Vol. 7. Basel: Schwabe, 1989. 81–90.

Ruesch, Jürgen, and Gregory Bateson. *Communication: The Social Matrix of Psychiatry.* New York: Norton, 1951.

Schkommodau, Hans. *Thematik des Paradoxes in der Aufklärung.* Wiesbaden. 1972.

Schulz-Buschhaus, Ulrich. "Vom Lob der Pest und vom Lob der Perfidie: Burleske und politische Paradoxographie in der italienischen Renaissance-Literatur." Gumbrecht and Pfeiffer 259–73.

Serres, Michel. *Le Parasite.* Paris: Grasset, 1980.

Spencer Brown, George. *Laws of Form.* 2nd ed. New York: Dutton, 1979.

Stone, Lawrence. *The Crisis of the Aristocracy 1558–1641.* Oxford: Clarendon, 1965.

Thomas, Keith. *Vergangenheit, Zukunft, Lebensalter: Zeitvorstellungen im England der frühen Neuzeit.* Berlin: Wagenbach, 1988.

Tiryakian, Edward A. "The Changing Centers of Modernity." *Comparative Social Dynamics: Essays in Honor of S. N. Eisenstadt.* Ed. Erik Cohen et al. Boulder: Westview, 1985. 121–47.

von Foerster, Heinz. *Observing Systems.* Seaside: Intersystems, 1981.

———. "Principles of Self-Organization—In a Socio-Managerial Context." *Self-Organization and Management of Social Systems: Insights, Promises, Doubts, and Questions.* Ed. Hans Ulrich and Gilbert J. B. Probst. Berlin: Springer, 1984. 2–24.

Williams, Raymond. *Culture and Society 1780–1950.* New York: Columbia UP, 1958.

HYPATIA

A JOURNAL OF FEMINIST PHILOSOPHY

► **Hypatia**, edited by Linda Lopez McAlister, Joanne Bell Waugh, and Cheryl A. Hall, is the only journal for scholarly research at the intersection of philosophy and women's studies and is a leader in reclaiming the work of women philosophers. It is an indispensable tool for anyone interested in the rapidly expanding and developing scholarship in feminist philosophy and provides the best single access to the latest research.

► ## ISSUES OF SPECIAL INTEREST

Feminist Ethics and Social Policy 2, Edited by Linda Lopez McAlister (Vol. 10, no. 2)

Feminist Ethics and Social Policy 1, Edited by Patrice DiQuinzio and Iris Marion Young (Vol. 10, no. 1)

Feminist Philosophy of Religion, Edited by Marilyn Thie and Nancy Frankenberry (Vol. 9, no. 4)

Feminism and Peace, Edited by Karen J. Warren and Duane Cady (Vol. 9, no. 2)

Feminism and Pragmatism, Edited by Charlene Haddock Seigfried (Vol. 8, no. 2)

Lesbian Philosophy, Edited by Claudia Card (Vol. 7, no. 4)

Philosophy and Language, Edited by Dale Bauer and Kelly Oliver (Vol. 7, no. 2)

Ecological Feminism, Edited by Karen J. Warren (Vol. 6, no. 1)

Subscriptions (4 issues)
Individuals: $35.00
Institutions: $60.00
Foreign surface post
outside USA: $12.50

Single Issues
$12.95 each
Postage & handling:
$1.75 each

Indiana University Press Journals Division
601 North Morton, Bloomington, IN 47404 USA
Telephone: 812-855-9449, Fax: 812-855-8507
Email: Journals@Indiana.Edu

On Environmentality: Geo-Power and Eco-Knowledge in the Discourses of Contemporary Environmentalism

Timothy W. Luke

This study examines how discourses of nature, ecology, or the environment, as disciplinary articulations of "eco-knowledge," might be reinterpreted as efforts to generate systems of "geo-power" over, but also within and through, Nature for the governance of modern economies and societies. The thinking of Michel Foucault, particularly his notions of sexuality and bio-power as mediations for discursively formed discipline, provides a basis for this reinterpretation, because many of the terms associated with "the environment" are perplexing until one puts them under a genealogical lens. These dynamics have been at play for nearly a hundred and thirty years—or at least since self-consciously ecological discourses were formulated by George Marsh (1885) or Ernst Haeckel (1866) in the nineteenth century—but their operations are particularly apparent today.

While many examples of such tendencies might be mobilized here, this examination of geo-power systems as a mediation of

© 1995 by *Cultural Critique*. Fall 1995. 0882-4371/95/$5.00.

environmentality will center upon only one—the work of the Worldwatch Institute. The continuous attempt to reinvent the forces of Nature in the economic exploitation of advanced technologies, linking structures in Nature to the rational management of its energies as geo-power, is an ongoing supplement to the disciplinary construction of various modes of bio-power in promoting the growth of human populations (Foucault, *History of Sexuality* I 140–41). Directed at generating geo-power from the more rational insertion of natural and artificial bodies into the machinery of production, discourses of environmentality can be seen fabricating disciplinary environments where power/knowledge operate as ensembles of geo-power and eco-knowledge.

In and of itself, Nature arguably is meaningless until humans assign meanings to it by interpreting some of its many signs as meaningful (Bramwell, Eckersley). The outcomes of this activity, however, are inescapably indeterminate. Because different human beings will observe its patterns, choosing to accentuate some while deciding at the same time to ignore others, Nature's meanings always will be multiple and unfixed. Only these interpretive acts can construct contestable textual fields, which can then be read on various levels of expression for their many manifest or latent meanings. Before technologies turn its matter and energy into products, Nature already is transformed discursively into "natural resources." And, once it is rendered intelligible through these discursive processes, it can be used to legitimize almost anything. Therefore, this analysis will look into the discursive uses and conceptual definitions of some common theoretical notions, like "the environment," "environmentalism," and "environmentalist," to reconsider how many contemporary environmentalists are giving a new look to "the environment," as a concept, by transforming its identity in the practices of "environmentality." Finally, as these preliminary navigational bearings indicate, doubts are raised here about the apparently benign intentions of environmental actions, given the disciplinary propensities of the practices embedded in this new regime of environmentality.

For more concrete evidence to justify such caution, this study of geo-power and eco-knowledge will look at the work of the Worldwatch Institute. Established in 1974 amidst the economic and political panic sparked by the OPEC oil crisis of 1973, the

Worldwatch Institute might be dismissed as just another nest of D.C. policy wonks, turning out position papers on water scarcity, reforestation, windmill economics, and overpopulation. This image of the Worldwatchers is accurate, but incomplete. And, given this incompleteness, worldwatching ought not to be quickly ignored or easily dismissed. Such activities can be the essence of power/knowledge formation, because much of what policy wonks do basically boils down to defining, creating, and enforcing discursive regimes of disciplinary truth. Consequently, this analysis carefully re-reads one recent Worldwatch Institute publication, *Saving the Planet: How to Shape an Environmentally Sustainable Society* (1991) by Lester Brown, Christopher Flavin, and Sandra Postel, to illustrate how the eco-knowledge generated by the Worldwatch Institute might be seen as a mediation of environmentality in a new regime of geo-power.

1. Eco-Diction: Making Nature Speak as "Environment"

Many individuals who are intent upon turning the world into "a better place to live" often turn today to "the environment" in order to make their improvements. Believing that they must do anything and everything to protect "the environment," they transform this undertaking into a moral crusade. Their struggles, however, are often hobbled by a fundamental lack of clarity about what "the environment" actually *is*. This lack of certainty or centeredness in the meaning of environments is intriguing, because so many contemporary ecological discourses articulate their visions of moral value, political organization, and social control by stressing the salience of solving "environmental problems" for contemporary society.

"Environment," "environmentalism," and "environmentalist" are words used and accepted so broadly now that it is difficult to remember how recently they came into such wide currency. Before 1965, their use in ordinary discussions actually was quite rare in most policy discourses. More suggestive terms, like "Nature," "conservation," or "ecology," typically were deployed in making references about the characteristics of the environmental. Now, a generation later, in the 1990s, Nature in these discourses occasionally will speak as "Nature," but increasingly its presence is marked as "the environment." This twist is interesting inasmuch as the various meanings of Nature, while remaining fully contestable, are somewhat clearer than a generation ago. At the same time, the meanings of the "environment," which are essentially uncontested, remain very unclear. Documenting this shift in usage is not an exact practice, but to start, one might look briefly through newspaper indices or expert discourses to develop a sense of the shift.

In 1960, or the year Rachel Carson's *New Yorker* essays on how pesticides were despoiling wildlife first drew broad public attention, there is only one story in *The New York Index* about environmental science, and it ties the topic to "astronautics." Five years earlier, in 1955, the word is not even registered in the index, but by 1965 there are four entries about "the environment," one of them about a speech by President Johnson on the need for greater efforts at conservation and beautification in preserving the environment. By 1970, there are almost two and a half entire pages of citations. And, more importantly, the concept remains a significant feature in the index during every year after 1970: one and two-thirds pages in 1975, one and a third in 1980, two pages in 1985, and three and a third in 1990. Even though increasing attention is being allotted in *The New York Times* to concerns that are broadly labeled as "environmental" or "environmentalistic," what "the environment" means to the press is much less clear. It encompasses Nature, conservation, and ecology as well as pollution, deforestation, and contamination.

Despite all of the talk about its central importance, "the environment" constantly escapes exacting definition, even in expert "environmentalist" discourses (Worster). For almost any given ecological writer, the significance of the environment and environmentalism is now apparently assumed to be so obvious that precise definitions are superfluous. ReVelle and ReVelle in their text *The Environment: Issues and Choices for Society* (1988), for example, name their book after the environment, but they fail to include any definition of what it means in their book's glossary or analysis. Buchholz in *Principles of Environmental Management: The Greening of Business* (1993) does not define the environment as a vital concept in ecology, even though he recounts standard dictionary definitions, presenting it as the surroundings that are natural organisms' ecological settings (29–30). When the environment is defined by experts, it basically encompasses everything. Nebel, for example, in his *Environmental Science: The Way the World Works* (1990) follows this fashion by identifying the environment as "the combination of all things and factors external to the individual or population of organisms in question" (576). Given such nonexistent, derivative, or vague understandings of the environment, it becomes more interesting as to how and why "Nature," "the biosphere," or all "ecological systems" easily can circulate as conceptual equivalents in rough-and-ready exchange as a loose understanding of what "the environment" might mean.

Interestingly, this tendency also marks the work of explicitly political analyses of the environment (Paehlke). Even Barry Commoner, whose political thinking on environmental problems from the 1960s through the 1990s has won wide respect, takes this analytical path. Commoner does not directly confront the concept of the environment; instead, he divides Nature into "two worlds: the natural ecosphere, the thin skin of air, water, and soil and the plants and animals that live in it, and the man-made technosphere," which now has become

> sufficiently large and intense to alter the natural processes that govern the ecosphere. And in turn, the altered ecosphere threatens to flood our great cities, dry up our bountiful farms, contaminate our food and water, and poison our bodies—catastrophically diminishing our ability to provide for basic human needs. (*Making Peace* 7)

Ultimately, Commoner depicts these two worlds as being "at war." As humans in the technosphere disrupt the ecosphere, the ecosphere responds with equally or more disruptive secondary effects in the technosphere. In some sense, the environment is "Nature" for Commoner, but it is also "Society," or, more accurately, Nature-as-transformed-by-Society. The prospect of something like "geo-power," in turn, is foreshadowed by expert intellectual interventions typified by his critiques. In fact, geo-power might be seen as the means of productively fusing the technosphere with the biosphere through the right codes of eco-knowledge. He stresses this interpretation in *The Closing Circle* (1971) when he claims "the environment is, so to speak, the house created on the earth *by* living things, *for* living things" (32). This representation of the environment as life's house, however, does little more than reduce it to a biophysical housing of all living things—or, again, the setting that surrounds organisms. Hence, environmentalism becomes the practice of running this house created by living things for living things more rationally or justly.

This curious absence of clear definition can be tracked back beyond Commoner to Carson's original call for greater environmental awareness. *Silent Spring,* as it appeared in *The New Yorker* in 1960, and as a book in 1962, largely directed its analysis at "the web of life" rather than "the environment." Still, in reexamining how unregulated application of chemical pesticides adversely affected biotic communities in the world's overlapping and interconnecting food chains, Carson constructed a provisional reading of "the environment." That is, some substances from the technosphere (chemical pesticides) were invented to kill something in the biosphere (animal pests). While their application was intended to control only those animals that ate crops, carried disease, and infested dwellings, their impact was much broader. Pesticides soon spread through everything in the ecosphere—both human technosphere and nonhuman biosphere—returning from the "out there" of natural environments back into plant, animal, and human bodies situated at the "in here" of artificial environments with unintended, unanticipated, and unwanted effects. By using zoological, toxicological, epidemiological, and ecological insights, Carson generated a new sense of how "the environment" might be seen. However, she never based her analysis directly upon a formalized notion of "the environment" or "environmental damage."

Of course, any concept, like "the environment," "environmentalism," or "environmentalist," can be deployed as indistinctly as all of these patterns of use indicate. In noting how the words are used, one sees what we might ordinarily expect: namely, that they tend to mean various things to many people in several different contexts. Another approach to the problem would be to develop a provisional genealogy of the term's early origins to reveal other more embedded understandings of "the environment" that could be more suggestive than the sense of "environment" which encompasses *all* surroundings, *every* factor that affects organisms, the *totality* of circumstances, or the *sum* complex of conditions. A return to the semantic origins of environment, then, might illuminate some of these ambiguities and clarify how environmentalistic concepts actually work in the present.

2. On Environing

The separation of organisms from their environments is the primary epistemological divide cutting through reality in the rhetorics of ecology. This discursive turn goes back to Haeckel's initial 1866 identification of ecology as the science that investigates all of the relations of an organism to its organic and inorganic environments. Nonetheless, there are differences among ecologists over what these "environments" might be. Because the expanse of the organic and inorganic environment is so broad, it often is defined in terms delimiting what it *is* by looking at what it *is not*. In other words, it is the organism, or biotic community, or local ecosystem that ecologists place at the center of their systems of study, while the environment is reduced to everything outside of the subject of analysis. With these maneuvers, environments are often transformed rhetorically into silences, backgrounds, or settings. In this manner, they also are studied and understood not directly as such, but more indirectly in terms of the objective relations and effects they register upon the subjects of study they surround.

Even so, this inversion of *one* thing, like an organism or society, into *everything*, or the environment, might disclose the nature of the environment only in relation to this one thing. After all, environmental analysis must reduce "everything" to measures of "anything" available for measurement (like temperature levels, gas concentrations, molecular dispersions, resource variations, or growth rates) to track variations in "something" (like an organism's, a biome's, or a river's responses to these factors). But is it "the environment" that is being understood here, or is its identity being evaded in reducing it to a subset of practicable measurements? Does this vision of "environment" really capture the actual quality or true quantity of all human beings' interrelations with all of the terrains, waters, climates, soils, architectures, technologies, societies, economies, cultures, or states surrounding them? In its most expansive applications, then, the environment becomes a strong but sloppy force: it is anything out there, everything around us, something affecting us, nothing within us, but also a thing upon which we act. Despite its formal definitions, however, the environment is not, in fact, everything. Many environmental discourses look instead at *particular* sites or at *peculiar* forces. The discursive variations and conceptual confrontations of the "environment" really begin to explode when different voices accentuate this or that set of things in forming their environmental analysis. On the one side, they may privilege forces in the ecosphere, or, on the other side, they might stress concerns from the technosphere. But in either case, each rhetoric which operates as an agency protecting "the environment" struggles to site "the environmental" as a somewhere affected by or coming from everything.

Perhaps the early origins of "the environment" as a concept—its historical emergence and original applications—might prove more helpful. In its original sense, which is borrowed by English from Old French, an environment is an action resulting from, or the state of being produced by a verb: "to environ." And environing as a verb is, in fact, a type of strategic action. To environ is to encircle, encompass, envelop, or enclose. It is the physical activity of surrounding, circumscribing, or ringing around something. Its uses even suggest stationing guards around, thronging with hostile intent, or standing watch over some person or place. To environ a site or a subject is to beset, beleaguer, or besiege that place or person.

An environment, as either the means of such activity or the product of these actions, now might be read in a more suggestive manner. It is the encirclement, circumscription, or beleaguerment of places and persons in a strategic disciplinary policing of space. An environmental act, in turn, is already a disciplining move, aimed at constructing some expanse of space—a locale, a biome, a planet as biospherical space, or, on the other hand, some city, any region, the global economy in technospherical territory—in a discursive envelope. Within these enclosures, environmental expertise can arm environmentalists who stand watch over these surroundings, guarding the rings that include or exclude forces, agents, and ideas.

If one thinks about it, this original use of "the environment" is an accurate account of what is, in fact, happening in many environmental practices today. Environmentalized places become sites of supervision, where environmentalists see from above and from without through the enveloping designs of administratively delimited systems. Encircled by enclosures of alarm, environments can be disassembled, recombined, and subjected to the disciplinary designs of expert management. Enveloped in these interpretive frames, environments can be redirected to fulfill the ends of other economic scripts, managerial directives, and administrative writs. Environing, then, engenders "environmentality," which embeds instrumental rationalities in the policing of ecological spaces.

3. Environmentality and Governmentality

These reflections on "the environment" reframe its meanings in terms of the practices of power, allowing us to turn to Michel Foucault for additional insight. The bio-power formation described by Foucault was not historically closely focused upon the role of Nature in the equations of biopolitics (Foucault, *History of Sexuality* I 138–42). For Foucault, the whole point of the controlled tactics of inserting human bodies into the machineries of industrial and agricultural production as part and parcel of strategically adjusting the growth of human populations to the development of industrial capitalism was to bring "life and its mechanisms into the realm of explicit calculations," making the disciplines of knowledge and discourses of power into many agencies as part of the "transformation of human life" (143). Once this threshold of bio-power was crossed, human economics, politics, and technologies continually placed all human beings' existence into question.

Foucault notes that these industrial transformations implicitly raised ecological issues as they disrupted and redistributed the understandings provided by the classical episteme of defining human interactions with Nature. Living became "environmentalized," as humans related to their history and biological life in new ways from within growing artificial cities and mechanical modes of production, which positioned this new form of human being "at the same time outside history, in its biological environment, and inside human historicity, penetrated by the latter's techniques of knowledge and power" (143). Here we can begin to locate the emergence of "the environment" as a nexus for knowledge formation and as a cluster of power tactics. As human beings began to consciously wager their life as a species on the outcomes of these biopolitical strategies and technological systems, it became clear that they also were wagering the lives of other (or all) species as well. While Foucault regards this shift as one of many lacunae in his analysis, it is clear there is much more going on here than he realizes. Once human power/knowledge formations become the foundation of industrial society's economic development, they also become the basis for the physical survival of all terrestrial life forms. Here, ecological analysis emerges as a productive power formation that reinvests human bodies—their means of health, modes of subsistence, and styles of habitation integrating the whole space of existence—with bio-historical significance by framing them within their various bio-physical environments filled with various animal and plant bodies.

Foucault can be read as dividing the environment into two separate, but interpenetrating spheres of action: the biological and the historical. For most of human history, the biological dimension, or forces of Nature working in the forms of disease and famine, dominated human existence with the ever-present menace of death. Developments in agricultural technologies as well as in hygiene and health techniques, however, gradually provided some relief from starvation and plague by the end of the eighteenth century. As a result, the historical dimension began to grow in importance as "the development of the different fields of knowledge concerned with life in general, the improvement of agricultural techniques, and the observations and measures relative to man's life and survival" averted some of the imminent risks of death (142). In other words, "the historical" starts to envelop, circumscribe, and surround "the biological." Hence, environmentalized settings emerged "in the space of movement thus conquered, and broadening and organizing that space, methods of power and knowledge assumed responsibility for the life processes and undertook to control and modify them" (142). While he does not explicitly define these spaces, methods, and knowledges as such as being "environmental," it appears that such maneuvers were crucial to the emergence of environmentalization. As biological existence was refracted through economic, political, and technological existence, "the facts of life" passed into fields of control for eco-knowledge and spheres of intervention for geo-power.

Environments then emerged with bio-power as part and parcel of the regulation of life via biopolitics, and, for nearly a century, ecology apparently remained another ancillary correlate of bio-power, inhabiting discourses about species extinction, resource conservation, and overpopulation. Until the productive regime of biopolitics became fully globalized (because Nature itself is not entirely encircled), ecology was a fairly minor voice in the disciplinary chorus organizing development and growth. Things changed, however, once the extensive expansionist strategies of development and growth employed in the eighteenth and nineteenth centuries collapsed around 1914, promoting conservationist ethics in Europe and North America that fretted over conserving resources for resource-driven intensive modes of production. And, as new mediations of development and growth were constructed after 1945, the geo-power/eco-knowledge nexus of environmentalization came to comfortably supplement the high technology, capital intensive development strategies that have since been implemented.

Thus, the environment, if one follows Foucault's line of reasoning (105–06), must not be understood as the naturally given sphere of ecological processes which human powers try to keep under control, nor should it be viewed as a mysterious domain of obscure terrestrial events which human knowledge works to explain. Instead, it emerges as a historical artifact that is openly constructed, not an occluded reality that is difficult to comprehend. In this great network, the simulation of spaces, the intensification of resources, the incitement of discoveries, the formation of special knowledges, the strengthening of controls, and the provocation of resistances can all be linked to one another.

The immanent designs of Nature, when and where they are "discovered" in environments, closely parallel the arts of government. One might ask if the two are not inseparable in geo-power/eco-knowledge systems. As Foucault sees the arts of government, they essentially are concerned with how to introduce economy into the political practices of the state. Government becomes in the eighteenth century the designation of a "level of reality, a field of intervention, through a series of complex processes" in which "government is the right disposition of things" ("Governmentality" 93). Governmentality applies techniques of instrumental rationality to the arts of everyday management. It evolves as an elaborate social formation, or "a triangle, sovereignty-discipline-government, which has as its primary target the population and as its essential mechanism the apparatuses of security" (102).

Most significantly, Foucault sees rulers and authorities mobilizing governmentality to bring about "the emergence of population as a datum, as a field of intervention and as an objective of governmental techniques" (102) so that now "the population is the object that government must take into account in all its observations and *savoir*, in order to be able to govern effectively in a rational and conscious manner" (100). The networks of continuous, multiple, and complex interaction between populations (their increase, longevity, health), territory (its expanse, resources, control), and wealth (its creation, productivity, distribution) are sites of governmentalizing rationality to manage the productive interaction of these forces.

Foucault invites social theorists not to reduce all ensembles of modernizing development to the "statalization" of society wherein "the state" becomes an expansive set of managerial functions, discharging its effects in the development of productive forces, the reproduction of relations of production, or the organization of ideological superstructures. Instead he argues in favor of investigating the "governmentalization" of the economy and society whereby individuals and groups are enmeshed within the tactics and strategies of a complex form of power whose institutions, procedures, analyses, and techniques loosely manage mass populations and their surroundings in a highly politicized symbolic and material economy (103). Because governmental techniques are the central focus of political struggle and contestation, the interactions of populations with their natural surroundings in highly politicized economies compel states constantly to redefine what is within their competence throughout the modernizing process. To survive after the 1960s in a world marked by decolonization, global industrialization, and nuclear military confrontation, it is not enough for states merely to maintain legal jurisdiction over their allegedly sovereign territories. As ecological limits to growth are either discovered or defined, states are forced to guarantee their populations' fecundity and productivity in the total setting of the global political economy by becoming "environmental protection agencies."

Governmental discourses methodically mobilize particular assumptions, codes, and procedures in enforcing specific understandings about the economy and society. As a result, they generate "truths" or "knowledges" that also constitute forms of power with significant reserves of legitimacy and effectiveness. Inasmuch as they classify, organize, and vet larger understandings of reality, such discourses can authorize or invalidate the possibilities for constructing particular institutions, practices, or concepts in society at large. They simultaneously frame the emergence of collective subjectivities (nations as dynamic populations) and collections of subjects (individuals) as units in such nations. Individual subjects as well as collective subjects can be reevaluated as "the element in which are articulated the effects of a certain type of power and the reference of a certain type of knowledge, the machinery by which the power relations give rise to a possible corpus of knowledge, and knowledge extends and reinforces the effects of this power" (Foucault, *Discipline and Punish* 29). Therefore, an environmentalizing regime must advance eco-knowledges to activate its command over geo-power as well as to re-operationalize many of its notions of governmentality as environmentality. Like governmentality, the disciplinary articulations of environmentality must center upon establishing and enforcing "the right disposition of things."

4. Green Governmentality as Resource Managerialism

The script of environmentality embedded in new notions like "the environment" is rarely made articulate in scientific and technical discourses. Yet, there are politics in these scripts. The advocates of deep ecology and social ecology dimly perceive this in their frustrations with "reform environmentalism," which weaves its logics of geo-power in and out of the resource managerialism that has defined the mainstream of contemporary environmental protection thinking and traditional natural resource conservationism (Luke, "Green Consumerism"). Resource managerialism can be read as the eco-knowledge of modern governmentality. While voices in favor of conservation can be found in Europe early in the nineteenth century, the real establishment of this stance comes in the United States with the Second Industrial Revolution from the 1880s through the 1920s and the closing of the Western Frontier in the 1890s (Noble). Whether one looks at John Muir's preservationist programs or Gifford Pinchot's conservationist codes, an awareness of modern industry's power to deplete natural resources, and hence the need for systems of conservation, is well established by the early 1900s (Nash, *Wilderness*). President Theodore Roosevelt, for example, organized the Governor's Conference in 1907 to address this concern, inviting the participants to recognize that the natural endowments upon which "the welfare of this nation rests are becoming depleted, and in not a few cases, are already exhausted" (Jarrett 51).

Over the past nine decades, the fundamental premises of resource managerialism have not changed significantly. In fact, this code of eco-knowledge has only become more formalized in bureaucratic applications and legal interpretations. Paralleling the managerial logic of the Second Industrial Revolution, which empowered technical experts on the shop floor and professional managers in the main office, resource managerialism imposes corporate administrative frameworks upon Nature in order to supply the economy and provision society through centralized state guidance. These frameworks assume that the national economy, like the interacting capitalist firm and household, must avoid both overproduction (excessive resource use coupled with inadequate demand) and underproduction (inefficient resource use in the face of excessive demand) on the supply side as well as overconsumption (excessive resource exploitation with excessive demand) and underconsumption (inefficient resource exploitation coupled with inadequate demand) on the demand side.

To even construct the managerial problem in this fashion, Nature must be reduced—through the encirclement of space and matter by national as well as global economies—to a cybernetic system of biophysical systems that can be dismantled, redesigned, and assembled anew to produce "resources" efficiently and in adequate amounts when and where needed in the modern market-place. In turn, Nature's energies, materials, and sites are redefined by the eco-knowledges of resource managerialism as the source of "goods" for sizable numbers of some people, even though greater material and immaterial "bads" also might be inflicted upon even larger numbers of other people who do not reside in or benefit from the advanced national economies that basically monopolize the use of world resources at a comparative handful of highly developed regional and municipal sites. Many of these eco-knowledge assumptions and geo-power commitments can be seen at work in the discourses of the Worldwatch Institute as it develops its own unique vision of environmentality for a global resource managerialism.

5. New Power/Knowledge

The Worldwatch Institute provides a curious instantiation of how regimes of environmentality might be seen at work in the processes of developing a geo-power/eco-knowledge formation. Taking the world as one ecological site, the Worldwatch Institute aptly typifies a green power/knowledge center in the play of current-day environmental politics. Seeing the path of untrammeled industrial development as the cause of environmental crises, a recent Worldwatch Institute book by Brown, Flavin, and Postel attributes the prevailing popular faith in material growth to "a narrow economic view of the world" (21). Any sense of constraint on further growth is cast by economics "in terms of inadequate demand growth rather than limits imposed by the earth's resources" (22). Ecologists, however, study the allegedly complex changing relationships of organisms with their environments, and, for them, "growth is confined by the parameters of the biosphere" (22). For Brown, Flavin, and Postel, economists ironically regard ecologists' concerns as "a minor subdiscipline of economics—to be 'internalized' in economic models and dealt with at the margins of economic planning," while "to an ecologist, the economy is a narrow subset of the global ecosystem" (23). To end this schism, the Worldwatch Institute pushes for melding ecology with economics to infuse environmental studies with economic instrumental rationality and defuse economics with ecological systems reasoning. Once this is done, the roots of economic growth no longer can be divorced from "the natural systems and resources from which they ultimately derive," and any economic process that "undermines the global ecosystem cannot continue indefinitely" (23).

With this rhetorical maneuver, the Worldwatch Institute articulates its vision of geo-power/eco-knowledge as the instrumental rationality of resource managerialism working on a global scale. Nature, now reinterpreted as a cybernetic system of biophysical systems, reappears among nation-states in those "four biological systems—forests, grasslands, fisheries, and croplands—which supply all of our food and much of the raw materials for industry, with the notable exceptions of fossil fuels and minerals" (Brown, Flavin, and Postel 73). As a result, the performance of these systems might be monitored in analytical spreadsheets written in bioeconomic terms, and then judged in equations balancing increased human population and highly constrained base ecosystem outputs. When looking at these four systems, one must recognize that Nature is merely a system of energy-conversion systems:

> Each of these systems is fueled by photosynthesis, the process by which plants use solar energy to combine water and carbon dioxide to form carbohydrates. Indeed, this process for converting solar energy into biochemical energy supports all life on earth, including the 5.4 billion members of our species. Unless we manage these basic biological systems more intelligently than we now are, the earth will never meet the basic needs of 8 billion people.
>
> Photosynthesis is the common currency of biological systems, the yardstick by which their output can be aggregated and changes in their productivity measured. Although the estimated 41 percent of photosynthetic activity that takes place in the oceans supplies us with seafood, it is the 59 percent occurring on land that supports the world economy. And it is the loss of terrestrial photosynthesis as a result of environmental degradation that is undermining many national economies. (73–74)

Photosynthetic energy generation and accumulation, then, is to become the accounting standard for submitting such geo-power to environmentalizing discipline. It imposes upper limits on economic expansion; the earth is only so large. The 41 percent that is aquatic and marine as well as the 59 percent that is terrestrial are actually decreasing in magnitude and efficiency due to "environmental degradation." Partly localized within many national territories and partly globalized as transboundary pollution, the system of systems needs global management—a powerful, all-knowing world watch—to mind its environmental resources.

Such requirements arise from the convergence of dangerous trends identified by such bioeconomic accounting:

> 40 percent of the earth's annual net primary production on land now goes directly to meet human needs or is indirectly used or destroyed by human activity—leaving 60 percent for the millions of other land-based species with which humans share the planet. While it took all of human history to reach this point, the share could double to 80 percent by 2030 if current rates of population growth continue; rising per capita consumption could shorten the doubling time considerably. Along the way, with people usurping an ever larger share of the earth's life-sustaining energy, natural systems will unravel faster. (74)

To avoid this collapse, human beings must stop increasing their numbers so rapidly, halt increasingly resource-intensive modes of production, and limit increasing levels of material consumption. All of these ends require a measure of surveillance and degree of steering beyond the modern nation-state, but perhaps *not* beyond some postmodern worldwatch engaged in the disciplinary tasks of equilibrating the "net primary production" of solar energy fixed by photosynthesis in the four systems. Natural resources in the total solar economy of food stocks, fisheries, forest preserves, and grass lands are rhetorically ripped from Nature only to be returned as environmental resources, enveloped in accounting procedures and encircled by managerial programs. Worldwatching presumes to know all of this, and in knowing it, to have mastered all of its economic/ecological implications through authoritative technical analysis. By questioning the old truth regime of mere economic growth, a new regime of truth for attaining sophisticated ecological economy stands ready to reintegrate human production and consumption in the four biological systems.

The Worldwatch Institute writers here are engaged in a

struggle "for truth" in economic and environmental discourse. By simultaneously framing economics with the bad rap of growth fetishism and twinning ecology with the high purpose of documenting environmental interconnectedness, the Worldwatchers are striving to transform fields of knowledge as bands of power. Inasmuch as today's decentered networks of power operate through relations of truth "linked in a circular relation with systems of power which produce and sustain it, and to effects of power it induces and which extend it" (Foucault, *History of Sexuality* I 144), these discursive alterations are the requisite moves for prevailing in a disciplinary struggle for discursive authority. By shifting the authorizing legitimacy of truth claims used in policy analysis away from *economic* terms to *ecological* terms (as they are cast in these thermodynamic allusions), the Worldwatch Institute's experts are working to reframe the power/knowledge systems of advanced capitalist societies.

6. The Environment as Disciplinary Space

No longer Nature nor even ecosystem, the world under this kind of watch is truly becoming "an environment," ringed by many eco-knowledge centers dedicated to the rational eco-management of its geo-powers. Being "an environmentalist" quickly becomes a power expression of the eco-knowledge formations of environmentality in which the geo-powers of the global ecosystem can be mobilized through the disciplinary codes of green operational planning. The health of global populations as well as the survival of the planet itself allegedly necessitate that a bioeconomic spreadsheet be draped over Nature, generating an elaborate set of accounts for a terrestrial eco-economy of global reach and scope. Hovering over the world in a scientifically centered surveillance machine built out of the disciplinary grids of efficiency and waste, health and disease, poverty and wealth as well as employment and unemployment discourses, Brown, Flavin, and Postel declare "the once separate issues of environment and development are now inextricably linked" (25). Indeed, they are in the discourses of Worldwatch Institute as its organizational expertise surveys Nature-in-crisis by auditing levels of topsoil depletion, air pollution, acid rain, global warming, ozone destruction, water pollution, forest reduction, and species extinction.

Environmentality, then, would govern by restructuring to-day's ecologically unsound society through elaborate managerial designs to realize tomorrow's environmentally sustainable econ-omy. The shape of an environmental economy would emerge from a reengineered economy of environmentalizing shapes vetted by worldwatching codes. The individual human subject of today, and all of his or her unsustainable practices, would be reshaped through this environmentality, redirected by practices, discourses, and ensembles of administration that more efficiently synchronize the bio-powers of populations with the geo-powers of environ-ments. Traditional codes defining human identity and difference would be reframed by systems of environmentality in new equa-tions for making comprehensive global sustainability calculations as the bio-power of populations merges with the ecopower of envi-ronments. To police global carrying capacity, in turn, this environ-mentalizing logic bids each human subject to assume the much less capacious carriage of disciplinary frugality instead of affluent sub-urban consumerism. All of the world will come under watch, and the global watch will police its human charges to dispose of their things and arrange their ends—in reengineered spaces using new energies at new jobs and leisures—around these environing agendas.

Sustainability, however, cuts both ways. On the one hand, it can articulate a rationale for preserving Nature's biotic diversity in order to maintain the sustainability of the biosphere. But, on the other hand, it also can represent an effort to reinforce the prevail-ing order of capitalistic development by transforming sustainabil-ity into an economic project. To the degree that modern subjectiv-ity is a two-sided power/knowledge relation, scientific-professional declarations about sustainability essentially describe a new mode of environmentalized subjectivity. In becoming enmeshed in a worldwatched environ, the individual subject of a sustainable soci-ety could become simultaneously "subject to someone else by con-trol and dependence," where environmentalizing global and local state agencies enforce their codes of sustainability, and police a self-directed ecological subject "tied to his own identity by a conscience or self-knowledge" (Foucault, "Afterword" 12). In both manifestations, the truth regime of ecological sustainability draws up criteria for what sort of "selfness" will be privileged with political identity and social self-knowledge.

Sustainability, like sexuality, becomes a discourse about exerting power over life. How power might "invest life through and through" (Foucault, *History of Sexuality* I 139) becomes a new challenge, once biopolitical relations are established as environmentalized systems. Moreover, sustainability more or less presumes that some level of material and cultural existence has been attained that is indeed worth sustaining. This formation, then, constitutes "a new distribution of pleasures, discourses, truths, and powers; it has to be seen as the self-affirmation of one class rather than the enslavement of another: a defense, a protection, a strengthening, and an exaltation . . . as a means of social control and political subjugation" (123).

The global bio-accounting systems of the Worldwatch Institute conceptually and practically exemplify the project of environmentality with their rhetorics of scientific surveillance. How Nature should be governed is not a purely administrative question turning upon the technicalities of scientific "know-how." Rather, it is essentially and inescapably political. The discourses of Worldwatching that rhetorically construct Nature also assign powers to new global governors and governments, who are granted writs of authority and made centers of organization in the Worldwatchers' environmentalized specifications of managerial "who-can" and political "how-to."

7. Instituting a Worldwatch: The Eco-Panopticon

Not surprisingly, then, the various power/knowledge systems of instituting a Worldwatch environmentality appear to be a practical materialization of panoptic power. The Worldwatch Institute continually couches its narratives in visual terms, alluding to its mission as outlining "an ecologically defined vision" of "how an environmentally sustainable society would look" in a new "vision of a global economy." As Foucault claims, "whenever one is dealing with a multiplicity of individuals on whom a particular form of behavior must be imposed, the panoptic schema may be used"

(*Discipline and Punish* 205) because it enables a knowing center to reorganize the disposition of things and redirect the convenient ends of individuals in environmentalized spaces. As organisms operating in the energy exchanges of photosynthesis, human beings can become environed on all sides by the cybernetic system of biophysical systems composing Nature.

Worldwatching, in turn, refixes the moral specification of human roles and responsibilities in the enclosed spaces and segmented places of ecosystemic niches. And, in generating this knowledge of environmental impact by applying such powers of ecological observation, the institutions of Worldwatch operate as a green panopticon, enclosing Nature in rings of centered normalizing super-vision where an eco-knowledge system identifies Nature as "the environment." The notational calculus of bioeconomic accounting not only can, but in fact must reequilibrate individuals and species, energy and matter, inefficiencies and inequities in an integrated panel of globalized observation. The supervisory gaze of normalizing control, embedded in the Worldwatch Institute's panoptic practices, adduces "the environmental," or enclosed, segmented spaces, "observed at every point, in which the individuals are inserted in a fixed place, in which the slightest movements are supervised, in which all events are recorded, in which an uninterrupted work of writing links the centre and periphery, in which power is exercised without division, according to a continuous hierarchical figure, in which each individual is constantly located, examined, and distributed among the living beings, the sick and the dead" (Foucault, *Discipline and Punish* 197). To save the planet, it becomes necessary to environmentalize it, enveloping its system of systems in new disciplinary discourses to regulate population growth, economic development, and resource exploitation on a global scale with continual managerial intervention.

Many contemporary environmental movements, particularly those inspired by the Worldwatch Institute's analyses, push governmentality to a global rather than a national level of control. The biosphere, atmosphere, and ecosphere are all reintegrated into the truth regime of political economy to serve more ecological ends, but they are also made to run along new economic tracks above and beyond the territorial spaces created by nation-states. By touting the necessity of recalibrating society's logics of governmentality in new spatial registers at the local and global level, the geo-power politics of environmentality aim to rewrite the geographies of national stratified space with new mappings of bioregional economies knitted into global ecologies—complete with environmentalized zones of "dying forests," "regional desertification," "endangered bays," or "depleted farmland."

If Foucault's representation of governmentality accounts for the practices of power mobilized by centered national sovereigns in the era of capitalist modernization and national state-building after 1648, the Worldwatch Institute's approach to environmentality perhaps foreshadows the practices of power being adduced by multicentric alliances of transnational capital or loose coalitions of highly fragmented local sovereignties, following the collapse of the old Cold War competitions in the early 1990s. New spatial domains are being created in the world today, on the one hand, by pollution, nuclear contamination, and widespread rapid deforestation, and, on the other, by telecommunications, jet transportation, and cheap accessible computerization. Nation-states are not answering effectively the challenges posed within their borders by these new spaces. But a variety of new organizations in the contemporary environmental movement (Luke, "Ecological Politics"), like the Worldwatch Institute, Earth First!, The World Wildlife Federation, or Greenpeace, at least are addressing, if not answering, how these spaces are developing, what impact they have in today's political economy, and who should act to respond to the challenge. In the bargain, they also are interposing their own environmentalizing conceptual maps, technical disciplines, and organizational orders on these spaces as they urge local citizen's groups or global supranational agencies to move beyond the constraints imposed by national sovereignty to construct new sustainable spaces for human habitation.

The cybernetic system of biophysical systems, once known as Nature, has now been reduced to "the environment," so that it might be remapped to police the provinces of photosynthesis and bind the borders of bioeconomics which these spaces constitute. Logics of sovereignty, imposing military-administrative jurisdiction over bits and pieces of these global systems in irrationally drawn territories through governmentality, must be supplanted by larger logics of environmentality. As Fredric Jameson notes, if these changes can be understood as the historical expression of what is regarded as "postmodern," then this postmodernity must be confronted "since the modernization process is complete and Nature is gone for good" (ix). That is, where the times of modernity end, the spaces of environmentality perhaps begin.

Of course, it is possible to define the environment in codes that are not entirely wound up within the power/knowledge regime of technoscience, like those of the Worldwatch Institute. In their own ways, the discourses of many Earth First! activists, some ecofeminist writers, and a few deep ecology thinkers are working to develop understandings of Nature that stand outside of the bio-economic accounting standards used by so many mainstream environmental organizations and quite a few radical ecology groups (see Fox; Devall and Sessions; and Nash, *Wilderness*). These alternative discursive frameworks, however, tend to exclude such voices from any effective participation in policy-making (Luke, "Dreams of Deep Ecology"). And, even when some token access might be granted to the members of these movements for registering some policy-related input, their discursive understandings are either pardoned as metaphysical excess or translated into latent policy-relevant prescriptions. Otherwise, the dominant regime of power/knowledge expects its critics, even fairly effective ones like those in the Worldwatch Institute, to accept the technoscientific codes of bureaucratic address which drive environmentality.

In many ways, these contemporary maneuvers to construct an eco-panopticon which re-envisions Nature by environmentalizing its workings as a system of systems can be traced back to the power/knowledge provided in a photographic image (captured initially by the Apollo 8 astronauts) of the Earth in space as it was seen from a NASA spacecraft traveling to the Moon. From its popularization in the 1960s to its banalization in the 1990s, many have put the image to pernicious uses. The dust jacket of another worldwatching manifesto, *Earth in the Balance: Ecology and the Human Spirit* (1992) by Vice President Al Gore, continues this practice with its iconic presentation of a composite photograph of a cloudless earth reduced to crystalline perfection by digital photography. Inside the book, Gore walks down many of the Worldwatch Institute's paths in touting the merits of an "eco-nomics" to underpin his visions for a Global Marshall Plan to save "the environment" with carefully targeted Strategic Environmental Initiatives operated by post–Cold War Washington bureaucracies. Framing the planet in computer-controlled photography serves as his rhetorical pretext for saving the planet through the operations of the green power/knowledge of Gore's "eco-nomic" environmentality.

The pretense of human agency actually engaging in some sort of worldwatch becomes a credible possibility, technologically and administratively, only with this image. Technological power is now so great that even Nature can be reduced to an eco-panoptic snapshot. Armed with the first photos of the earth in space, many people began rethinking their foundational images of the planet in the late 1960s. As the Earth was enveloped for the first time in photography, bringing it under control, into focus, and within reach for ordinary human beings, mythologies changed. For some, the image conveyed the precious fragility of a tiny planet in the immense cosmos. For others, it provided a compelling representation of the world's biggest managerial challenge—generating geo-power via eco-knowledge. Humanity's role must become one of watching over or policing all of the natural systems at work in the skies, oceans, and continents depicted by such photographs as encircled manageable space. Once one can watch the world in eco-panoptic videotapes and photographs, the worldwatching project begins, turning photographic images into political practices and ideological ideals aimed at environing Nature by disciplining its spaces.

Note

A preliminary version of this paper was prepared for the annual meeting of the Society for Human Ecology, April 22–23, 1994, at Michigan State University in East Lansing, Michigan, and some passages of it appear in *Telos* 97 (1993) and *Capitalism Nature Socialism* 18 (1994).

Works Cited

Bramwell, Anna. *Ecology in the 20th Century: A History.* New Haven: Yale UP, 1989.
Brown, Lester, Christopher Flavin, and Sandra Postel. *Saving the Planet: How to Shape an Environmentally Sustainable Global Economy.* New York: Norton, 1991.

Buchholz, Rogene. *Principles in Environmental Management: The Greening of Business.* Englewood Cliffs: Prentice-Hall, 1993.

Carson, Rachel. *Silent Spring.* Boston: Houghton Mifflin, 1962.

Commoner, Barry. *Making Peace with the Planet.* New York: Pantheon, 1990.

———. *The Closing Circle: Nature, Man and Technology.* New York: Knopf, 1971.

Devall, Bill, and George Sessions. *Deep Ecology: Living as if Nature Mattered.* Salt Lake City: Peregrine Smith, 1985.

Eckersley, Robyn. *Environmentalism and Political Theory: Toward an Ecocentric Approach.* Albany: SUNY P, 1992.

Foucault, Michel. "Afterword: The Subject and Power." *Michel Foucault: Beyond Structuralism and Hermeneutics.* 2nd ed. Ed. Hubert L. Dreyfus and Paul Rabinow. Chicago: U of Chicago P, 1982. 208–26.

———. *Discipline and Punish: The Birth of the Prison.* Trans. Alan Sheridan. New York: Vintage, 1979.

———. "Governmentality." *The Foucault Effect: Studies in Governmentality.* Ed. Graham Burchell, Colin Gordon, and Peter Miller. Chicago: U of Chicago P, 1991. 87–104.

———. *The History of Sexuality, Vol. I: An Introduction.* Trans. Robert Hurley. New York: Vintage, 1980.

Fox, Warwick. *Toward a Transpersonal Ecology: Developing New Foundations for Environmentalism.* Boston: Shambhala, 1990.

Gore, Al. *Earth in the Balance: Ecology and the Human Spirit.* Houghton Mifflin, 1992.

Haeckel, Ernst. *Generalle Morphologie der Organismen.* Berlin: Reimer, 1866.

Jameson, Fredric. *Postmodernism, or, The Cultural Logic of Late Capitalism.* Durham: Duke UP, 1991.

Jarrett, Henry, ed. *Perspectives on Conservation: Essays on America's Natural Resources.* Baltimore: Resources for the Future, 1958.

Luke, Timothy W. "The Dreams of Deep Ecology." *Telos* 78 (1988): 65–92.

———. "Ecological Politics and Local Struggles: Earth First! as an Environmental Resistance Movement." *Current Perspectives in Social Theory* 14 (1994): 241–67.

———. "Green Consumerism: Ecology and the Rise of Recycling." *The Nature of Things: Language, Politics and the Environment.* Ed. Jane Bennett and William Chaloupka. Minneapolis: U of Minnesota P, 1993. 154–72.

Marsh, George. *The Earth as Modified by Human Action.* New York: Scribner's, 1985.

Nash, Roderick. *The Rights of Nature: A History of Environmental Ethics.* Madison: U of Wisconsin P, 1989.

———. *Wilderness and the American Mind.* 3rd ed. New Haven: Yale UP, 1982.

Nebel, Bernard J. *Environmental Science: The Way the World Works.* 3rd ed. Englewood Cliffs: Prentice-Hall, 1990.

Noble, David. *America by Design: Science, Technology and the Rise of Corporate Capitalism.* New York: Knopf, 1977.

Oelschlaeger, Max. *The Idea of Wilderness: From Prehistory to the Age of Ecology.* New Haven: Yale UP, 1991.

Paehlke, Robert. *Environmentalism and the Future of Progressive Politics.* New Haven: Yale UP, 1989.

ReVelle, Penelope, and Charles ReVelle. *The Environment: Issues and Choices.* Boston: Jones and Bartlett, 1988.

Worster, Donald. *Nature's Economy: The Roots of Ecology.* Garden City: Anchor Books, 1977.

The Autonomy of Affect

Brian Massumi

I

A man builds a snowman on his roof garden. It starts to melt
in the afternoon sun. He watches. After a time, he takes the
snowman to the cool of the mountains, where it stops melting.
He bids it good-bye, and leaves.

Just images, no words, very simple. It was a story depicted in a
short shown on German TV as a fill-in between programs. The
film drew complaints from parents reporting that their children
had been frightened. That drew the attention of a team of researchers. Their study was notable for failing to find much of what
it was studying: cognition.

Researchers, headed by Hertha Sturm, used three versions of
the film: the original wordless version and two versions with voice-
overs added. The first voice-over version was dubbed "factual." It
added a simple step-by-step account of the action as it happened.
A second version was called "emotional." It was largely the same as
the "factual" version, but included at crucial turning points words
expressing the emotional tenor of the scene under way.

Sets of nine-year-old children were tested for recall and asked to rate the version they saw on a scale of "pleasantness." The factual version was consistently rated the least pleasant and was also the worst remembered. The most pleasant was the original wordless version, which was rated just slightly above the emotional. And it was the emotional version that was best remembered.

This is already a bit muddling. Something stranger happened when the subjects of the study were asked to rate the individual scenes in the film simultaneously on a "happy-sad" scale and a "pleasant-unpleasant" scale. The "sad" scenes were rated the *most pleasant*, the sadder the better.

The hypothesis that immediately suggests itself is that in some kind of precocious anti-Freudian protest, the children were equating arousal with pleasure. But this being an empirical study, the children were wired. Their physiological reactions were monitored. The factual version elicited the highest level of arousal, even though it was the most unpleasant (i.e., happy) and made the least long-lasting impression. The children, it turns out, were physiologically split: factuality made their heart beat faster and deepened their breathing, but it made their skin resistance fall. The original nonverbal version elicited the greatest response from their skin. Galvanic skin response measures *autonomic* reaction.

From the tone of their report, it seems that the researchers were a bit taken aback by their results. They contented themselves with observing that the difference between sadness and happiness is not all that it's cracked up to be, and worrying that the difference between children and adults was also not all that it was cracked up to be (judging by studies of adult retention of news broadcasts). Their only positive conclusion was *the primacy of the affective* in image reception (Sturm 25–37).

Accepting and expanding upon that, it could be noted that the primacy of the affective is marked by a gap between *content* and *effect*: it would appear that the strength or duration of an image's effect is not logically connected to the content in any straightforward way. This is not to say that there is no connection and no logic. What is meant here by the content of the image is its indexing to conventional meanings in an intersubjective context, its socio-linguistic qualification. This indexing fixes the *quality* of the image; the strength or duration of the image's effect could be

called its *intensity*. What comes out here is that there is no correspondence or conformity between quality and intensity. If there is
a relation, it is of another nature.

To translate this negative observation into a positive one: the
event of image reception is multi-leveled, or at least bi-level. There
is an immediate bifurcation in response into two seemingly autonomous systems. One, the level of intensity, is characterized by a
crossing of semantic wires: on it, sadness is pleasant. The level of
intensity is organized according to a logic that does not admit of
the excluded middle. This is to say that it is not semantically or
semiotically ordered. It does not fix distinctions. Instead, it vaguely
but insistently connects what is normally indexed as separate.
When asked to signify itself, it can only do so in a paradox. There
is disconnection of signifying order from intensity—which constitutes a different order of connection operating in parallel. The gap
noted earlier is not only between content and effect. It is also between the form of content—signification as a conventional system
of distinctive difference—and intensity. The disconnection betwen
form/content and intensity/effect is not just negative: it enables a
different connectivity, a different difference, in parallel.

Both levels, qualification and intensity, are immediately embodied. Intensity is embodied in purely autonomic reactions most
directly manifested in the skin—at the surface of the body, at its
interface with things. Depth reactions belong more to the form/
content (qualification) level, even though they also involve autonomic functions such as heartbeat and breathing. The reason may
be that they are associated with expectation, which depends on
consciously positioning oneself in a line of narrative continuity.
Modulations of heartbeat and breathing mark a reflux of consciousness into the autonomic depths, coterminous with a rise of
the autonomic into consciousness. They are a conscious-autonomic
mix, a measure of their participation in one another. Intensity is
beside that loop, a nonconscious, never-to-conscious autonomic remainder. It is outside expectation and adaptation, as disconnected
from meaningful sequencing, from narration, as it is from vital
function. It is narratively de-localized, spreading over the generalized body surface, like a lateral backwash from the function-
meaning interloops traveling the vertical path between head and
heart.

Language, though head-strong, is not simply in opposition to intensity. It would seem to function differentially in relation to it. The factual version of the snowman story was dampening. Matter-of-factness dampens intensity. In this case, matter-of-factness was a doubling of the sequence of images with a narration expressing in as objective a manner as possible the common-sense function and consensual meaning of the movements perceived on screen. This interfered with the images' effect. The emotional version added a few phrases that punctuated the narrative line with qualifications of the emotional content, as opposed to the objective-narrative content. The qualifications of emotional content enhanced the images' effect, as if they resonated with the level of intensity rather than interfering with it. An emotional qualification breaks narrative continuity for a moment to register a state—actually re-register an already felt state (for the skin is faster than the word).

The relationship between the levels of intensity and qualification is not one of conformity or correspondence, but of resonance or interference, amplification or dampening. Linguistic expression can resonate with and amplify intensity at the price of making itself functionally redundant. When on the other hand it doubles a sequence of movements in order to add something to it in the way of meaningful progression—in this case a sense of futurity, expectation, an intimation of what comes next in a conventional progression—then it runs counter to and dampens the intensity. Intensity would seem to be associated with nonlinear processes: resonation and feedback which momentarily suspend the linear progress of the narrative present from past to future. Intensity is qualifiable as an emotional state, and that state is static—temporal and narrative noise. It is a state of suspense, potentially of disruption. It's like a temporal sink, a hole in time, as we conceive of it and narrativize it. It is not exactly passivity, because it is filled with motion, vibratory motion, resonation. And it is not yet activity, because the motion is not of the kind that can be directed (if only symbolically) toward practical ends in a world of constituted objects and aims (if only on screen). Of course the qualification of an emotion is quite often, in other contexts, itself a narrative element that moves the action ahead, taking its place in socially recognized lines of action and reaction. But to the extent that it is, it is not in resonance with intensity. It resonates to the exact degree to which it is in excess of any narrative or functional line.

In any case, language doubles the flow of images, on another level, on a different track. There is a redundancy of resonation that plays up or amplifies (feeds back disconnection, enabling a different connectivity), and a redundancy of signification that plays out or linearizes (jumps the feedback loop between vital function and meaning into lines of socially valorized action and reaction). Language belongs to entirely different orders depending on which redundancy it enacts. Or, it always enacts both more or less completely: two languages, two dimensions of every expression, one superlinear, the other linear. Every event takes place on both levels—and between both levels, as they themselves resonate to form a larger system composed of two interacting subsystems following entirely different rules of formation. For clarity, it might be best to give different names to the two halves of the event. In this case: *suspense* could be distinguished from and interlinked with *expectation*, as superlinear and linear dimensions of the same image-event, which is at the same time an expression-event.

Approaches to the image in its relation to language are incomplete if they operate only on the semantic or semiotic level, however that level is defined (linguistically, logically, narratologically, ideologically, or all of these in combination, as a Symbolic). What they lose, precisely, is the expression *event*—in favor of structure. Much could be gained by integrating the dimension of intensity into cultural theory. The stakes are the new. For structure is the place where nothing ever happens, that explanatory heaven in which all eventual permutations are prefigured in a self-consistent set of invariant generative rules. Nothing is prefigured in the event. It is the collapse of structured distinction into intensity, of rules into paradox. It is the suspension of the invariance that makes happy happy, sad sad, function function, and meaning mean. Could it be that it is through the expectant suspension of that suspense that the new emerges? As if an echo of irreducible excess, of gratuitous amplification, piggy-backed on the reconnection to progression, bringing a tinge of the unexpected, the lateral, the unmotivated, to lines of action and reaction. A change in the rules. The expression-event is the system of the inexplicable: emergence, into and against (re)generation (the re-production of a structure). In the case of the snowman, the unexpected and inexplicable that emerged along with the generated responses had to do with the differences between happiness and sadness, children and adults, not being all they're cracked up to be, much to our scientific chagrin: a change in the rules. Intensity is the unassimilable.

For present purposes, intensity will be equated with affect. There seems to be a growing feeling within media and literary and art theory that affect is central to an understanding of our information- and image-based late-capitalist culture, in which so-called master narratives are perceived to have foundered. Fredric Jameson notwithstanding, belief has waned for many, but not affect. If anything, our condition is characterized by a surfeit of it. The problem is that there is no cultural-theoretical vocabulary specific to affect.[1] Our entire vocabulary has derived from theories of signification that are still wedded to structure even across irreconcilable differences (the divorce proceedings of poststructuralism: terminable or interminable?). In the absence of an asignifying philosophy of affect, it is all too easy for received psychological categories to slip back in, undoing the considerable deconstructive work that has been effectively carried out by poststructuralism. Affect is most often used loosely as a synonym for emotion.[2] But one of the clearest lessons of this first story is that emotion and affect—if affect is intensity—follow different logics and pertain to different orders.

An emotion is a subjective content, the socio-linguistic fixing of the quality of an experience which is from that point onward defined as personal. Emotion is qualified intensity, the conventional, consensual point of insertion of intensity into semantically and semiotically formed progressions, into narrativizable action-reaction circuits, into function and meaning. It is intensity owned and recognized. It is crucial to theorize the difference between affect and emotion. If some have the impression that it has waned, it is because affect is unqualified. As such, it is not ownable or recognizable, and is thus resistant to critique.

It is not that there are no philosophical antecedents to draw on. It is just that they are not the usual ones for cultural theory. Spinoza is a formidable philosophical precursor on many of these points: on the difference in nature between affect and emotion; on the irreducibly bodily and autonomic nature of affect; on affect as a suspension of action-reaction circuits and linear temporality in a sink of what might be called "passion," to distinguish it both from passivity and activity; on the equation between affect and effect; on the form/content of conventional discourse as constituting an autonomous or semi-autonomous stratum running counter to the full registering of affect and its affirmation, its positive development, its expression as and for itself. The title of Spinoza's central work suggests a designation for the project of thinking affect: Ethics.[3]

II

Another story, about the brain: the mystery of the missing half-second.

Experiments were performed on patients who had been implanted with cortical electrodes for medical purposes. Mild electrical pulses were administered to the electrode and also to points on the skin. In either case, the stimulation was felt only if it lasted more than half a second: half a second, the minimum perceivable lapse. If the cortical electrode was fired a half-second before the skin was stimulated, patients reported feeling the skin pulse first. The researcher speculated that sensation involves a "backward referral in time"—in other words, that sensation is organized recursively before being linearized, before it is redirected outwardly to take its part in a conscious chain of actions and reactions. Brain and skin form a resonating vessel. Stimulation turns inward, is folded into the body, except that there is no inside for it to be in, because the body is radically open, absorbing impulses quicker than they can be perceived, and because the entire vibratory event is unconscious, out of mind. Its anomaly is smoothed over retrospectively to fit conscious requirements of continuity and linear causality.[4]

What happens during the missing half second? A second experiment gave some hints.

Brain waves of healthy volunteers were monitored by an electroencephalograph (EEG) machine. The subjects were asked to flex a finger at a moment of their choosing, and to note the time

of their decision on a clock. The flexes came 0.2 seconds after they
clocked the decision. But the EEG machine registered significant
brain activity 0.3 seconds *before* the decision. Again, a half-second
lapse between the beginning of a bodily event and its completion
in an outwardly directed, active expression.

Asked to speculate on what implications all this might have
for a doctrine of free will, the researcher, Benjamin Libet, "proposes that *we may exert free will not by initiating intentions but by vetoing,
acceding or otherwise responding to them after they arise*" (Horgan).

In other words, the half-second is missed not because it is
empty, but because it is overfull, in excess of the actually performed action and of its ascribed meaning. Will and consciousness
are *subtractive*. They are *limitative, derived functions* which reduce a
complexity too rich to be functionally expressed. It should be
noted in particular that during the mysterious half-second, what
we think of as "higher" functions, such as volition, are apparently
being performed by autonomic, bodily reactions occurring in the
brain but outside consciousness, and between brain and finger, but
prior to action and expression. The formation of a volition is necessarily accompanied and aided by cognitive functions. Perhaps
the snowman researchers of the first story couldn't find cognition
because they were looking for it in the wrong place—in the
"mind," rather than in *the body* they were monitoring. Talk of intensity inevitably raises the objection that such a notion inevitably involves an appeal to a pre-reflexive, romantically raw domain of
primitive experiential richness—the nature in our culture. It is not
that. First, because something happening out of mind in a body
directly absorbing its outside cannot exactly said to be experienced. Second, because volition, cognition, and presumably other
"higher" functions usually presumed to be in the mind, figured as
a mysterious container of mental entities that is somehow separate
from body and brain, are present and active in that now not-so-
"raw" domain. Resonation assumes feedback. "Higher functions"
belonging to the realm of qualified form/content, in which identified, self-expressive persons interact in conventionalized action-
reaction circuits following a linear time-line, are fed back into the
realm of intensity and recursive causality. The body doesn't just
absorb pulses or discrete stimulations; it infolds *contexts*, it infolds

volitions and cognitions that are nothing if not situated. Intensity is asocial, but not presocial—it *includes* social elements, but mixes them with elements belonging to other levels of functioning, and combines them according to different logic. How could this be so? Only if the *trace* of past actions *including a trace of their contexts* were conserved in the brain and in the flesh, but out of mind and out of body understood as qualifiable interiorities, active and passive respectively, directive spirit and dumb matter. Only if past actions and contexts were conserved and repeated, autonomically *reactivated*, but not accomplished; begun, but not completed. Intensity is *incipience*, incipient action and expression. Intensity is not only incipience, but the incipience of mutually exclusive pathways of action and expression that are then reduced, inhibited, prevented from actualizing themselves completely—all but one. Since the crowd of pretenders to actualization are tending toward completion in a new context, their incipience cannot just be a conservation and reactivation. They are *tendencies*—in other words, pastnesses opening onto a future, but with no present to speak of. For the present is lost with the missing half-second, passing too quickly to be perceived, too quickly, actually, to have happened.

This requires a complete reworking of how we think about the body. Something that happens too quickly to have happened, actually, is *virtual*. The body is as immediately virtual as it is actual. The virtual, the pressing crowd of incipiencies and tendencies, is a realm of *potential*. In potential is where futurity combines, unmediated, with pastness, where outsides are infolded, and sadness is happy (happy because the press to action and expression is life). The virtual is a lived paradox where what are normally opposites coexist, coalesce, and connect; where what cannot be experienced cannot but be felt—albeit reduced and contained. For out of the pressing crowd an individual action or expression *will* emerge and be registered consciously. One "wills" it to emerge, to be qualified, to take on socio-linguistic meaning, to enter linear action-reaction circuits, to become a content of one's life—by dint of inhibition.

Since the virtual is unlivable even as it happens, it can be thought of as a form of superlinear abstraction that does not obey the law of the excluded middle, that is organized differently but is inseparable from the concrete activity and expressivity of the body.

The body is as immediately abstract as it is concrete; its activity and expressivity extend, as on their underside, into an incorporeal, yet perfectly real, dimension of pressing potential.

It is Bergson who stands as a philosophical precursor on many of these points: on the brain as a center of indetermination; on consciousness as subtractive and inhibitive; on perception as working to infold extended actions and expressions, *and* their situatedness, into a dimension of intensity or *in*tension as opposed to extension; on the continual doubling of the actual body by this dimension of intensity, understood as a superlinear, superabstract realm of potential; on that realm of the virtual as having a different temporal structure, in which past and future brush shoulders with no mediating present, and as having a different, recursive causality; on the virtual as cresting in a liminal realm of emergence, where half-actualized actions and expressions arise like waves on a sea to which most no sooner return.

Bergson could profitably be read together with Spinoza. One of Spinoza's basic definitions of affect is an "affection of (in other words an impingement upon) the body, *and at the same time the idea of the affection*." This starts sounding suspiciously Bergsonian if it is noted that the body, when impinged upon, is described by Spinoza as being in a state of passional suspension in which it exists more outside of itself, more in the abstracted action of the impinging thing and the abstracted context of that action, than within itself; and if it is noted that the idea in question is not only not conscious but is not in the first instance in the "mind."

In Spinoza, it is only when the idea of the affection is doubled by an *idea of the idea of the affection* that it attains the level of conscious reflection. Conscious reflection is a doubling over of the idea on itself, a self-recursion of the idea that enwraps the affection or impingement, at two removes. For it has already been removed once, by the body itself. The body infolds the *effect* of the impingement—it conserves the impingement minus the impinging thing, the impingement abstracted from the actual action that caused it and actual context of that action. This is a first-order idea produced spontaneously by the body: the affection is immediately, spontaneously doubled by the repeatable trace of an encounter, the "form" of an encounter, in Spinoza's terminology (an infolding, or contraction, of context in the vocabulary of this essay). The trace determines a tendency, the potential, if not yet the appetite, for the autonomic repetition and variation of the impingement. Conscious reflection is the doubling over of this dynamic abstraction on itself. The order of connection of such dynamic abstractions among themselves, on a level specific to them, is called mind. The autonomic tendency received second-hand from the body is raised to a higher power to become an activity of the mind. Mind and body are seen as two levels recapitulating the same image/expression event in different but parallel ways, ascending by degrees from the concrete to the incorporeal, holding to the same absent center of a now spectral—and potentialized—encounter. Spinoza's Ethics is the philosophy of the becoming-active, in parallel, of mind and body, from an origin in passion, in impingement, in so pure and productive a receptivity that it can only be conceived as a third state, an excluded middle, prior to the distinction between activity and passivity: affect. This "origin" is never left behind, but doubles one like a shadow that is always almost perceived, and cannot but be perceived, in effect.

In a different but complementary direction, when Spinoza defines mind and body as different orders of connection, or different regimes of motion and rest, his thinking converges in suggestive ways with Bergson's theories of virtuality and movement.

It is Gilles Deleuze who reopened the path to these authors, although nowhere does he patch them directly into each other. His work and theirs could profitably be read together with recent theories of complexity and chaos. It is all a question of *emergence*, which is precisely the focus of the various science-derived theories which converge around the notion of self-organization (the spontaneous production of a level of reality having its own rules of formation and order of connection). Affect or intensity in the present account is akin to what is called a critical point, or a bifurcation point, or singular point, in chaos theory and the theory of dissipative structures. This is the turning point at which a physical system paradoxically embodies multiple and normally mutually exclusive potentials, only one of which is "selected." "Phase space" could be seen as a diagrammatic rendering of the dimension of the virtual. The organization of multiple levels that have different logics and temporal organizations but are locked in resonance with each other and recapitulate the same event in divergent ways, recalls the fractal ontology and nonlinear causality underlying theories of complexity.

The levels at play could be multiplied to infinity: already mentioned are mind and body, but also volition and cognition, at least two orders of language, expectation and suspense, body depth and epidermis, past and future, action and reaction, happiness and sadness, quiescence and arousal, passivity and activity. . . . These could be seen not as binary oppositions or contradictions, but as resonating levels. Affect is their point of emergence, in their actual specificity; and it is their vanishing point, in singularity, in their virtual coexistence and interconnection—that critical point shadowing every image/expression-event. Although the realm of intensity that Deleuze's philosophy strives to conceptualize is transcendental in the sense that it is not directly accessible to experience, it is not transcendent and it is not exactly outside experience either. It is immanent to it—always in it but not of it. Intensity and experience accompany one another, like two mutually presupposing dimensions, or like two sides of a coin. Intensity is immanent to matter and to events, to mind and to body and to every level of bifurcation composing them and which they compose. Thus it also cannot but be experienced, in effect—in the proliferations of levels of organization it ceaselessly gives rise to, generates and regenerates, at every suspended moment. Deleuze's philosophy is the point at which transcendental philosophy flips over into a radical immanentism, and empiricism into ethical experimentation. The Kantian imperative to understand the conditions of possible experience as if from outside and above transposes into an invitation to recapitulate, to repeat and complexify, ground level, the real conditions of emergence, not of the categorical, but of the unclassifiable, the unassimilable, the never-yet felt, the felt for less than half a second, again for the first time—the new. Kant meets Spinoza, where idealism and empiricism turn pragmatic, becoming a midwifery of invention—with no loss in abstractive or inductive power. Quite the contrary—both are heightened. But now abstraction is synonymous with an unleashing of potential, rather than its subtraction. And the sense of induction has changed, to a triggering of a process of complexifying self-organization. The implied ethics of the project is the value attached—without foundation, with desire only—to the multiplication of powers of existence, to ever-divergent regimes of action and expression.

Feedback (Digression)

The work of Gilbert Simondon is an invaluable resource for this kind of project.[5] An example is his treatment of the feedback of atoms of "higher" modes of organization into a level of emergence. He sees this functioning even on the physical level, where "germs" of forms are present in an emergent dimension along with unformed elements such as tropisms (attractors), distributions of potential energy (gradients defining metastabilities), and nonlocalized relations (resonance). According to Simondon, the dimension of the emergent—which he terms the "preindividual"—cannot be understood in terms of form, even if it infolds forms in a germinal state. It can only be analyzed as a continuous but highly differentiated *field* that is "out of phase" with formed entities (has a different topology and causal order from the "individuals" which arise from it and whose forms return to it). A germinal or "implicit" form cannot be understood as a shape or structure. It is more a bundle of potential functions localized, as a differentiated region, within a larger field of potential. The regions are separated from each other by dynamic thresholds rather than by boundaries. Simondon calls these regions of potential "quanta," even as they appear on the macrophysical level, and even on the human level (99) (hence the atomic allusion). Extrapolating a bit, the "regions" are obviously abstract, in the sense that they do not define boundaried spaces, but are rather differentiations within an open field characterized by action at a distance between elements (attractors, gradients, resonation). The limits of the region, and of the entire field (the universe), are defined by the reach of its elements' collective actions at a distance. The limit will not be a sharp demarcation, more like a multidimensional fading to infinity. The field is open in the sense it has no interiority or exteriority: it is limited *and* infinite.

"Implicit" form is a bundling of potential functions, an infolding or contraction of potential interactions (intension). The playing out of those potentials requires an *unfolding* in three-dimensional space and linear time—extension as actualization; actualization as *expression*. It is in expression that the fade-out occurs. *The limits of the field of emergence are in its actual expression.* Implicit form may be thought of as the effective presence of the sum total of a things's interactions, minus the thing. It is a thing's relationality autonomized as a dimension of the real. This *autonomization of relation* is the condition under which "higher" functions feed back. Emergence, once again, is a two-sided coin: one side in the virtual (the autonomy of relation), the other in the actual (functional limitation). What is being termed affect in this essay is precisely this two-sidedness, the simultaneous participation of the virtual in the actual and the actual in the virtual, as one arises from and returns to the other. Affect is this two-sideness *as seen from the side of the actual thing*, as couched in its perceptions and cognitions. Affect is *the virtual as point of view*, provided the visual metaphor is used guardedly. For affect is synaesthetic, implying a participation of the senses in each other: the measure of a living thing's potential interactions is its ability to transform the effects of one sensory mode into those of another (tactility and vision being the most obvious but by no means only examples; interoceptive senses, especially proprioception, are crucial).[6] Affects are *virtual synaesthetic perspectives* anchored in (functionally limited by) the actually existing, particular things that embody them. The *autonomy* of affect is its participation in the virtual. *Its autonomy is its openness.* Affect is autonomous to the degree to which it escapes confinement in the particular body whose vitality, or potential for interaction, it is. Formed, qualified, situated perceptions and cognitions fulfilling functions of actual connection or blockage are the *capture* and closure of affect. Emotion is the intensest (most contracted) expression of that capture—and of the fact that something has always and again escaped. Something remains unactualized, inseparable from but unassimilable to any *particular*, functionally anchored perspective. That is why all emotion is more or less disorienting, and why it is classically described as being outside of oneself, at the very point at which one is most intimately and unshareably in contact with oneself and one's vitality. If there were no escape, no excess or remainder, no fade-out to infinity, the universe would be without potential, pure entropy, death. Actually existing, structured things live in and through that which escapes them. Their autonomy is the autonomy of affect.

The escape of affect *cannot but be perceived, alongside* the perceptions that are its capture. This side-perception may be punctual, localized in an event (such as the sudden realization that happiness and sadness are something besides what they are). When it is punctual, it is usually described in negative terms, typically as a form of *shock* (the sudden interruption of functions of actual connection).[7] But it is also continuous, like a background perception that accompanies every event, however quotidian. When the continuity of affective escape is put into words, it tends to take on positive connotations. For it is nothing less than *the perception of one's own vitality*, one's sense of aliveness, of changeability (often signified as "freedom"). One's "sense of aliveness" is a continuous, nonconscious *self-perception* (unconscious self-reflection). It is the perception of this self-perception, its naming and making conscious, that allows affect to be effectively analyzed—as long as a vocabulary can be found for that which is imperceptible but whose escape from perception cannot but be perceived, as long as one is alive.[8]

Simondon notes the connection between self-reflection and affect. He even extends the capacity for self-reflection to all living things (149)—although it is hard to see why his own analysis does not constrain him to extend it to all *things* (is not resonation a kind of self-reflection?). Spinoza could be read as doing this in his definition of the idea of the affection as a trace—one that is not without reverberations. More radically, he sees ideas as attaining their most adequate (most self-organized) expression not in us but in the "mind" of God. But then he defines God as Nature (understood as encompassing the human, the artificial, and the invented). Deleuze is willing to take the step of dispensing with God. One of the things that distinguishes his philosophy most sharply from that of his contemporaries is the notion that ideality is a dimension of matter (also understood as encompassing the human, the artificial, and the invented) (see in particular *Difference and Repetition*).

The distinction between the living and the nonliving, the biological and the physical, is not the presence or absence of reflection, but its directness. Our brains and nervous systems effect the autonomization of relation, in an interval smaller than the smallest perceivable, even though the operation arises from perception and returns to it. In the more primitive organisms, this autonomization is accomplished by organism-wide networks of interoceptive and exteroceptive sense-receptors whose impulses are not centralized in a brain. One could say that a jelly-fish *is* its brain. In all living things, the autonomization of relation is effected by a center of indetermination (a localized or organism-wide function of resonation that de-linearizes causality in order to re-linearize it with a change of direction: from reception to reaction). At the fundamental physical level, there is no such mediation.[9] The place of physical nonmediation between the virtual and the actual is explored by quantum mechanics. Just as "higher" functions are fed back—all the way to the subatomic (i.e., position and momentum)—quantum indeterminacy is fed forward. It rises through the fractal bifurcations leading to and between each of the superposed levels of reality. On each level, it appears in a unique mode adequate to that level. On the level of the physical macrosystems analyzed by Simondon, its mode is potential energy and the margin of "play" it introduces into deterministic systems (epitomized by the three-body problem so dear to chaos theory). On the biological level, it is the margin of undecidability accompanying every perception, which is one with a perception's transmissibility from one sense to another. On the human level, it is that same undecidability fed forward into thought, as evidenced in the deconstructability of every structure of ideas (as expressed, for example, in Gödel's incompleteness theorem and in Derrida's *différance*). Each individual and collective human level has its peculiar "quantum" mode (various forms of undecidability in logical and signifying systems are joined by emotion on the psychological level, resistance on the political level, the specter of crisis haunting capitalist economies, etc.). These modes feed back and feed forward into one another, echoes of each other one and all.

The use of the concept of the quantum outside quantum mechanics, even as applied to human psychology, is not a metaphor. For each level, it is necessary to find an operative concept for the objective indeterminacy that echoes what on the subatomic level goes by the name of quantum. This involves analyzing every formation as participating in what David Bohm calls an *implicate order* cutting across all levels and doubled on each (Bohm and Hiley; I would like to thank Timothy Murphy for pointing out the parallels between Deleuze and Bohm). Affect is as good a general term as any for the interface between implicate and explicate order.[10] Turning to the difference between the physical and the biological, it is clear that there can be no firm dividing line between them, nor between them and the human. Affect, like thought or reflection, could be extended to any or every level, providing that the uniqueness of its functioning on that level is taken into account. The difference between the dead, the living, and the human is not a question of form or structure, nor of the properties possessed by the embodiments of forms or structures, nor of the qualified functions performed by those embodiments (their utility or ability to do work). The distinction between kinds of things and levels of reality is a question of degree: of the way in which modes of organization (such as reflection) are differentially present on every level, bar the extremes. The extremes are the quantum physical and the human inasmuch as it aspires to or confuses itself with the divine (which occurs wherever notions of changelessness, eternity, identity, and essence are operative). Neither extreme can be said to exist, although each could be said to be real, in entirely different ways (the quantum is productive of effective reality, and the divine is effectively produced, as a fiction). In between lies a continuum of existence differentiated into levels, or regions of potential, between which there are no boundaries, only dynamic thresholds.

As Simondon notes, all of this makes it difficult to speak of either transcendence or immanence (156). No matter what one does, they tend to flip over into each other, in a kind of spontaneous Deleuzian combustion. It makes little difference if the field of existence (being plus potential; the actual in its relation with the virtual) is thought of as an infinite interiority or a parallelism of mutual exteriorities. You get burned either way. Spinoza had it both ways (an indivisible substance divided into parallel attributes). To the extent that the terms transcendence and immanence connote spatial relations—and they inevitably do—they are inadequate to the task. A philosophical sleight of hand like Spinoza's is always necessary. The trick is to get comfortable with productive paradox.

All of this—the absence of a clear line of demarcation between the physical, the vital, the human, and the superhuman; the unde-cidability of immanence and transcendence—also has important implications for ethical thought. A common thread running through the varieties of social constructivism currently dominant in cultural theory holds that everything, including nature, is con-structed in discourse. The classical definition of the human as the rational animal returns in new permutation: the human as the chattering animal. Only the animal is bracketed: the human as the chattering of culture. This reinstates a rigid divide between the human and the nonhuman, since it has become a common-place, after Lacan, to make language the special preserve of the human (chattering chimps notwithstanding). Now saying that the quantum level is transformed by our perception is not the same as saying that it is only *in* our perception; saying that nature is discursively constructed is not necessarily the same as saying that nature is *in* discourse. Social constructivism easily leads to a cul-tural solipsism analogous to subjectivist interpretations of quan-tum mechanics. In this worst case solipsist scenario, nature appears as immanent to culture (as its construct). At best, when the status of nature is deemed unworthy of attention, it is simply shunted aside. In that case it appears, by default, as transcendent to culture (as its inert and meaningless remainder). Perhaps the difference between best and worst is not all that it is cracked up to be. For in either case, nature as naturing, nature as having its own dyna-mism, is erased. Theoretical moves aimed at ending the Human end up making human culture the measure and meaning of all things, in a kind of unfettered anthropomorphism precluding—to take one example—articulations of cultural theory and ecology. It is meaningless to interrogate the relation of the human to the nonhuman if the nonhuman is only a construct of human culture, or inertness. The concepts of nature and culture need serious re-working, in a way that expresses the irreducible *alterity* of the non-human in and through its active *connection* to the human, and vice versa. It is time that cultural theorists let matter be matter, brains be brains, jellyfish be jellyfish, and culture be nature, in irreducible alterity and infinite connection.

A final note: the feedback of "higher" functions can take such forms as the deployment of narrative in essays about the break-down of narrative.

III

Next story.

The last story was of the brain. This one is of the brainless. His name is Ronald Reagan. The story comes from a well-known book of pop-neurophysiology by Oliver Sacks (76–80).

Sacks describes watching a televised speech by the "Great Communicator" in a hospital ward of patients suffering from two kinds of cognitive dysfunction. Some were suffering from global aphasia, which rendered them incapable of understanding words as such. They could nonetheless understand most of what was said, because they compensated by developing extraordinary abilities to read extraverbal cues: inflection, facial expression, and other gesture—body language. Others on the ward were suffering from what is called tonal agnosia, which is the inverse of aphasia. The ability to hear the expressiveness of the voice is lost, and with it goes attention to other extraverbal cues. Language is reduced to its grammatical form and semantic or logical content. Neither group appeared to be Reagan voters. In fact, the speech was universally greeted by howls of laughter and expressions of outrage. The "Great Communicator" was failing to persuade. To the aphasics, he was functionally illiterate in extraverbal cueing; his body language struck them as hilariously inept. He was, after all, a recycled bad actor, and an ageing one at that. The agnosics were outraged that the man couldn't put together a grammatical sentence or follow a logical line to its conclusion. He came across to them as intellectually impaired. (It must be recalled that this is long before the onset of Reagan's recently announced Alzheimer's disease—what does that say about the difference between normality and degeneration?)

Now all of this might have come as news to those who think of Reagan and other postmodern political stars on the model of charismatic leadership, in which the fluency of a public figure's gestural and tonal repertoire mesmerizes the masses, lulling them into bleary-eyed belief in the content of the mellifluous words. On the contrary, what is astonishing is that Reagan wasn't laughed and jeered off the campaign podium and was swept into office not once but twice. It wasn't that people didn't hear his verbal fumbling or recognize the incoherence of his thoughts. They were the butt of constant jokes and news stories. And it wasn't that what he lacked on the level of verbal coherence was glossed over by the seductive fluency of his body image. Reagan was more famous for his polyps than his poise, and there was a collective fascination with his faltering health and regular shedding of bits and pieces of himself. The only conclusion is that Reagan was an effective leader not in spite of but because of his double dysfunction. He was able to produce ideological effects by non-ideological means, a global shift in the political direction of the United States by falling apart. His means were affective. Once again: affective, as opposed to emotional. This is not about empathy or emotive identification, or any form of identification for that matter.[11]

Reagan politicized the power of mime. That power is in interruption. A mime decomposes movement, cuts its continuity into a potentially infinite series of submovements punctuated by jerks. At each jerk, at each cut into the movement, the potential is there for the movement to veer off in another direction, to become a different movement. Each jerk suspends the continuity of the movement, for just a flash, too quick really to perceive—but decisively enough to suggest a veer. This compresses into the movement under way potential movements that are in some way made present without being actualized. In other words, each jerk is a critical point, a singular point, a bifurcation point. At that point, the mime almost imperceptibly intercalates a flash of virtuality into the actual movement under way. The genius of the mime is also the good fortune of the bad actor. Reagan's gestural idiocy had a mime effect. As did his verbal incoherence, in the register of meaning. He was a communicative jerk. The two levels of interruption, those of linear movement and conventional progressions of meaning, were held together by the one Reagan feature that did, I think, hold positive appeal—the timbre of his voice, that beautifully vibratory voice. Two parallel lines of abstractive suspense resonated together. His voice embodied the resonation. It embodied the abstraction. It was the embodiment of an asignifying intensity doubling his every actual move and phrase, following him like the shadow of a mime. It was the continuity of his discontinuities.[12]

Reagan operationalized the virtual in postmodern politics. Alone, he was nothing approaching an ideologue. He was nothing, an idiocy musically coupled with an incoherence. That's a bit unfair. He was an incipience. He was unqualified and without content. But the incipience that he was, was prolonged by technologies of image transmission, and then relayed by apparatuses, such as the family or the church or the school or the chamber of commerce, which in conjunction with the media acted as part of the nervous system of a new and frighteningly reactive body politic. It was on the receiving end that the Reagan incipience was qualified, given content. Receiving apparatuses fulfilled the inhibitory, limitative function. They selected one line of movement, one progression of meaning, to actualize and implant locally. That is why Reagan could be so many things to so many people; that is why the majority of the electorate could disagree with him on every major issue, but still vote for him. Because he was actualized, in their neighborhood, as a movement and a meaning of their selection—or at least selected for them, with their acquiescence. He was a man for all inhibitions. It was commonly said that he ruled primarily by projecting an air of confidence. That was the emotional tenor of his political manner, dysfunction notwithstanding. Confidence is the emotional translation of affect as *capturable* life potential; it is a particular emotional expression and becoming-conscious of one's side-perceived sense of vitality. Reagan transmitted vitality, virtuality, tendency, in sickness and interruption. ("I am in control here," cried the general, when Reagan was shot. He wasn't, actually.) The actualizations relaying the Reagan incipience varied. But with the exception of the cynical, the aphasic, and the agnosic, they consistently included an overweening feeling of confidence—that of the supposedly sovereign individual within a supposedly great nation at whose helm idiocy and incoherence reigned. In other words, Reagan was many things to many people, but within a general framework of affective jingoism. Confidence is the apotheosis of affective capture. Functionalized and nationalized, it feeds directly into prison construction and neo-colonial adventure.

What is of dire interest now, post-Reagan, is the extent to which he contracted into his person operations that might be argued to be endemic to late-capitalist, image- and information-based economies. Think of the image/expression-events in which we bathe. Think interruption. Think of the fast cuts of the video clip or the too-cool TV commercial. Think of the cuts from TV programming to commercials. Think of the cuts across programming and commercials achievable through zapping. Think of the distractedness of televsion viewing, the constant cuts from the screen to its immediate surroundings, to the viewing context where other actions are performed in fits and starts as attention flits. Think of the joyously incongruent juxtapositions of surfing the Internet. Think of our bombardment by commercial images off the screen, at every step in our daily rounds. Think of imagistic operation of the consumer object, as turnover time increases as fast as styles can be recycled. Everywhere, the cut, suspense—incipience. Virtuality, perhaps?

Affect holds a key to rethinking postmodern power after ideology. For although ideology is still very much with us, often in the most virulent of forms, it is no longer encompassing. It no longer defines the global mode of functioning of power. It is now one mode of power in a larger field that is not defined, overall, by ideology.[13] This makes it all the more pressing to connect ideology to its real conditions of emergence. For these are now manifest, mimed by men of power. One way of conceptualizing the non-ideological means by which ideology is produced might deploy the notions of *induction* and *transduction*—induction being the triggering of a qualification, of a containment, an actualization; and transduction being the transmission of an impulse of virtuality from one actualization to another, and across them all (what Guattari calls transversality). Transduction is the transmission of a force of potential that cannot but be felt, simultaneously doubling, enabling, and ultimately counteracting the limitative selections of apparatuses of actualization and implantation.[14] This amounts to proposing an *analog* theory of image-based power: images as the conveyors of forces of emergence, as vehicles for existential potentialization and transfer. In this, too, there are notable precursors. In particular, Walter Benjamin, whose concept of shock and image bombardment, whose analyses of the unmediated before-after temporality of what he called the "dialectical image," whose fascination with mime and mimickry, whose connecting of tactility to vision, all have much to offer an affective theory of late-capitalist power.[15]

At this point, the impression may have grown that affect is being touted here as if the whole world could be packed into it. In a way, it can, and is. The affective "atoms" that overfill the jerk of the power-mime are monads, inductive/transductive virtual perspectives fading out in all directions to infinity, separated from one another by dynamic thresholds.[16] They are autonomous, not through closure but through a singular openness. As unbounded "regions" in an equally unbounded affective field, they are in contact with the whole universe of affective potential, as by action at a distance. Thus they have no outside, even though they are differentiated according to which potentials are most apt to be expressed (effectively induced) as their "region" passes into actuality. Their passing into actuality is the key. Affect *is* the whole world: from the precise angle of its differential emergence. How the element of virtuality is construed—whether past or future, inside or outside, transcendent or immanent, sublime or abject, atomized or continuous—is in a way a matter of indifference. It is all of these things, differently in every actual case. Concepts of the virtual in itself are important only to the extent to which they contribute to a pragmatic understanding of emergence, to the extent to which they enable triggerings of change (induce the new). It is the edge of virtual, where it leaks into actual, that counts. For that seeping edge is where potential, actually, is found.

Resistance is manifestly not automatically a part of image reception in late-capitalist cultures. But neither can the effect of the mass media and other image- and information-based media simply be explained in terms of a lack: a waning of affect, or a decline in belief, or alienation. The mass media are massively potentializing—but the potential is inhibited, and both the emergence of the potential and its limitation are part and parcel of the cultural-political functioning of the media, as connected to other apparatuses. Media transmissions are breaches of indetermination. For them to have any *specific* effect they must be determined to have that effect by apparatuses of actualization and implantation that plug into them and transformatively relay what they give rise to (family, church, school, chamber of commerce, to name but a few). The need actively to actualize media transmission is as true for reactive politics as it is for a politics of resistance, and requires a new understanding of the body in its relation to signification and the ideal or incorporeal. In North America at least, the far right is far more attuned to the imagistic potential of the postmodern body than the established left, and has exploited that advantage for the last decade and a half. Philosophies of affect, potential, and actualization may aid in finding counter-tactics.

IV

Last story:

> A man writes a health-care reform bill in his White House. It starts to melt in the media glare. He takes it to the Hill, where it continues to melt. He does not say goodbye.

Although economic indicators show unmistakable signs of recovery, the stock market dips. By way of explanation, TV commentators cite a second-hand feeling. The man's "waffling" on other issues has undermined the public's confidence in him, and is rebounding on the health-care initiative. The worry is that Clinton is losing his "presidential" feel. What does that have to do with the health of the economy? The prevailing wisdom among the same commentators is that *passage* of the health-care would harm the economy. It is hard to see why the market didn't go *up* at the news of the "unpresidential" falter of what many "opinion-makers" considered a costly social program inconsistent with basically sound economic policy inherited from the previous administration, credited with starting a recovery. However, the question does not even arise, because the commentators are operating under the assumption that the stock market registers affective fluctuations in adjoining spheres more directly than properly economic indicators. Are they confused? Not according to certain economic theorists who, when called upon to explain to a nonspecialist audience the ultimate foundation of the capitalist monetary system, answer "faith."[17] And what, in the late-capitalist economy, is the base cause of inflation, according to the same experts? A "mindset," they say, in which feelings about the future become self-fulfilling prophesies capable of reversing "real" conditions (Heilbroner and Thurow 151).

The ability of affect to produce an economic effect more swiftly and surely than economics itself means that affect is itself a real condition, an intrinsic variable of the late-capitalist system, as infrastructural as a factory. Actually, it is beyond infrastructural, it is everywhere, in effect. Its ability to come second-hand, to switch domains and produce effects across them all, gives it a meta-factorial ubiquity. It is beyond infrastructural. It is transversal.

This fact about affect—this matter-of-factness of affect—needs to be taken seriously into account in cultural and political theory. Don't forget.

Notes

1. The thesis on the waning of affect in Jameson's classic essay on postmodernism ("Cultural Logic") powerfully raised the issue of affect for cultural theory. The most sustained and successful exploration of affect arising from subsequent debates is in Grossberg. The present essay shares many strands with Grossberg's work, including the conviction that affect has become pervasive rather than having waned. Differences with Grossberg will be signaled in subsequent notes.

2. Grossberg slips into an equation between affect and emotion at many points, despite distinguishing them in his definitions. The slippage begins in the definition itself, where affect is defined quantitatively as the strength of an investment and qualitatively as the nature of a concern (82). This is done in order to avoid the perceived trap of asserting that affect is unformed and unstructured, a move which Grossberg worries makes its analysis impossible. It is argued here that affect is indeed unformed and unstructured, but that it is nevertheless highly organized and effectively analyzable (it is not entirely containable in knowledge, but is analyzable in effect, as effect). The crucial point is that form and structure are not the only conceivable modes of differentiation. Here, affect is seen as prior to or apart from the qualitative, and its opposition with the quantitative, and therefore not fundamentally a matter of investment (if a thermodynamic model applies, it is not classical but quantum and far-from-equilibrium; more on this later). For more on the relation between affect and quality/quantity, see Massumi.

3. The reference to conventional discourse in Spinoza is to what he calls "universal notions" (classificatory concepts that attribute to things defining structural properties and obey the law of the excluded middle) and "transcendental notions" (teleological concepts explaining a thing by reference to an origin or end in some way contained in its form). See *The Ethics*, book 2, proposition 40, scholium 1 in Volume 1 of *The Collected Works*.

4. The retrospective character of attributions of linear causality and logical consistency was analyzed by Henri Bergson under the rubric of the "retrograde movement of truth." See *The Creative Mind*.

5. See in particular chapter 2 (an analysis of the chemistry of crystallization). Simondon carries out throughout his work a far-reaching critique of concepts of form and structure in philosophy and the natural and social sciences.

6. On proprioception and affect, see Massumi.

7. A connection could be made here with the work of Walter Benjamin on shock and the circulation of images. Susan Buck-Morss (312) quotes from Benjamin's *Passagen-werk* on the "monadological structure" of "dialectical images." This structure is a "force-field" manifesting a nonlinear temporality (a conflict between "fore-history" and "after-history" in direct connection with one another, skipping over the present without which the conflict would nevertheless not take place: "in

order for a piece of the past to be touched by present actuality, there must be no connection between them").

8. For a brilliant analysis of affect in terms of intensity, vitality, synaesthesia ("amodal perception"), and nonconscious sense of self, see Stern.

9. Deleuze discusses perception, the brain, and matter in *Cinema 1*, chapters 1 and 3 (in relation to Bergson). Deleuze and Guattari make the connection between the brain and chaos in *What Is Philosophy?*, conclusion.

10. The main difference between this perspective and that of Lawrence Grossberg is that his approach does not develop a sustainable distinction between implicate and explicate orders (between virtuality and actuality, intension and extension). Although Meaghan Morris does not use the term affect, her analysis of the function of the TV screen brings her approach to the mass media into close philosophical affinity with the one being developed here. In "Ecstasy and Economics (A Portrait of Paul Keating)," she describes the screen image as triggering a "phase of empowerment" that is also a "passage" and "transport," not between two places but between a place and a non-place, an "elsewhere": "the screen . . . is not a border between comparable places or spaces . . . What visibly 'exists' there, 'bathed' in glow, is merely a 'what'—a relative pronoun, a bit of language, that *relation* 'your words describe'" (Morris 70–72).

11. On these and other topics, including gory detail of Reagan's crumblings, see Dean and Massumi. The statement that ideology—like every actual structure—is produced by operations that do not occur on its level and do not follow its logic is simply a reminder that it is necessary to integrate implicate order into the account. This is necessary to avoid capture and closure on a plane of signification. It signals the measure of openness onto heterogeneous realities of every ideological structure, however absolutist. It is a gesture for the conceptual enablement of resistance in connection with the real. Ideology is construed here in both the common-sense meaning as a structure of belief, and in the cultural-theoretical sense of an interpellative subject positioning.

12. On mime, see José Gil.

13. For one account of how this larger field functions, see Deleuze, "Postscriptum" 240–47.

14. The concept of transduction is taken, with modifications, from the work of Gilbert Simondon.

15. In addition to the quotes in Buck-Morss cited in note 7 above, see in particular Benjamin 160–63. See also Michael Taussig 141–48. Bakhtin also develops an analog theory of language and image, in which synaesthesia and the infolding of context discussed earlier in this essay figure prominently.

16. Bohm and Hiley (353–54) use a holographic metaphor to express the monadic nature of the "implicate order" as "enfolded" in the explicate order.

17. Heilbroner and Thurow 138: "Behind [currency], rests the central requirement of faith. Money serves its indispensable purposes as long as we believe in it. It ceases to function the moment we do not."

Works Cited

Bakhtin, Mikhail. "The Problem of Content, Material, and Form in Verbal Art." *Art and Answerability: Early Philosophical Essays.* Ed. Michael Holquist and Vadim Liapunov. Trans. Vadim Liapunov. Austin: U of Texas P, 1990. 257–325.

Benjamin, Walter. *One Way Street*. London: Verso, 1985.

Bergson, Henri. *The Creative Mind*. Trans. Mabelle L. Audison. New York: Philosophical Library, 1946.

———. *Matter and Memory*. Trans. N. M. Paul and W. S. Palmer. New York: Zone, 1988.

Bohm, David, and B. J. Hiley. *The Undivided Universe*. New York: Routledge, 1993.

Buck-Morss, Susan. "Dream-world of Mass Culture: Walter Benjamin's Theory of Modernity and the Dialectics of Seeing." *Modernity and the Hegemony of Vision*. Ed. Michael Levin. Berkeley: California UP, 1993.

Dean, Kenneth, and Brian Massumi. *First and Last Emperors: The Absolute State and the Body of the Despot*. New York: Autonomedia/Semiotexte, 1992.

Deleuze, Gilles. *Cinema 1: The Movement-Image*. Trans. Hugh Tomlinson and Barbara Habberjam. Minneapolis: Minnesota UP, 1986.

———. *Difference and Repetition*. Trans. Paul Patton. New York: Columbia UP, 1994.

———. "Post-scriptum sur les sociétés de contrôle." *Pourparlers*. Paris: Minuit, 1990. (Forthcoming in English, New York: Columbia UP.)

Deleuze, Gilles, and Félix Guattari. *What Is Philosophy?* New York: Columbia UP, 1993.

Gil, José. *Métamorphoses du corps*. Paris: Editions de la Différence, 1985. (Forthcoming in English as *Metamorphoses of the Body*. Trans. Stephen Muecke. Minneapolis: Minnesota UP.)

Grossberg, Lawrence. *We Gotta Get Out of This Place: Popular Conservatism and Postmodern Culture*. New York: Routledge, 1992.

Heilbroner, Robert, and Lester Thurow. *Economics Explained: Everything You Need to Know About How the Economy Works and Where It Is Going*. New York: Simon and Schuster, 1994.

Horgan, John. "Can Science Explain Consciousness?" *Scientific American* July 1964: 76–77.

Jameson, Fredric. "The Cultural Logic of Late Capitalism." *Postmodernism, or, The Cultural Logic of Late Capitalism*. Durham: Duke UP, 1991. 1–54.

Massumi, Brian. "The Bleed: Where Body Meets Image." *Rethinking Borders*. Ed. John Welchman. London: Macmillan, forthcoming.

Morris, Meaghan. *Ecstasy and Economics: American Essays for John Forbes*. Sydney: Empress Publishing, 1992.

Sacks, Oliver. *The Man Who Mistook His Wife for a Hat*. London: Picador, 1985.

Simondon, Gilbert. *L'individu et sa genèse physico-biologique*. Paris: PUF, 1964.

Spinoza, Baruch. *The Collected Works of Spinoza*. Ed. and trans. Edwin Curley. Princeton: Princeton UP, 1985.

Stern, Daniel. *The Interpersonal World of the Infant: A View from Psychoanalysis and Developmental Psychology*. New York: Basic, 1985.

Sturm, Hertha. *Emotional Effects of Media: The Work of Hertha Sturm*. Ed. Gertrude Joch Robinson. Working Papers in Communications. Montreal: McGill U Graduate Program in Communications, 1987. 25–37.

Taussig, Michael. "Tactility and Vision." *The Nervous System*. New York: Routledge, 1992. 141–48.

Pre- and Post-Dialectical Materialisms: Modeling Praxis Without Subjects and Objects

Marjorie Levinson

I begin with three quotations, serving as something between topic sentences and course-headings.[1] One is from Marx, the other two from the more recent tradition of materialist social thought. Together, they point up what I see as some general interests and aims governing the effort on the part of today's radical thinkers to reconceive both the practical and the categorical relations between culture and nature, the human and the nonhuman, the biological and the mechanical. These statements should also help to distinguish that project from the ecological critiques of industrial and postindustrial capitalism which develop from a conservative humanist position. I refer to writers like Jonathan Bate, who use the rhetoric of intervention to revive the primitivist, essentializing, aestheticizing, and protectionist views of nature that arose in the early 19th century in response to despoliations brought about by industrial capitalism as well as to changes in consciousness promoted by that economic and social transformation.[2] Romantic period writing, many canonically definitive forms of which launch an internal critique of bourgeois competitive individualism by way of what

© 1995 by *Cultural Critique*. Fall 1995. 0882-4371/95/$5.00.

used to be called "nature worship," has for obvious reasons become something of a resource and touchstone for conservative ecology. It is my feeling that much of this poetry, when its reading is informed by concepts materially intimated in the technologies of the present, may release a very different picture of the human in its physical environments—or, one could say, of the physical environments which compose the human. This picture promises to be less constrained by notions of subjective priority than the models articulated by both the traditional and the revisionist readings of Romantic poetry. Rather than shore up the anthropocentric form of the subject embedded in the conservative critique of capitalism and its exploitation of natural resources, this picture could assist the general project of critique of the subject, an exercise in social transformation.

I take my first coordinate from *Dialectic of Enlightenment*. Here, Max Horkheimer and Theodor Adorno describe their task "not as the conservation of the past but as the redemption of the hopes of the past." My second heading, from Marx's *Eighteenth Brumaire*, urges the Revolution to take its poetry from the future, and not, as in 1789, from the storehouse of antiquity. Last, I repeat a parenthetical remark from T. J. Clark's essay on Clement Greenberg and the avant-garde. Questioning some classic accounts of modernism's practices of negation (specifically, its foregrounding of the physical medium in order to block bourgeois identification with and entry into the picture), Clark pauses to wonder more generally "Why, after all, *should* matter be 'resistant'? It is a modernist piety with a fairly dim ontology appended" (152–53). As usual, Clark is a model of understatement. The alleged resistance of matter could be described as more than a piety and earlier than modernism and its ontology sharpens if we conceive it in social terms, much as Clark proceeds to do in that essay. The task as he and others conceive it is to pin down the connections between, on the one hand, the broad range of needs entailed by particular social and economic formations, and, on the other, the special experiences and ideas of the human (and of subjectivity and inwardness as its privileged forms) that meet or challenge those needs. Matter, as a trope of resistance to the human in general and thought in particular will turn out to have specific constitutive functions with respect to particular social formations and ideals.

The Adorno-Horkheimer distinction between conserving and redeeming the past could also be expressed as the difference between historicism and dialectics, between repetition and remembering, and between two kinds of violence: the violence of repression and the violence of reinvention. The statement also draws a line between the past and the hopes of the past, which do not lie ready to hand, empirically self-evident, *in* that past. Glossed by the caution from Marx and applied to the politics of criticism, the Frankfurt School project of redemptive historiography can be read as the confessedly impossibilist attempt to realize the hopes of the *present* rather than wait for history to redeem them. In order to do that, the critic must shape her practice not *to* that present but to a future that is somehow (in some coded, partial, obscure, and un–self-conscious way) sealed up in contemporary material conditions. A politics or a criticism thus conceived will understand that the unreflected survey of the present scene—the object riddled with error—cannot of itself furnish a critical perspective. This is the lesson of the past.

The chief distinction made by both the Adorno-Horkheimer quotation and the slogan from Marx is between a conservative and a critical restoration, or between what Seyla Benhabib has called a politics of fulfillment and a politics of transfiguration. These terms distinguish two critical orientations that are often conflated or confused: on the one hand, humanly liberating actions governed by ethics and agendas based on empirical observation and designed to secure or reform existing identity forms, and on the other, action and thought oriented toward the as yet incompletely thinkable conditions and potentials of those given arrangements and assumptions. No amount of self-inspection or sociological analysis will yield the concepts that would organize those possibilities into knowable forms. Since there is no breaking with the intellectual processes of the present, what is needed is some kind of break *within* those processes, some critical opening onto their historicity.

Tim Clark's question introduces just such an opening. It raises the possibility that the seemingly axiomatic resistance of matter to mind and by extension, nature to culture (however the content of these terms is defined) may, instead of restricting the human endowment, in fact prop it up. As I will explain, Clark's question has implications for practices of critical knowing once nature, like the unconscious, has been subjected to a "new and historically original penetration and colonization," such that its "last vestiges . . . which survived on into classical capitalism are at length eliminated" (Jameson 49). That description is Fredric Jameson's and it helps to define what he, following Ernest Mandel, designates late or postindustrial capitalism, the situation of the western critical practices today.

Lately, students of Romantic period writing have been looking at styles, forms, and values long considered peripheral, epiphenomenal, or epochally anomalous. In such literary modes as the gothic and the sentimental, for example, readers are finding figures of subject-object, inside-outside, self-other, intention-action, individual-group relations that do not match up with the more familiar patterns of difference and identity, patterns that tend to involve some sort of prolifically oppositional dynamics. What I shall call the weak forms of Romanticism (to distinguish them from the so-called "strong" or Oedipally and dialectically organized writing of the period), when focused through the lens of the many critiques of the subject associated with poststructuralist thinking, embody affective, existential, economic, social, political, and even biological possibilities toward which contemporary theory is reaching. The textualities I have mentioned challenge the work model of activity on which the philosophies of the subject, of reflection, and of praxis are based. This model, which supports the wide range of discourses associated with the project of modernity, features the profitable transformation of nature and matter by a human (e.g., cultural, social, national) agency which is both materially empowered by this process and refined into ever increasing self-awareness and self-possession.[3] By contrast, the figures and narratives that organize a good deal of gothic and sentimental writing do not conform to a mechanical, organic, dialectical, or deconstructive model of subject-object relations, all as it were solutions to the mind-body problem. In an essay entitled "Romantic Poetry: The State of the Art," I explore one such departure in the context of a minor Wordsworth poem, a lyrical ballad that revolves around an image and a narrative of indifference. As in the "impoverished art" of Samuel Beckett, "nothing happens, nobody comes, nobody goes" (Bersani and Dutoit). In Wordsworth's poem, however, the thematization and valorization of the negative (the mechanism of the modernist transumption of banality) does not happen either, and that is to say that the poem's rhetorical and philosophical indifference is of a different order than that which characterizes the significant insignificances of the modern. My effort in the essay is to explore the potentials of a representational practice that does not participate in economies of subjectivization and of value, economies entailed by the qualitative and philosophically founding distinction between subjects and objects.[4] In the case of the dominant varieties of Romanticism and also modernism, these economies tend to neutralize the poetry's subversive gestures.

It is my feeling that forms and effects such as these launch a second-order resistance to the dominative reason of Enlightenment, a resistance that may help us in our own struggles with various present-day forms of Enlightenment. I refer to the limits of the various critical operations, all of which feature some kind of transformative and valorizing interest in the object of study. Underlying the formal parallel is a broad, objective convergence, connecting Romanticism's fraught relation to Enlightenment, or to modernity in its first full-dress appearance, to the postmodernism that obtains in certain ways and places today, a challenge to the realizing and in effect affirmative negativity of the great modernisms, or, one could say, of the great critiques of modernity, for often these amount to the same thing. The "second-order" resistance presently discernible in certain Romantic sites today differs from the reactive, antithetical, and to that extent, formally absorbed critique embodied in Romantic nature worship, the program which Bate and other conservative critics hope to revive. In other words, both movements, the Romantic and postmodern, can be seen as connected-in-difference to the modernity they negate. At the same time, or by another reading, both intimate a critique that is *not* so embedded. Both, at certain moments or under certain conditions, break free not just of analytic and skeptical reason but also of the more fundamental subject-object problematic and its dialectical overcomings, symbolic fusions, and dialogic reciprocities. Both manage to refigure mind-matter, self-other, human-natural ratios by way of, in the case of Romanticism, pre- or non-Cartesian paradigms, and in postmodern critique, by embracing the category transgressions entailed by the new sciences and technologies. Both contain practices of difference or apartness (as opposed to negation, opposition, intervention) which avoid bringing forth through their confrontational coherence another and yet more total humanism.[5]

The postmodernist exercise in transfigurative thinking follows from widely experienced difficulties in continuing to perform a subjectivity that is externally bounded by hierarchies of identity-difference ratios, and that is internally structured, stratified, and driven by conflict arising from contradictions between purpose and instinct and desire and need, both of those duos reflecting the master binary of self and other. The reasons for this felt deconstruction of the classical as well as dialectical categories of difference and identity are too many and too various to recount here. Let me cite one commonly explored phenomenon—the absorption of the political and the ideological by the economic, or the chiasmic relationship between what were once conceived as distinct domains related to each other by a linear, mechanical, or reflective causality—to signal the size and complexity of the changes involved.

The change that interests me both for its own sake and for its capacity to mobilize otherwise inert strains in Romantic period writing is the changed function of nature in the present. By function, I mean action potentials, drawing on Vladimir Propp's early structuralist distinction between function and content in narrative economies. The assumed structural, material, and even ontological otherness of nature was the enabling condition for that model of the self and of the human conventionally traced to Enlightenment and its philosophic ancestors (Bacon, Locke, and Newton). It can be seen, however, that nature's resistance to the human took a human form. In its way of asserting its otherness, it respected modes of action, opposition, and self-definition associated with the human community. Something basic in that picture and experience of the self and of humanness must change once nature begins to demonstrate a distinctive kind of agency, one that formally departs from the modalities of impulse, action, and effectivity associated with the human or cultural context. I refer to action forms that do not prolifically oppose the human in the ways familiar to us from the Hegelian, Romantic, Marxist, and also Freudian accounts. Nature is no longer that substantial resistance invoked by Kant in his preface to the *Critique of Pure Reason,* lacking which the dove of thought could not take flight. A growing number of biological and physical processes (such as weather anomalies, new diseases and epidemiological behaviors, genetic mutations) reveal a randomness (and often, an imponderable mixture of randomness and determinisms) that the available constructs of entity and environment, chance and necessity, organ and system, and even time and space cannot conceptually seize much less control. Chaos and complexity theories represent one kind of effort to frame these nonrational, nonlinear, and irreversible patterns of change.[6] The keen and surprisingly widespread interest in these theories shown by humanists of many stripes suggests some general dissatisfaction with mainstream explanatory paradigms, and also, related to this, a general sense that the natural world has changed both in a substantive way and relationally to the human and social worlds over the last decade.[7] These natural actions do not add up to an equal and opposite subject-form, the sort of monolithic and either deified or demonized otherness that once (in the age of belief that, according to Horkheimer and Adorno, was already the beginning of Enlightenment) called forth the mythic identities of gods and heroes. Rather, these freakish natural behaviors suggest a *mutation* of agency and this puts our own agency as well as our concepts of it at risk. The boundaries between the human and the natural, the biological and the physical, the organism and the machine, the mind and the body, are now, at strategic points, breached. A degree of self-deconstruction, betraying the interdependence or imbrication of the received categories, seems to have occurred at the level of technology and scientific practice.

Finally, nature seems for the first time ever a finite domain which we are well on our way to exhausting. Like the other changes I have mentioned, this one challenges classical models of the human in a deep and qualitative way. Lacking an irreducible and as it were, self-perpetuating otherness in nature, structurally guaranteeing the ongoing recognition of the human, our transformative encounters with the physical environment cannot do the subject-making work they once did. They cannot yield the same dividends.

My response to this situation is nearly the opposite of those who advocate revival of the nature-worship that marked the earliest responses to industrial capitalism. Rather than seek to conserve or restore the past, I would like to imagine what a "redemption of the hopes of the past" might look like. The plan is to return to Romanticism through the western gate, through "the poetry of the future," or, through a postmodern figure of nature and thus culture, of the other and thus the self, that looks nothing like Romanticism's high arguments but very much like some of its more retiring representational effects, or what I termed above the weak forms of Romantic period writing.

Even as I affirm this interest and urge others to pursue it, let me qualify it by stating the obvious: namely, that one would be mad not to be terrified by the changes in the structure and behaviors of the environment. In a more personal vein, I must also confess that I for one very much miss the assured interiority I remember from my own past and from the pasts available to me through many works of literature. But I also believe in the historicity of the choices available to us and in the dependence of critique on the real conditions of physical and social life and their modes of reproduction. Romanticism's discourse of nature had a critical, a utopian, and a transfigurative value in its own day, but it will not work the same magic two hundred years later and within a cultural formation that is not dominated by the commodity form, not sustained by colonial expansion, not defined by the reorganization of agrarian labor into the patterns of industrial manufacture, and not faced with a nature that patiently abides our actions and gives predictable returns on our investments.

For me, then, it is not a question of *deciding* to conduct a presentist reading of the past, nor is presentism a matter of relevant topics and remedial values. It is a question, rather, of the forms that define knowledge, objects, and experience in the present. One returns to Romanticism—or, one undertakes to redeem the hopes of the past—because the pre-Enlightenment imagination students of the period are now finding in that body of writing gives a concretely sensuous and in some ways more advanced form to the post-Enlightenment stirrings and strivings that characterize the present scene.[8]

The two discourses that have structured my efforts to articulate Romanticism's postanthropological, postdialectical perspectives are Spinoza and some work in the field of theoretical biology. In the context of Romanticism's philosophical critique of Enlightenment, Spinoza provided a theory of knowledge not implicated in the Cartesian relations that defined the age's normal science, nor was this theory consistent with the Kantian and Hegelian structures (troping particular economic and social forms) that governed the age's approved oppositional modes, its licensed subversions. I invoke Spinoza to signify a mode of representation not based on rupture, scission, or negation, and not subject to reappropriation. Not, that is, organized along the lines of material production and reproduction in their classic agrarian, industrial, and sexual (patriarchal) forms.

The unique place Spinoza holds in the history of philosophy traces to his postulate of a reality that is one substance, given in or as the infinite attributes of mind and matter, thought and extension. This assault on Cartesian dualism breaks proleptically with all the familiar idealist and materialist philosophies, with their "for itself" of thought, their "in itself" of sheerly existent material reality, and the difference-in-identity of their reflective or dialectical synthesis. Spinoza builds a universe which is nothing but the thought which is god or nature ("*Deus sive natura*"). His account acknowledges the reality and the force of material and historical conditions along with the whole realm of imagination or ideology, or empirical self-evidence. At the same time, he advances the claims of a critical reason that calls such knowledge into question. The authority of this reason does not, however, derive from either external or internal referents, as in, respectively, correspondence and constructivist epistemologies. Its truth is strictly a function of the coherence, complexity, and combinatory power of its articulation and its products. In brief, what Spinoza offers is a nondualistic but nonreductive materialism, very different from the Kantian analytic which negotiates the subject-object split by positing the subjective constitution of experience and the objective regulation of the subject via the categories and the transcendental time-space intuitions. Spinoza's double-aspect monism also differs from the Hegelian *aufhebung* which, like Kant's analytic, draws the objective term into the dialectic by rewriting it as a displaced, disguised, or undeveloped form of subjectivity (or, Spirit). For Spinoza, nature is not the delimiting and thus instrumental negation of the human nor is its otherness a mere ideological illusion, masking the contentious realities of social practice. (That is a view which effectively dissolves difference into an artifact of human activity, where the human amounts to an essentialist postulate of self-realizing activity.) Spinoza's argument for the immanence of knowledge to its object—his proposition that the mind is nothing but the idea of the body, itself a modification of that larger body which is nature as a whole—stands behind Althusser's argument for scientific knowledge of a system as one possible product of and element in that system (and thus, as both truth and illusion at the same time, or as Spinoza might say, under different aspects and at different levels).

Interestingly, Gilles Deleuze claims Spinoza as the ancestor of his post-rationalist (that is, non-logocentric) theory of excess, affects, and speed (as opposed to containment, thought, and structure) as defining formal properties. As read by Deleuze, Spinoza provides a grammar for articulating a subjectless thinking and a theory of affects that displaces traditional ethics. Affect is traced to the combinatory energy within and between individual entities, and "goodness," like "joy," is defined as "a matter of dynamism, power, and the composition of powers" (Deleuze, *Spinoza* 23).

Spinoza is also named by the deep ecology movement as its philosophical source. This movement takes issue with the anthropocentrism of the various protectionist or "stewardship" approaches to the environment. For deep ecology, protection is nothing more than long range and displaced production. Human stewardship objectifies nature in the sense of converting it conceptually, if not literally, into "resources" that are valorized by reference to long-term availability for development of a material or spiritual kind. Deep ecology considers these two modes of development equally exploitative—their imagination of the human, moreover, no less restrictive than their concept of nature. Deep ecology is curious to imagine entities, or what Gregory Bateson calls "units of purpose," in terms of complexity, coherence, aggregative capacity, and energy, rather than structures, boundaries, linear causalities, and intentions.

This is the point of intersection with some studies in theoretical biology. In the work of Francisco Varela and Humberto Maturana, Richard Dawkins, Rupert Sheldrake, and, from a different angle, Donna Haraway, one finds a rejection of the mind-matter, culture-nature ratios developed by the critical philosophies, reflection theories, and philosophies of praxis, all of which define nature, however socially produced, as the bounding outline to the human.

Richard Dawkins, for example, redefines the meaningful biological entity as the DNA material, shifting the emphasis from the individual organism and the cell. He reconceives natural selection at this level and by reference to what he calls "the selfish gene," whose only drive is to launch itself into the next generation through any body that will get it there. In effect, Dawkins takes Darwin's critique of fixed and ahistorical species to the next, or rather more basic, level. Pursuing the implications of this shift, Dawkins considers the external products or behavioral effects of the discrete and bounded organism as, in a strict sense, its phenotypic expression. Many of these so-called "animal artifacts" (e.g., termite mounds, beehives) are collectively produced. Often, the producing community is one whose genetic material or that part of it relevant to the artifact is distributed among many discrete bodies in a fashion no different from the distribution of genetic material among organs and systems within individual bodies. In tandem then with his challenge to traditional notions of phenotypic integrity, Dawkins draws on the parallel cited above to extend his description of the *genotype* beyond the classically defined individual organism. Further, through an enlarged but conceptually conservative description of the parasite-host relationship, Dawkins challenges the notion of genetic purity within the individual body and its organs and cells. Finally, he disputes the accepted distinction between growth and reproduction, calling the question on individual entities in a diachronic way, or with respect to discrete generations.

Maturana and Varela challenge the traditional distinction between context and organism by defining cognition not as "a grasping of an external reality, but as the specification of one."[9] In a way that seems contrary to Dawkins' extension of the geno- and phenotype into the environment but that results in a comparable dismantling of the received binaries, these authors conceive discrete systems within and between organisms as both autonomous and recursive, triggered by the environment to release internally determined activity. The autonomy of the system, thus, is that of a *composite* unity. It is realized through neighborhood relations, one component of which is the system's behavioral or performative specifications of that unity. This is the meaning of "recursive" as used by these authors. The question they put is not, how does the organism obtain information about its environment, but how does it happen that the organism has the structure that permits it to specify (i.e., operate effectively in) the medium in which it exists. This amounts to a question of representation as survival, or, "auto-poiesis," a word they coin. The organization of an autopoietic system is nothing but its domain of interactions and this domain can survive the change of every single property and element in the system. The ghost in the rationalist and materialist machine is shown to be nothing but the survival of a form of organization in the real world as perceived by another system in that world, a system perforce specified by that organization and thus included in it. This is a radically simple and, for most of us, counter-intuitive way to conceive the identity of living systems, of the relations within and between them, and between system and environment.

Rupert Sheldrake proposes the concept of morphic fields organized by morphic resonance as a way of overcoming another kind of dualism inaugurated by modern science, namely, its recognition of evolution based on genetic memory for the biological kingdom but not for the physical universe. Sheldrake tries at once to liberate the concept of formative memory from the spatially bounded organism (positing something very like action at a distance and across temporal divides) and to propose for the physical and, by convention, inanimate universe "habits" or predispositions to behavior based on past behavior patterns rather than on eternal and immutable laws. Morphic fields, like the known fields of physics, are nonmaterial regions of influence extending in space and continuing in time. They are localized in and around the systems they organize. According to Sheldrake, they are the reason why we can speak rigorously of an evolutionary and historical universe governed by probabilities influenced by past events, all of which develop within nature and history. The structure of the fields within which organisms and the physical world develop depends on what has happened before. They represent a kind of pooled or collective memory of the species, based on the mechanism of morphic resonance, itself based on similarity: "The more similar an organism to previous organisms, the greater their influence on it by morphic resonance" (Sheldrake 108). Unlike the familiar kinds of field-influence, however, there is no actual transfer of energy. Sheldrake describes morphogenetic fields as probability structures in which the influence of the most common past types combines to increase the probability that such types will occur again.

The anti-instrumentalist and literally poststructuralist models of nature advanced by these writers draw on the observation common to a range of sciences that the boundaries between the human and the natural, the animate and inanimate, are weakening, thereby undoing the defining closures of those binary terms. Bill McKibben, an environmental journalist, calls this state of affairs the *second* end to nature. According to McKibben, nature came to its first end as far back as the 1930s, with the ecological disaster of a pollution reaching right into the basic physical conditions of human life. The second apocalypse comes into being with the profound ontological changes suggested and in some cases already realized by the new reproductive technologies, such that the very laws whereby the biological and physical worlds perpetuate themselves can be altered by genetic engineering. It is not just that we know how to make new things and new classes of things. Rather, we have developed modes of production capable of dissolving the classical groundplot of making and of self-making, of objects and of subjects, other and self, matter and mind, nature and culture.

This development, its potential for abuse terrible beyond all imagining, is a material fact of our moment and is the most epochally specific fact of our times. For that reason alone, the descriptive, projective, and theory accounts that try to factor it in (the work of Donna Haraway is exemplary of this movement) are an improvement on the wishful thinking built into many of our forms of intellectual production, especially those cultural critiques that put the question of otherness and appropriation. If there is any descriptive value left in Marxism's structural analysis, it may be here that it is seen: namely, in the emergence of a mode of production that incorporates and surpasses biological reproduction. To be sure, this infrastructural element coexists with historically residual but still robust modes of production (for example, industrial, monopoly, and semiotic or simulacral capitalism). What we are perhaps witnessing is something comparable to the untidy but in retrospect sharply revolutionary emergence of the commodity form, that philosopher's stone which turns labor and use-value, human histories of making and doing, into petrified things that paradoxically immortalize the living value which they ceaselessly consume. In the strange world of deep environmental pollution and of genetic engineering, we have made technology and its byproducts immanent in the natural world in a most literal way. In effect, we have undermined the very concept of raw material, not just by reference to histories of the social production of nature but by altering the structure of biological forms and processes. Could this set the material conditions for the collapse or surpassing of the subject-object problematic, an end that is also in some way a return to a pre-Enlightenment episteme—cyborgs converging on gargoyles?

That is a coupling which sends us back, via Fredric Jameson, to Marx's injunction against the taking of moral positions, and which underlines yet again the difference between a conservative and a redemptive use of nature and of the past. Jameson urges materialist critique to do the impossible: to think the cultural evolution of capitalism dialectically, as catastrophe and progress, baleful and liberating, all together (47). In the context under discussion here, the task would involve searching out ways to reinvent value, intention, production, and even survival in the absence of that relational identity which the human had enjoyed through its assured engagements with a nature that symbolized "*das ganz Andere*," the entirely Other. Paradoxically, the deepest assault on the human may be the experience of its unboundedness and unstoppability. Quantity changes quality; in a world where the human is everywhere, how can re-appropriation, the action classically constitutive of humanness and its effects, proceed? From what *site* would it proceed and what body, what boundaries, would this process enlarge? The second end to nature is also the second end to man, one that makes the Foucauldian farewell look like another myth of Enlightenment.

Notes

1. This essay was written for a public debate with Jonathan Bate, author of *Romantic Ecology: Wordsworth and the Environmental Tradition*. I have revised the paper so as to liberate it from that polemical context, but the broad strokes and the telegraphic style of the essay remain unchanged.

2. Bate wants to recover Romanticism's antithetical critique of Enlightenment,

its argument for an idea of nature that opposes the utilitarian, commercial, and progressivist values and tendencies of the age, or what we might call its economic and cultural dominants, both of them organized around the commodity form. This argument has stood demystified, or at the least heavily qualified, ever since Geoffrey Hartman exposed the Hegelian but nontriumphalist groundplot of Wordsworth's poetry, its negative dialectics. Bate justifies his attempt to revive what is in essence M. H. Abrams' natural-supernaturalist argument in several, deeply questionable ways it is not worth disputing here. The strongest and most sustained defense Bate offers centers on the present environmental crisis. That phrase describes a situation in which the most basic resources and conditions of human life on this planet (or more modestly, of the social organization of human life that has become normative over the past 60 years) will probably be exhausted or irreversibly contaminated in the lifetime of persons now alive. In other words, the conditions are set for a practical transcendence of regional, classist, national, and even economic self-interest. Clearly, the argument runs, this is the moment to usher back in the most universalizing claims of Romantic nature worship, with its advocacy of a reverential stewardship of the environment as the distinctively, essentially, and ennoblingly human attitude.

For Bate, today's world badly needs the deep-structure limits within which Romanticism's acts of mind took place. Through the revisionist readings of the past decade and the skeptical or deconstructive work that preceded it, we have learned how those consecrating acts, despite their humanizing intentions and effects, ultimately reinforced the ontological difference between nature and mind in order to confirm the latter—and a distinctively productivist form of the latter—in its scope and priority. This is exactly the effect Bate hopes to recover.

For me, the category slippage that seems so widespread and definitive an experience of life in our times has no choice but to move forward into a yet more dangerously blended and labile future. My interest in Romanticism is the opposite of Bate's.

3. The processes of value production as articulated through Hegelian, Marxist, and also Freudian theory may be read as confirming a specifically gendered construct of sexual reproduction. I refer to the way in which the dynamics of self-enriching alienation recapitulate an allegory of insemination. A substance that is figured as an essential and definitive because generative human element is alienated from its source, incarnated through its mixture with an ontologically "other" substance (that is to say, the ahistorical, as it were, given material body of the woman), and reappropriated in its developed, valorized state by the original male agent, with the twofold effect of enlarging and enriching the male body and humanizing, in the sense of conferring a more realized form upon, the female. In light of this homology, the biological creativity of woman—as close to a universal stereotype as one gets—may be read as an ideologically pressured denial of the primary genetic productivity assigned to men.

4. One postmodern figure for a nondialectical model of difference and identity is Deleuze's "fold." Instead of a subject and object, an inside and an outside when these are conceived as structurally distinct and (however infinitessimally) separated domains, the fold allows us to think differentiation, orientation, position, and therefore identity in terms of topological variation: not objects and events but ceaseless self-relation. "The outside is not a fixed limit but a moving matter animated by peristaltic movements, folds and foldings that together make up an inside: they are not something other than the outside, but precisely the inside *of* the outside." Invagination, chiasmus, and the more traditional moebius strip are metaphors that belong under this concept (*Foucault* 96, 97).

5. There are overlaps here with strains of feminist work in Romantic studies which focus on writing that does not share the transformational and valorizing ambitions of the canonical verse. One thinks, too, of Paul Hamilton's current study of literalism in Romantic writing, a zero-degree discourse that is documentary without being mimetic, exemplifying a performative poetics of which he finds instances in Dorothy Wordsworth's journals. Or there is Alan Liu's work on detail that does not accumulate into picture or design but that remains extravagant, excessive, ornamental, redundant, erotic, nonrelational.

Another related project is the effort in postcolonial studies to articulate cultural otherness without in the same stroke assimilating it by orientalizing it, the end-result being the subordination of the other to the privileged identity-term of the system in question. One example of this would be Ashis Nandy's construction of a critical traditionalism drawing on premodern cultural practices as well as a theorized resistance politics: as it were, pairing Gandhi and Gramsci. See Nandy's *The Intimate Enemy*.

6. See the recent discussions of complexity theory by Lewin, Waldrop, and Prigogine and Stengers.

7. In addition, many of the new imaging technologies (MRI for example) are prompting a reappraisal of anatomical structures and structuration processes, such that topology rather than surface-depth, exterior-interior relations provides the cognitive schema.

8. See, for example, Kroker, Sloterdijk, Taussig, and Mann.

9. Maturana and Varela, xv. See also Wolfe for a discussion of the bearing of autopoiesis on Niklas Luhmann's systems theory. Also, for a generous sampling of new mind-body paradigm exploration, see Crary and Kwinter.

Works Cited

Adorno, Theodor, and Max Horkheimer. *Dialectic of Enlightenment*. Trans. John Cumming. New York: Continuum, 1986.

Bate, Jonathan. *Romantic Ecology: Wordsworth and the Environmental Tradition*. London: Routledge, 1991.

Bateson, Gregory. *Steps to an Ecology of Mind*. New York: Ballantine, 1972.

Benhabib, Seyla. *Critique, Norm, and Utopia: A Study of the Foundations of Critical Theory*. New York, Columbia UP, 1986.

Bersani, Leo, and Ulysse Dutoit. *Arts of Impoverishment: Beckett, Rothko, Resnais*. Cambridge: Harvard UP, 1993.

Clark, T. J. "Clement Greenberg's Theory of Art." *Critical Inquiry* 9.1 (Fall 1982): 139–56.

Crary, Jonathan, and Sanford Kwinter, eds. *Incorporations*. New York: Zone, 1992.

Dawkins, Richard. *The Extended Phenotype*. Oxford: Oxford UP, 1982.

———. *The Selfish Gene*. Oxford: Oxford UP, 1976.

Deleuze, Gilles. *Foucault*. Trans. Sean Hand. Minneapolis: U of Minnesota P, 1988.

———. *Spinoza: Practical Philosophy*. Trans. Robert Hurley. San Francisco: City Lights, 1988.

Haraway, Donna J. *Simians, Cyborgs, and Women: The Reinvention of Nature*. New York: Routledge, 1991.

Jameson, Fredric. *Postmodernism, or, The Cultural Logic of Late Capitalism*. Durham: Duke UP, 1991.

Kroker, Arthur. *The Possessed Individual: Technology and the French Postmodern*. New York: St. Martin's, 1992.

Levinson, Marjorie. "Romantic Poetry: The State of the Art." *MLQ* 54.2 (1993): 183–214.

Lewin, Roger. *Complexity: Life at the Edge of Chaos*. New York: Macmillan, 1992.

Mann, Paul. *The Theory-Death of the Avant-Garde*. Bloomington: Indiana UP, 1991.

Marx, Karl. *The Eighteenth Brumaire of Louis Bonaparte*. New York: International, 1963.

Maturana, Humberto, and Francisco Varela. *Autopoiesis and Cognition: The Realization of the Living*. Dordrecht: D. Reidel, 1980.

McKibben, Bill. *The End of Nature*. New York: Doubleday, 1989.

Nandy, Ashis. *The Intimate Enemy: Loss and Recovery of Self Under Colonialism*. Delhi: Oxford UP, 1983.

Prigogine, Ilya, and Isabelle Stengers. *Order Out of Chaos: Man's New Dialogue with Nature*. New York: Bantam, 1984.

Sheldrake, Rupert. *The Presence of the Past: Morphic Resonance and the Habits of Nature*. New York: Random House, 1988.

Sloterdijk, Peter. *Critique of Cynical Reason*. Trans. Michael Eldred. Minneapolis: U of Minnesota P, 1987.

Taussig, Michael. *The Nervous System*. New York: Routledge, 1992.

Waldrop, M. Mitchell. *Complexity: The Emerging Science at the Edge of Order and Chaos*. New York: Simon and Schuster, 1992.

Wolfe, Cary. "Making Contingency Safe for Liberalism: The Pragmatics of Epistemology in Rorty and Luhmann." *New German Critique* 61 (1994): 101–27.

Adorno, Ellison, and the Critique of Jazz

James M. Harding

All totaled, Theodor Adorno wrote seven essays on jazz: three in the thirties, two in the forties, and two in the early fifties. His portrait of jazz was never flattering and was highly idiosyncratic. In the thirties, Adorno's criticisms of jazz functioned as the negative critical movement in what can be described as his dialectical embrace of Walter Benjamin's classic essay "The Work of Art in the Age of Mechanical Reproduction" (Arato and Gebhardt 270; Daniel 41–42). For while a polemic against technology endures throughout Adorno's subsequent writing on jazz, extending well into the sixties and framing his discussion of jazz in *Dissonanzen* (1962), Thomas Levin has recently noted that even as far back as the thirties, Adorno was simultaneously calling for a reading of popular music that was "sensitive to both its reified and its utopian dimensions," and he began to acknowledge the didactic and "decidedly progressive" advantages offered by phonographs and radio programs (Schönherr 85; Adorno, *Dissonanzen* 6; Levin 28, 47). Despite this call, Adorno lingered on the "reified" and never ventured into the "utopian dimensions" of jazz. Even Adorno's defenders concede that his criticisms are marked by an almost fanati-

© 1995 by *Cultural Critique*. Fall 1995. 0882-4371/95/$5.00.

cal rigidity and that the criticisms tend to "flatten out the dynamic contradictions of popular culture" (Jay, "America" 122). Two comparable tendencies to "flatten out" surface in Adorno scholarship on jazz: those who criticize Adorno the strongest examine neither all of his essays on jazz nor the historical context of his arguments, and those who sympathize with Adorno ignore the vast amount of research on jazz that is at their disposal.[1] In both cases, jazz is handled as a homogeneous collective entity, which thus obscures the internal dynamics of jazz and attributes to it a privileged ahistorical status.

To understand Adorno's criticisms of jazz requires situating them in a social history that considers the internal (dynamic) tensions within the jazz tradition. One means of highlighting the socio-historical complexities of this tradition is to juxtapose Adorno's criticisms with the representations of jazz in Ralph Ellison's *Invisible Man* (1952). In his essays, Ellison has proven himself to be a formidable jazz critic in his own right. Bringing the two writers into the same discussion not only confronts Adorno's arguments with those of a critic who had first-hand experience of the formative years of jazz, but also, because of the important role that African-American musical traditions have in Ellison's novel, discussion of it side-by-side with discussion of Adorno places Adorno's criticisms within a context of the social complexities of the jazz tradition.[2] My goal in pursuing such considerations is to demonstrate Adorno's place in the history of jazz criticism and to give a much needed historical grounding to the debate on Adorno, jazz, and popular music. In particular, I want to focus on the pivotal position that Louis Armstrong plays in *Invisible Man*'s prologue and epilogue. What emerges from this focus is a surprising correlation between the attitudes of the narrator in Ellison's novel and of Adorno in his criticisms of jazz.

During the thirty years that span Adorno's writings on jazz, his only major discursive shift resulted from his encounter with two books which, save for numerous earlier discussions in Frankfurt with the jazz critic Mátyás Seiber, were to become the intellectual sources of all his subsequent writing on jazz: Winthrop Sargeant's *Jazz: Hot and Hybrid* (1938) and Wilder Hobson's *American Jazz Music* (1938). In one respect, the review which Adorno wrote of these books in 1941, and which is marred by misquotations and misrepresentations of Sargeant's and Hobson's arguments, only widens Adorno's frame of reference for opinions he already had about classical music and about jazz. Written roughly two years after Adorno's arrival in America, the review, interestingly enough, criticizes the defenders of jazz not because they equate jazz with classical music, but rather because in doing so— to invert Jay's phrase—they "flatten out the dynamic contradictions of" classical music. By reaffirming the internal disparities of classical music, Adorno begins in his review to dismantle what two years earlier he argued was an obsolete distinction between classical and popular music. Adorno believed that the culture industry had long since appropriated the distinction and thus undermined the presumptions of both Sargeant's and Hobson's arguments.

Jazz: Hot and Hybrid and *American Jazz Music* became fixed diametrical points of reference for Adorno, and the arguments Adorno formulated for his review resurface in his last three essays. Though critical of Sargeant's "naive" defense of jazz, Adorno admired him as a fellow musician and critic. Sargeant was a Viennese trained violinist with the New York Philharmonic, and his book was, according to Adorno, of "much more serious scientific intentions and . . . much more adequate to the subject matter" than Hobson's (Adorno, "Review" 168). The fact that Adorno twists many of Sargeant's arguments against him did not stop Adorno from later frequently appealing to Sargeant as a "scientific" authority to substantiate his own arguments. The appeals span twenty years: from Adorno's short contribution to Runes' and Schrickel's *Encyclopedia of the Arts* (1946), to his article "Perennial Fashion" (1953) and his little-known published polemic with Joachim-Ernst Berendt (1953), to his *Introduction to the Sociology of Music* (1962).

Adorno's handling of Hobson, on the other hand, was curt if not abusive. He attacked Hobson's attempt to define jazz as America's classical music, reacted negatively to Hobson's understanding of how jazz had found its way into modern classical composition, and challenged Hobson's uncritical conception of modern classical music. In his equation of jazz and classical music, Hobson fails to distinguish between Viennese schools which understood themselves in terms of rivalry and opposition, and Adorno's disapproval derives in large part from the strong personal investment that he

had in maintaining the clarity of these oppositions. By citing both
Alban Berg's "Wozzeck" and Krenek's "Jonny Spielt Auf" (in the
same sentence) as examples of jazz-influenced concert music, Hobson merges the avant-garde atonal school of Schönberg with the
Gebrauchsmusik of composers like Hindemith, Krenek, and Weill
(Hobson 82–83; Craig 475). Adorno associated Hindemith's circle
with *Neue Sachlichkeit,* which was the subject of much of his aesthetic criticism and which was, temperamentally at least, incompatible with Schönberg's atonal philosophy.

It is safe to say that as far as Adorno was concerned, if jazz
was associated with *Neue Sachlichkeit* or *Gebrauchsmusik,* so much the
worse for jazz. Indeed, as early as his 1936 essay "On Jazz," Adorno
had rejected jazz because of its association with *Neue Sachlichkeit*
and the movement's ideological undertones (49). It is no small co-
incidence then that after his review of *American Jazz Music,* Adorno
subtly revises Hobson's argument in his contribution to Runes' and
Schrickel's *Encyclopedia of the Arts* (1946). He cites all the examples
given by Hobson, but replaces the reference to Berg with one to
Stravinsky, who, in *The Philosophy of Modern Music* (1949), was to
become the central figure of contrast which Adorno used in his
praise of Schönberg. Four years later, in Adorno's published polemic with the German jazz critic Joachim-Ernst Berendt, "Für
und Wider den Jazz" (1953), Adorno turns the tables on Berendt,
who in defense of jazz notes the similarities it bears to the composi-
tions of Stravinsky and Hindemith. Adorno responds that whoever
believes Stravinsky and Hindemith to be the vanguard of the new
and modern clearly is unfamiliar with Viennese atonality (Adorno
and Berendt, "Wider" 892).

Aside from how the two books summon Adorno's investment
in the rivalries of twentieth-century European music, Hobson's
and Sargeant's books are important to an understanding of
Adorno's views on jazz because, while both books trace the migration of jazz musicians from New Orleans to Chicago, they were
published prior to the advent of bebop. This is a source of enlight-
ening irony in "Perennial Fashion" and also in *Introduction to the
Sociology of Music,* since in both instances Adorno appeals to the
authority of Sargeant when he rejects both swing and bebop ("Perennial" 121; *Sociology* 33–34). Published when they were, Hobson's and Sargeant's books could provide no account of the period

of musical innovation and philosophical redefinition that occurred in jazz during the forties. Hobson's and Sargeant's arguments precede the period which Adorno used them to reject, and Adorno's appeal to Sargeant in his rejection of bebop suggests that Adorno's opinions about jazz were already solidified before the rise of the movement he slights in passing reference. With the exception of his categorical rejections in 1953 and 1962, Adorno displays no knowledge of bebop whatsoever.

There is little question about the inexcusable disservice that Adorno did to jazz and to his own arguments by relying so heavily in the forties, fifties, and sixties on jazz histories published in the thirties. But what this disservice means for Adorno's critique is another question. His arguments precede what has often been called the second half of jazz history. If we can accept Miles Davis's claim that the history of jazz is summed up in four words, "Louis Armstrong Charlie Parker," then it is worth considering the place and the significance that Adorno's opinions have in relation to the first half of that history. Despite his condemnation of bebop, Adorno's criticism focuses primarily on the early history of jazz, and philosophically, his criticism coincides frequently with the underpinnings of the first major movement in jazz history after Louis Armstrong's migration to Chicago.

Inasmuch as Adorno maintains that, in the aftermath of the culture industry's rise, a serious distinction can still be made in classical music between *Gebrauchsmusik* and Schönberg's avantgarde atonality, he concedes the possibility that other musical forms may sustain comparable critical disparities within the discourse of their own cultural traditions. Bebop's relation to swing, for example, can be understood in these terms, despite Adorno's having categorically rejected this interpretation. On this point, which is the logical baggage carried by Adorno's own arguments, it is helpful to apply to jazz Adorno's claim that works of art represent the last vestiges of critical resistance to social repression. Acknowledging the internal dynamics of the jazz tradition thus offers the possibility to heed Adorno's social and cultural critiques without succumbing to his penchant for totalizing concepts. Such an acknowledgment salvages Adorno's cultural theories by circumventing his monolithic conception of society and culture and by giving it a critical diversification and flexibility. To consider the dynamics of the jazz tradition facilitates an evaluation of jazz in terms of the "rigor," to follow Adorno, with which it established itself within a vast diversity of cultural contexts which Adorno passes over. The question thus arises concerning the extent to which jazz too is marked by dynamic disparities comparable to those whose integrity Adorno so vociferously defended with regard to modern European music. Pursuing this question provides a clear avenue into the workings of *Invisible Man* because Ellison draws heavily upon the disparities of jazz when constructing the essential tensions of his novel.

When Ellison's novel begins, the story has already ended, and the invisible man has retreated into hibernation, which he defines as "a covert preparation for a more overt action" (13). As a source of solace and inspiration, the invisible man listens to records by Louis Armstrong, who he says has "made poetry out of being invisible" and who has already moved into a realm of "overt action" comparable to that for which the invisible man is preparing and which takes form in the poetic structure of the story he narrates (8). For the invisible man, Armstrong's significance derives from an ability to create poetic meaning out of a situation with which the invisible man is only beginning to come to terms. Of central importance is the invisible man's distinction between the "covert" and "overt," because it is here that through literature he imitates Armstrong and develops what Deleuze and Guattari call a "minor literature" within the major cultural tradition which can afford him no visible recognition. In short, he begins to understand the revitalizing power of the vernacular amidst the dominant discourse which excludes him.

Briefly, Deleuze and Guattari argue that minorities (like the Czech/German Jews of Kafka's Prague) often construct a minor literature within a major language. Minor literatures emerge as a source of identity within an immediate political/cultural context. With regard to Adorno and the question of jazz, it is possible to modify Deleuze's and Guattari's arguments to accommodate a notion of a "minor culture" and to use this modification to examine two concurrent but disparate forms of cultural experience, what the invisible man calls the "overt" and "covert." The first instance falls under the scrutiny of Adorno's claim that resistance to uniformity demands the most rigorous critical activity. But the second becomes the minor cultural locus of identity and resistance which Deleuze and Guattari describe. A sense for the "covert" and "overt," or the "minor" and the "major," is implicit in the invisible man's act of self-naming, i.e., in the identity that he assumes while in hibernation.

"Jack-the-Bear," the name which the invisible man assumes for himself in his secluded basement room, belonged to an actual jazz musician and in the context of the invisible man's hibernation alludes to what in criticism has been acclaimed as the most vital element of jazz culture. Ostendorf recounts that Louis Armstrong learned his art in private sessions where jazz musicians gathered, competed with one another, and forged musical innovations in improvised "cutting contests" (Ostendorf 166). Jack-the-Bear was an avid participant in these sessions in Harlem during the thirties (Sales 74). In his own essays on jazz, Ellison describes the sessions as "a retreat, a homogeneous community where a collectivity of common experience could find continuity and meaningful expression" (*Shadow* 209). Even Sargeant notes in his revised edition of *Jazz: Hot and Hybrid* that jazz historians have frequently discussed the double life of jazz, that a covert or sub-cultural form of jazz existed "for the enjoyment of the players themselves" beneath the popular commercialized version criticized by Adorno (18). This duplicity in jazz culture is reflected in the name which the invisible man assumes for himself. Not only was Jack-the-Bear a legendary (covert) cutter, but his name later served as the title for one of Duke Ellington's greatest popular (overt) successes (Collier, *Making* 247).

The duplicity is also reflected in the structure of jazz music itself, and a momentary consideration of this structure suggests that the "covert" life of jazz is not merely a transitory respite to be discarded once the musician has prepared for "overt" action. The "covert" and "overt" exist concurrently, forming a social cultural parallel to the multilayered rhythms of jazz that are traceable to African influences and that are part of the religious cultural heritage of African Americans (Kofsky, "Folk Tradition" 3). In jazz a major beat in one line may simultaneously be a twelfth in another line, and thus jazz rhythm incorporates a notion of multiple meanings (Brown 117, 125–26).

Likewise, Amiri Baraka argues that in jazz improvisation the notes are not merely a departure from the score, but have multiple

mediations and hence multiple meanings (*Black Music* 15). What
in one setting constitutes the type of commercial exploitation for
which Armstrong was later criticized by beboppers and Adorno
alike, in another setting makes up the virtuosity upon which the
legend of Armstrong firmly rests. Certainly, "the improvisatory
skills of jazz musicians reflect the . . . flexibility and immediacy of
response" which have been necessary for black American survival
(Cowley 196). Later in the novel, this same type of flexibility enables the blues singer Trueblood, as Pancho Savery, Houston
Baker, Jr., and Berndt Ostendorf have noted, to reaffirm "his [folk]
identity" despite catastrophe, "translate his personal disaster into
a code of blues," and resist the "centralized [cultural] monologue"
which would condemn him (Savery 69; Baker, *Blues* 190; Ostendorf 151). The covert thus functions as a strategy for dealing with
the deficiencies of overt social experience. More importantly, however, in jazz a double cultural life emerges, and in its parallels to
the multilayered rhythms of African music, the duplicity of the jazz
social experience is a distinctly African contribution to American
culture. The duplicity is as much a part of the structures of the
music itself as it is reflective of the lives of jazz musicians.

Given that Hitler's stigmatization of jazz as non-Aryan belonged to the same ideology that forced Adorno, a German Jew,
to flee Nazi Germany, one would think that Adorno might have
developed a sensibility for the struggles for freedom within African
American folk culture—or, to follow Deleuze and Guattari, that, as
a member of one minor culture, Adorno might have felt strong
affinities for the articulated struggles of another. In fact, Adorno
claimed to have precisely such an affinity for black experience
when, shortly after he published "Perennial Fashion," Joachim-
Ernst Berendt accused him of implicit racism and suggested that
Langston Hughes would be a more appropriate spokesperson
than Adorno on behalf of black struggles for civil and cultural
equality. The tag of racism has plagued Adorno since his earliest
writings on jazz. Adorno reminds Berendt quite accurately that
he (Adorno) co-authored the most significant study of racism
in America in recent times, *The Authoritarian Personality* (1950).
Adorno explains to Berendt that he desires merely to point out
where blacks are being exploited as "eccentric clowns" and where
jazz subtly makes entertainment out of what has been done to Afri-

can Americans (Adorno and Berendt, "Wider" 892–93). In this respect, Adorno's response to Berendt corresponds with criticisms voiced in the African American community itself. In fact, Adorno's argument coincides almost verbatim with Ellison's argument in "Change the Joke and Slip the Yoke," where he claims that "the entertainment industry . . . [debases] all folk materials" and reduces blacks to grotesque comedy (*Shadow* 48). For Adorno, however, understanding of debasement and racism is inseparable from the forced experiential lessons he learned amidst the fascist rise to power in Weimar Germany. The seemingly racist undertones of his criticisms of jazz are a combination of abhorrence to both the culture or entertainment industry and the implementation of Nazi ideology.

Given the historical context of Nazi cultural politics, one can read, for example, the oft criticized grounds that Adorno uses for rejecting jazz in his first article on the subject, "Abschied vom Jazz" (1933), as a subtle defense of it. Adorno wrote this first article shortly after the Nazis outlawed the broadcasting of jazz on the radio. When one places Adorno's claims that jazz is "not Black, not powerful, not dangerous . . . [nor] emancipatory" in the context of fascist Germany, Adorno's arguments refute point by point the hysteria to which the Nazis appealed when they banned jazz music. As Marc Weiner has argued, it is thus "possible that [Adorno] intended . . . [his claims] to be read as a strategic response to the conservativism discernible in his contemporaries' reaction to the music" (Weiner 484).

The problem with Weiner's reading of "Abschied vom Jazz" is that, unless the article is placed within the general schema of Adorno's critique of fascist cultural ideology, it is equally possible to read "Abschied vom Jazz" as a defense of high culture, a reading which is encouraged by Adorno's scathing review of Wilder Hobson's book. This is the most frequent criticism of Adorno, typified by critics like Lorenzo Thomas, William Nye, or Peter Townsend who argue that, as a Eurocentric cultural elitist, Adorno had a deaf ear when it came to vernacular cultural expressions. Fredric Jameson subscribes to a similar position, although with a more apologetic tone, by simply redefining Adorno's writing on jazz as a critique not of "serious jazz" but of "Paul Whiteman" and by comparing Adorno's criticisms with a rejection of a "standard Hollywood Grade-B genre film" (141). In Adorno's defense, Martin Jay, Ulrich Schönherr, and Jamie Owen Daniel have noted that Adorno's controversial opinions on jazz employ the identical dialectical methodology that, a year after he published "On Jazz," Adorno used when criticizing Wagner in *In Search of Wagner* (Jay, *Adorno* 119; Schönherr 86; Daniel 40).[3] Two years later in "On the Fetish-Character in Music and the Regression of Listening" (1938) Adorno suggested that the Nazis' banning of jazz was as disgusting as their subsequent programmatic attempt to "cultivate" the masses by broadcasting the greatest achievements of German classical music.

The importance of "On the Fetish-Character in Music and the Regression of Listening" to any understanding of Adorno's concerns in his criticism of jazz cannot be underestimated. It undercuts the charges that Adorno was defending a high cultural elitism, because in it he asserts that "the differences in the reception of official 'classical' music and light music no longer have any real significance" (276). For Adorno "the real dichotomy . . . was not between 'light' and 'serious' music—he was never a defender of traditional cultural standards for their own sake—but rather between music that was market-oriented and music that was not" (Jay, *Imagination* 182). According to Adorno, the culture industry (and fascism is implicated here as well) had gained control of both classical and folk or popular music and employed similar mechanisms in both cases to manipulate the market. Although Adorno's favorable comments on music always refer to European music, to argue that Adorno's criticisms of jazz are a defense of high culture is to ignore his focus on the socio-historical tendencies which have rendered "the organization of culture into 'levels' . . . patterned after low, middle and highbrow," not only obsolete but also "reprehensible" (Adorno, "Perennial" 127).[4] Adorno's general critique of the commodity character of music as it has evolved under late capitalism challenges the survival of both classical music and jazz as forms of entertainment.

In *Adorno's Aesthetic Theory* Lambert Zuidervaart argues that in the early stages of capitalism "music was produced to be purchased, and it was purchased to be enjoyed." Adorno's objection was not against enjoyment, but rather that at the hands of the late-capitalist culture industry the use value of enjoyment had been

supplanted and exchange value was now presented as "as an en-
joyable use value" (Zuidervaart 77–78). When Adorno speaks
about the necessity of jazz's constantly promising "its listeners
something different [to] excite their attention," Adorno is not so
much talking about jazz itself as the industry that props it up ("Perennial" 126). But as a consequence, this industry seriously com-
promises the possibility for critical assessments of the quality of the
entertainment provided by the music, whether jazz or classical. On
this point Adorno is no voice in the wilderness. In *Black Nationalism
and the Revolution in Music* (1970), Frank Kofsky notes the conflict
of interest resulting from the fact that the critics of jazz are by and
large "dependent on the recording industry for their livelihood"
(75). They cannot afford to be critical because they are the same
people who earn their living by writing record jackets. More recently, John Gennari has explained that early jazz critics would
have had trouble avoiding these conflicts, that anyone "trying to
make a living as a jazz critic in the 1930s . . . would have had a hard
time *not* looking for the most remunerative possibilities available in
the practice of his craft" (475). To say that "Jazz, like everything
else in the culture industry, gratifies desires only to frustrate them
at the same time" refers to the advertising hype which redirects
"enjoyment" to the actual purchase and the often misleading
thought that one is getting something "new" and "innovative"
(Adorno, "Perennial" 126).[5]

Although Adorno's criticisms of modern music hinge on a dichotomy between market orientation and resistance to commodification, his reservations about jazz folk culture as a locus of struggle and liberation cannot entirely be linked to the abuses of the
entertainment or culture industry. They are also "tied . . . to his
revulsion with Nazi pseudo-folk culture" (Jay, *Adorno* 120). Martin
Jay has noted that for Adorno:

> Folk music was no longer alive, because the spontaneous *Volk*
> had been consumed in a process that left popular music, like
> all popular culture, the creature of manipulation and imposi-
> tion from above. (*Imagination* 185)

Inasmuch as the manipulations "from above" can be associated
with the entertainment industry, so too are Adorno's criticisms of

jazz inseparable from an intellectual opposition to the conditions which he believes led to the election of Hitler (Daniel 40). Adorno's apprehensions about jazz culture stem from his having observed the Nazis manipulate folklore to their own propagandistic ends.

Adorno's concern that jazz culture lends itself to appropriation does not appear to have been groundless. Scott DeVeaux observes in "Constructing the Jazz Tradition" that the history of jazz is a "struggle for possession of that history and the legitimacy that it confers" (DeVeaux 528–29). The struggle is often waged through definition by exclusion. Jazz has so frequently been coopted by groups with contradictory agendas that Amiri Baraka complained that white critics who seek to define "jazz as an art (or folk art)" often do so without giving consideration to the intelligent "socio-cultural philosophy" from which it stems (*Black Music* 14). During different periods, jazz has been embraced across the political spectrum. Cold Warriors and the State Department have used it as an avatar of American cultural values (Kofsky, *Revolution* 31, 111; De-Veaux 526; Gennari 478). In the twenties and thirties, the left too vied for possession of the jazz tradition in accordance with Lenin's general wishes that all branches of the party render "direct aid to all the revolutionary movements among the dependent and underprivileged nations (for example, Ireland, the American Negroes, etc.) and in the colonies" (Berry and Blassingame 416). Citing S. Frederick Starr's *Red and Hot,* James Lincoln Collier has noted that in 1928 "the Comintern decided . . . to treat American blacks as a 'colonized nation'" and that consequently critics like John Hammond, Otis Ferguson, Charles Edward Smith and B. H. Haggin represented jazz in left-oriented presses "as the 'folk music' of . . . [a] colonized race" ("Faking" 37; *Reception* 70–71). Incidentally, Collier himself has been the subject of much deserved criticism for his own selective revision of the jazz tradition.[6] But his argument on the subtleties of the left's interest in jazz offers some provocative insights into how *Invisible Man* questions the substantial theoretical support that black nationalists historically received from the Communist party. Lenin's insistence on "the right of subjugated peoples to self-determination" takes the ironic form of the Brotherhood's concern that the invisible man might not be black enough to represent their interests in Harlem and in the invisible man's being given "freedom of action" while remaining "under strict discipline to the committee" (Berry and Blassingame 416; Ellison, *IM* 351). Here, the irony emerges as it becomes increasingly evident to the invisible man that the Brotherhood will tolerate only its own limited preconception of what is black and what constitutes legitimate ethnic expression.

In his recent article "The Signifying Modernist," William Lyne observes that when the invisible man is asked by another member of the Brotherhood to sing a "Negro work song," the invisible man's mentor Jack rifles his ability to respond, subsumes it beneath the monologic interests of the Brotherhood, and thus disarms the "double-voiced tools [in jazz] that are supposed to undermine and transform . . . official hierarchies." In short, Jack, whose own expressions occasionally regress into a European tongue, appropriates "one of the most important parts of African American expressive culture" (Ellison, *IM* 304; Lyne 328). He can only understand enjoyment of African American musical traditions as degrading and as a remnant of racist attitudes. Collier's arguments suggest that a similar procedure marks the left's manipulation of jazz for its own political ends. On this point, he is in agreement with other historians, except that it is euphemistic to describe their view of jazz merely "as the 'folk music' of . . . [a] colonized race." Jack's disapproving retort, "the brother *does not sing*!," differs from the left's provisional embrace of jazz only in its frank rejection of the value of jazz traditions.

Scott DeVeaux has argued that Starr and Collier misperceive jazz and see it as a crippled articulation of a repressed people. Yet the same can be said of the left whose appreciation of jazz in the thirties was as often scurrilous as it was supportive (534). Examples abound. John Hammond was subjected to severe criticism in the *Daily Worker* when, after his "Spirituals to Swing" concert (1939), he claimed that "jazz music is uniquely American, the most important cultural exhibit we have given to the world" (Naison 22). Following the benefit given the next year for the Spaniards who were fighting against fascism, Hammond was so infuriated with the party's patronizing response to Fats Waller and Cab Calloway that "he demanded and received an apology from the *Daily Worker*" (Naison 3–4, 15). The source of the left's criticism of Hammond and of their patronizing attitudes toward jazz musicians lies in their assessment of jazz itself, an assessment which treated black folklore and jazz not as "important cultural exhibits" but rather as Eugene Gordon depicted them at the American Writers' Congress in 1935: "as a 'national psychosis' resulting from repression" (Strout 82). In this respect, Jack's blunt rejection of the request that the invisible man sing "a Negro work song" parallels the left's view of jazz: that it needed to be overcome.

At first glance Adorno's own position on jazz would appear to coincide with that expressed by Eugene Gordon and by the character Jack in Ellison's novel. In "Perennial Fashion," he argued that a "real unadulterated jazz" could not be distinguished from "the abuse of jazz" because abuse was an innate dimension of jazz itself. Negro spirituals, he argued, "were slave songs and as such combined the lament of unfreedom with its oppressed confirmation" ("Perennial" 122). To celebrate "Negro spirituals" now was also to celebrate the unfreedom that they confirm. However, Adorno's position differs from the left's provisional support of jazz specifically with regard to the question of abuse. Gordon's reservations about the aesthetic virtue of jazz did not hinder the left's appropriation of it as a tool for its own agenda.

Of particular interest to the left was the desire to dampen rivalries with black nationalists who had described themselves "as a nation within a nation" some seventy years prior to the Comintern's decision to adopt a similar line (Berry and Blassingame 397). In terms of improving the living standards of the African American community, the gains brought about by the left's activism in the 1930s had weakened support for black nationalist ideologies of Garveyism. Ellison portrays this competition in the Brotherhood's rivalry with the black nationalist Ras the Exhorter (Naison 2; Strout 82). Jazz fell within the scope of this agenda, in part, because the Nazi denouncement of it as degenerate galvanized black civil rights activists and the left in a common fight against the racist attitudes of fascism (Naison 3). But Jazz was not supported for jazz's sake. Rather the left's embrace of jazz further undermined black nationalism by coopting what Mary Berry and John Blassingame have called its cultural nationalistic program (388).

Ellison's novel parallels the left's use of jazz when, on the advice of the invisible man, the Brotherhood attempts to gain a consensus for its overall agenda by forging one on a specific community issue, the resistance to evictions. The strategy is to force Ras and his black nationalist followers into a position where the only way for them to keep from contradicting their own rhetoric is to give their support to the Brotherhood. Having gained community support for this specific goal, Jack then shifts focus from local issues to international ones (*IM* 355, 418). Likewise, specific support by the left for jazz music in the thirties was an attempt to gain consensus for a larger political agenda. Insofar as the left capitalized on the opportunity presented by the Nazi denouncement of jazz, their interest in jazz was as "unadulterated" as the Brotherhood's interest in pushing the issue of unjust evictions in Harlem; both serve to divert support from black nationalism and build consensus for their own program; both are part diversion and ploy.

In contrast to such political stratagems, Adorno's criticisms evince an unwillingness to pay disingenuous lip service, i.e., to abuse jazz, as a political strategy for forging consensus. Having witnessed how easy it was for the Nazis to manipulate folklore in a similar manner, Adorno approached jazz with apprehension and caution, recognizing that out of their element the artifacts of folk culture can become powerfully dangerous rhetorical tools. In this regard, Adorno's apprehensions have a subtle correspondence with the arguments of those whose defense of jazz emphasizes a cultural nationalism over the celebrated double life of jazz. Like Adorno, jazz critics who tend toward cultural separatism are most vehemently critical of the degrading abuse that jazz and jazz musicians have suffered and are skeptical of programmatic attempts to integrate them into a larger communal system.

Unlike Adorno, however, separatist critics attempt to circumvent the abusable dimensions of jazz by asserting its purity and value vis-à-vis environments that are prone toward abuse. Jazz becomes a music of "doing," whose vitality is lost in the recordings that document it (Williams 251). Or the vitality of jazz diminishes "the further jazz move[s] away from the stark blue reality of the blues continuum and the collective realities of Afro-American and American life" (Baraka, *Daggers* 271). In a new context, jazz becomes recoded, vitiated, reified. The vital literally becomes an object, manipulable and marketable. The separatist project, then, is to shelter jazz from abusive environments—except the problem with blaming abuse entirely on socio-historical mediations (i.e., the social context), exempting jazz itself, is that the two cannot be neatly separated. The fact that jazz readily glides from one context to next would suggest that it is fundamentally not as separatist as those who would "protect" it.

In reply to the unsympathetic analyses of black cultural nationalism that have dominated scholarship, Mary Berry and John Blassingame counter that, given the abysmal failures of integration, black separatism is no more "pathological," fantastic, or "unrealistic" as an idea than is integration (396). Yet neither is it any less problematic. If it were possible for jazz to thrive within a social vacuum, then perhaps apprehension would not have dominated Adorno's critique—and it is here that he parts ways with the majority of separatists. Whereas separatist critics often attack the abusers of jazz, Adorno pursues a radical critique aimed at eliminating the potential for abuse within cultural artifacts. His arguments presume that the potential for abuse (not just of jazz but of any cultural artifact) is one of the few areas of potential whose realization is virtually inevitable. This is no less true of jazz in the hands of the white jazz establishment than it is of communism in the hands of Stalin. The same is true of the Enlightenment philosophies which underlie the Brotherhood's ideology in Ellison's novel and which Adorno and Horkheimer subjected to a rigorous critique in *Dialectic of Enlightenment* precisely because, like jazz, the potential for abuse was part of their structure. For Adorno, the project of cultural criticism—however dubious its prospects might be—is to develop a discourse at whatever cultural level (high or low, aesthetic or philosophical) that cannot be appropriated, that cannot be abused. Not only does Adorno use the same dialectical method in his criticisms of Wagner and of jazz; but, insofar as jazz purports to be a voice of liberation (separatist or otherwise), it also falls within the scope of Adorno's dialectical critique of Enlightenment philosophy. In both cases the issue for Adorno is to point out where discourses of liberation perpetuate the domination that they ostensibly eliminate, to show where they generate the abuse they are supposed to prevent. To criticize jazz is simultaneously to criticize the social structures from which it seeks (or purports) to disentangle itself, structures which inevitably absorb, appropriate, and alter jazz almost as quickly as it appears.

Unlike those paying lip service, the invisible man's interest in jazz is not a strategy for building consensus. He turns to jazz and the recordings of Armstrong in disillusionment with the Brother-hood, once he realizes that their "words [can] no longer teach him anything" (de Romanet 113). At first one might argue that the turn coincides with sentiments of many jazzmen who, "unable to convey . . . [their] deepest emotions in the received idiom . . . , invented terms of . . . [their] own" (Leonard 152). The correspondence be-tween Armstrong's voice and his horn would suggest that in Arm-strong's musical riffs the invisible man seeks what the "Brother-hood's" idiom precludes (Schuller 100). Or along these same lines, the invisible man's shift from the Brotherhood to Armstrong coin-cides with Larry Neal's classic argument that Ellison is a counter-Marxian black nationalist, who develops, as Baker has added, "a theory of culture able to lend clarity to the quest for Afro-American liberation" (Baker, *Afro-American Poets* 153). But in Ellison's novel the recordings of Louis Armstrong are not merely a reinstatement of the "double-voiced" tools repressed by those whose interest in the black community was never more than a calculated ploy in a larger struggle for power. The invisible man's relation to Arm-strong is far more ambivalent and coincides with Adorno's own apprehensions about jazz—particularly with regard to the critique of jazz as a discourse of liberation.

Kimberly Benston argues that in his plight for recognition the invisible man "is drawn into . . . the Marxian (or more accurately, Hegelian) historical myth of progress through linear, spiralling de-velopment," in short, progress toward a teleological goal ("Histori-cism" 91). According to Benston, the invisible man's movement to-ward freedom necessitates a recognition that teleological history is a myth ("Historicism" 91; "Performing" 170). Yet this myth is pre-cisely what the invisible man finds repeated in Armstrong's music. In "The Poetics of Jazz," Ajay Heble explores how early jazz musi-cians, like Armstrong, relied on a diatonic scale. Structurally, the music resembles the "linear, spiralling development" cited by Ben-ston. Armstrong's music drives toward resolution. Always evolving toward a goal, viz. the tonic, the music "begs for completion," fos-ters the illusion of *telos* and "produce[s] a semblance of [the] social-ity" that has been denied the invisible man in his own experiences (Heble 53; Hullot-Kentor 100).

The *telos* reflected in Armstrong's music may explain why the invisible man listens to "What Did I Do To Be So Black And Blue," rather than to Armstrong's legendary "West End Blues" or "Weather Bird." Like Adorno himself, the invisible man recognizes that "in music, the concept of representation or imitation as a way of correlating art and reality is not particularly fruitful" (Hohendahl 66). Adorno is as apprehensive about jazz culture as he is about Enlightenment philosophy—so too is the invisible man as ambivalent with Armstrong's teleological diatonic music as he is with the Brotherhood's teleological, dialectical ideology.

The myth of progress has beaten and excluded the invisible man. In the novel's epilogue, he says he is uncertain whether his disillusionment "has placed him in the rear or in the avant-garde" (*IM* 599). This question of historical position, whether he is behind or ahead, reiterates the invisible man's relation to Armstrong. The position that he develops in relation to Armstrong not only resembles the ambivalence to jazz that Adorno expresses in his rejection of folk culture. It also expresses an attitude that only in retrospect has been called part of jazz history.

As is the case with Charlie Parker and bebop, the invisible man's personal history begins with his ambivalent relation to the diatonic music of Armstrong. When the invisible man says that he likes Louis Armstrong because "he's made poetry out of being invisible," his subsequent explanation of his "own grasp of invisibility" is a paraphrase of Charlie Parker. The invisible man explains: "Invisibility . . . gives one a slightly different sense of time, you're never quite on the beat. Sometimes you're ahead and sometimes behind" (*IM* 8). This is an explanation of the musical structure that Parker developed and that became the signature of bebop (Collier, *Making* 350, 353–54). Upon its arrival, bebop was called everything but jazz. The musical dimension of bebop responded to a long history of repression and the rejection of bebop by contemporary jazz critics fueled its momentum as a sub-cultural phenomenon. The subsequent placement of bebop in the jazz tradition was possible only by an improvised concept of history which, like the music of bebop itself, "denies system, closure, purity, abstract design" (Ostendorf 154). Like Schönberg's own rejection of late romanticism's organic development, continuity, and closure, bebop marks a departure from the organic musical structures that Adorno observed in the early forms of jazz. Insofar as the invisible man aligns himself with bebop's temporal and rhythmic revisions of Armstrong's music, he is also shifting conceptual modes of history. He shifts from a repressive systematic teleology to the unsystematic and also to un-totalizing historical improvisation.

Critics have argued that, viewed from its social aspect, bebop was a "manifesto of rebellious black musicians unwilling to submit to further exploitation" and "was a deliberate attempt to avoid playing the role of the flamboyant black entertainer, which whites had come to expect" (Kofsky, *Revolution* 57; Collier, *Jazz* 360). In this regard, Adorno's most vociferous attacks on the commercial jazz industry are contemporaneously as well as philosophically in harmony with the temperament of bebop. His criticisms coincided with a growing self-consciousness that occurred within African American communities as bebop was on the rise. Baraka argues that during the forties African Americans began to "consciously analyze and evaluate American society in many of that society's own terms." The crucial realization was that being black was not the only liability but rather that the society itself was also lacking. As the African American community grew increasingly self-conscious and confident, the general deficiencies of American society became more apparent (Baraka, *Blues People* 184–85). Like Adorno during his exile in the United States, black artists began to recognize the presence of these deficiencies specifically in entertainment, and they sought art forms in which they could distance themselves "from a cultural tradition that . . . [had] been integrated into the culture industry" (Hohendahl 65). Bebop was actively engaged in this search. So was Ellison.

For all its emphasis on racial identity and on resistance to exploitation, bebop still succumbed to the debasement which it tried to avoid. The reasons for this are complex; bebop succumbs not, as Frank Kofsky has argued, solely because whites controlled the "jazz establishment," and forced jazz musicians to conform because they found bebop's black nationalist undertones incompatible with their business interests ("Forerunners" 2). Rather the debasement resulted from dialectical tendencies in American society which were able to blunt "the sharp, ugly lines of . . . [the bebop] rebellion" (Ellison, *Shadow* 204). In short, black nationalist or anticapitalist sentiment has proven to be a lucrative product in the marketplace. "The culture industry can diffuse . . . rebellious sentiment . . . by repeating the same ideas and themes, even if they

speak to the deepest contradictions of capitalism, until they lack all
meaning" (Koval 2–3). Just as the invisible man turns to jazz when
the Brotherhood's words of liberation and freedom prove to be the
contrary, so too does the revolutionary promise of the jazz idiom
accommodate, indeed contain, its opposite.

The presence of this opposite is most immediately apparent
in bebop's point of departure, i.e., its attempted break from the
traditions that Armstrong was said to embody. Through the figure
of Armstrong in his novel, Ellison exposes the delusory, even contradictory, idealism that seethed beneath the beboppers' "rejection
of the traditional entertainer's role" (Ellison, *Shadow* 225). In his
essays Ellison expresses understanding for the desire of Parker's
contemporaries to move beyond the "heritage from the minstrel
tradition," viz. the tradition carried on by Armstrong, but at the
same time he notes that the beboppers were caught up in the contradiction of trying to get "rid of the role they demanded, [striving]
in the name of their racial identity . . . [for] a purity of status which
by definition is impossible for the performing artist" (*Shadow* 225).
Against the backdrop of "the thrust toward respectability exhib-
ited by the Negro jazzmen of Parker's generation," the invisible
man points out that Armstrong has not been superseded (Ellison,
Shadow 225). The breakup of a linear teleological history has pre-
served him. Armstrong, the invisible man says, "is still around with
his music and his dancing and his diversity, and I'll be up and
around with mine" (Ellison, *Shadow* 225; *IM* 568). Though clearly
not Armstrong's, neither is the invisible man's diversity that of
the beboppers.

An awareness of these contradictory tendencies—or deficiencies—pervades the writings of both Adorno and Ellison, and
it is the search for a form in which to critically articulate the awareness of them that finally places the two writers dialectically at odds
with both the deficiencies in American society to which bebop responded and to bebop itself. While Ellison's novel alludes sympa-
thetically to bebop, the novel is no mere apology for it—any more
than the unflattering portrayal of the Brotherhood is merely a criticism of the deficiencies of the communist party. First of all, inasmuch as bebop carries either a revolutionary or black nationalist
agenda, it too falls within the scope of Ellison's critical presentation
of the Brotherhood and of Ras. The invisible man does after all

spear the black nationalist in the jaw. Secondly, to argue that bebop has superseded the pitfalls into which Armstrong fell is to grant to jazz the teleological history with which the invisible man is at odds. Correspondingly, the more one examines where and how Adorno's arguments diverge from the general similarities that they bear to bebop, the more Adorno's arguments converge with the attitude that Ellison develops toward jazz and bebop in his novel.

In particular, the beboppers were "resentful of Louis Armstrong," as Ellison was later to argue, "confusing the spirit of his music with his clowning" (*Shadow* 211). If Ellison's depiction of the beboppers is accurate, then Adorno's association of jazz with the antics of an "eccentric clown" at first appears to have fallen into the same trap (Adorno, "Jazz" 512). In terms of general disposition, Adorno certainly had more in common with beboppers than he either realized or was willing to admit. How far this convergence extends beyond general disposition is another matter. Recently, Ulrich Schönherr has suggested implicitly that the convergence extends a great deal. Although Schönherr does not pursue the historical similarities between Adorno's arguments and those of bebop, he does argue that the contributions of musicians who followed in the wake of bebop have "largely fulfilled what Adorno had not seen realized in jazz" (93). But Schönherr has not gone unchallenged.

In the introduction to the volume in which Schönherr's article appears, Russell Berman and Robert D'Amico challenge Schönherr on the grounds that "to continue to defend jazz . . . through its later exponents and more 'artsy' performances vastly underestimates the force of Adorno's suspicion of emancipatory appearances" (73). Although it sounds as if Berman and D'Amico are addressing one issue and Schönherr another (i.e., as if Berman and D'Amico are reaffirming Adorno's dismissal of the notion that jazz is a source of liberation and Schönherr is merely concerned with musical innovations), the two are in fact intimately related, because the area in which jazz's most significant innovations have occurred is also the area in which jazz has traditionally expressed its emancipation: improvisation.

Schönherr's claim presupposes the position of critics like Bruce Baugh, who argues that Adorno relies too heavily on musical notation and thus fails to recognize the significance of the unscorable subtleties of jazz and blues improvisation (73–74). Yet, such assertions, which are standard criticism of Adorno, are premised upon a fundamental mis-perception about musical scores. Adorno points out that rather than producing mechanical acts, classical score establishes a sophisticated context for interpretation, the subtleties of which scoreless improvisations cannot provide and which are not part of notation anyway. Indeed, Adorno argues that "a performance of a Beethoven quartet that conveyed exclusively what was prescribed in the music would not make sense" ("Review" 168). "Inner transfiguration" and "paraphrases," traits which André Hodeir cites as hallmarks of improvisation, occur in every act of playing from the score (158–81). The point is this: reading a musical score is already an improvisatory act, just as reading a text is an act of construction. The inevitable improvisatory movements within the context established by the score may in fact be the only prospects of liberation which music offers. For Adorno, the exploitative, abusive wherewithal of the culture industry is so pervasive that only the most concerted effort can circumvent it (in this case only the musician's interpretative response to an already orchestrated context of resistance).

Adorno's defense of scored music coincides with his general views on the critical function of art and culture as a whole. Each genuine cultural artifact facilitates an interaction that in turn cultivates critical resistance. This is not to say that, collectively, cultural artifacts lead to a unified concept of resistance or even of liberation. Rather they comprise a diverse array of critical contexts, the individual mastery of which impedes abuse and appropriation in specific repressive situations. Nor is this to say that jazz music has never achieved the level of critical sophistication to which Adorno refers; it is merely the false dichotomy of "free" improvisation and "constrictive" musical notation that is reductive.

Adorno's position on context, resistance, and cultural artifacts helps to explain the disparate cultural repertoire that the invisible man employs in order to break the rhetorical bind that Jack places him in with the contradictory statement: "You will have freedom of action—and you will be under strict discipline to the committee" (Ellison, *IM* 351). The diverse field of reference in Ellison's novel provides "the resources of consciousness and imagination . . . [which the invisible man] brings to bear against the pressures of a changing environment" (Tanner 49). For the invisible man, the "changing environment" is reflected in the evolution of Jack's sentence, in the casual (almost un-observable) glide from "freedom" to "strictness." Perhaps the invisible man's single most significant accomplishment lies in marshaling his diverse interaction with cultural artifacts in a grand unmasking of the latent "strict" repression in each of the discourses of liberation in the novel.

Armstrong belongs to the invisible man's cultural repertoire and to his process of unmasking repressive "strictness" masquerading as liberation. Insofar as the invisible man is able to use Armstrong in this regard, Ellison provides a positive dialectical compliment to Adorno's claim in "Perennial Fashion" that "the organization of culture" in levels of high, middle, and lowbrow is anachronistic and "reprehensible." Most importantly, Ellison uses Armstrong to read bebop against the grain. He uses what Adorno describes as the obsolescence of high and lowbrow distinctions in order to undercut bebop's attempt to obtain liberation through a recognition by "high" culture. To undercut this appeal to high culture, Ellison embraces Armstrong and places improvisation in the most debasing light (*Shadow* 225). The most explicit example of this is to be found in the factory hospital attendants who, while trying to give the invisible man an electronic lobotomy, tell him— like fans encouraging a jazz player to improvise—to "Get hot, boy! Get hot!" (*IM* 232). The hotter he gets the more effect the lobotomy will have. Ellison thereby creates a position sensitive to the criticisms Parker and his contemporaries levied against Armstrong while at the same time subjecting bebop to critical scrutiny. In this respect, the invisible man is able to transform his original ambivalence for Armstrong into a critical negative dialectic.

This dialectic is manifest in the hospital scene as well because the scene can also be read as an allusion to the degrading side of the jazz tradition that Parker and his contemporaries were trying to circumvent. They sought to avoid not merely the entertainer's role but also the association of this role with the tradition of minstrelsy. Adorno shared this sentiment, repeatedly drawing attention to the continued presence of minstrelsy in modern jazz. In 1938 he echoed the stock leftist interpretation of jazz and argued that "the European-American entertainment business" had such control over jazz that its "triumph[s]" were "merely a confusing parody of colonial imperialism" ("On Jazz" 53). Nowhere was this colonial attitude more played out than in minstrelsy. Baker has noted that in minstrelsy white Americans "conceptualized a degraded, subhuman animal as a substitute for the actual African" (*Blues* 193).

The only way out of this degrading role is for Baker, like Ellison, to maintain that the private session of jazz and blues singers—when the white oppressor is absent—is where the real playing occurs (Baker, *Blues* 193–94). Baker's argument is compelling so long as one is of the opinion that there are adequate opportunities for the mask to be cast aside and so long as earlier role playing does not impair or constrain the player when he or she is alone. In these presumptions, Baker follows the arguments previously articulated by Robert B. Stepto in *From Behind the Veil* (1979). Both critics rely on an idealistic conception of the self whose integrity is immune from impairment despite the repeated "self-humiliation" and the "symbolic self-maiming," which according to Ellison is enacted by the minstrel (*Shadow* 49). Stepto, for example, claims that one of the great achievements of *Invisible Man* is "its brave assertion that there is a self and form to be discovered beyond the lockstep of linear movement within imposed definitions of reality" (168). Not merely the advent of poststructural theories of the self challenges Stepto's and Baker's claims. So too does the invisible man's relation to minstrelsy. His "improvisation" at the factory hospital questions the extent to which the formation of a vernacular theory compensates for the "maiming."

In "On the Fetish-Character in Music . . . ," Adorno begins his critique with an argument on the dissolution of the subject, a dissolution which arguably takes "humiliation" and "symbolic self-maiming" seriously and interprets such tendencies as having lasting debilitating consequences (276). According to these arguments, vernacular theory is purchased at great cost. More recently, Eric Lott has explored how Blackface Minstrelsy enacted a complex symbolic castration of black males (33–37). An allusion to this disturbing aspect of the jazz tradition occurs in the invisible man's dream when he is in the coal pit at the novel's end. Not only does he dream of castration, but he does so sleeping atop the material used to blacken faces in minstrelsy (*IM* 557). While Lott's exploration provides historical documentation for Adorno's infamous assertion that jazz has a "eunuchlike sound," the invisible man's dream graphically depicts what for Adorno were the most disturbing aspects of the blackfaced minstrelsy out of which jazz emerged. Indeed, Adorno was never able to see a function of jazz beyond the minstrelsy which he criticized in 1936 and 1938.

That the legacy of minstrelsy lies at the foundation of the jazz tradition is hardly subject to debate, but whether one can equate the colonialistic prejudices embodied in the figure of the minstrel with the late-capitalist enterprise embodied in the jazz musician is another question. What Adorno does in his reading of jazz is to presume that the interest of capital in culture is tantamount to the gross sub-human parodies of African Americans in minstrelsy. While the two are historically related, they are not the same, and to imply that they are succumbs to a blinding ahistoricism—with regard to minstrelsy but more significantly with regard to the historical consequences of late industrial capitalism. To undo this conflation is simultaneously to place Adorno in historical context and to uncover the dialectic at play in Ellison's novel. It is to apply the invisible man's break with the teleological historicism of the Brotherhood, his break with Armstrong's diatonic music, and his break with bebop's supposed evolution beyond swing; it is to apply all of these ruptures to the supposed continuity between minstrelsy and jazz. The question that jazz raises with regard to Adorno is whether the interest of the culture industry can really be reduced to a kiss of death for *all* cultural expression.

Scott DeVeaux has argued that jazz implicitly challenges traditional *agoraphobia,* the fear of the marketplace, which in cultural issues has manifested itself within an inflexible dialectic between "commercial" versus "artistic." Jazz challenges this dialectic because it "developed largely within the framework of modern mass market capitalism" (DeVeaux 530). Insofar as jazz has maintained a double life, this is perhaps where it is most readily to be found: in the forging of a space which is simultaneously commercial and aesthetically interesting. In fact, Adorno provides the basis for this argument in the peripheries of "On Jazz," where he concedes the need for quality jazz in order to promote mass consumption and to "allow the upper class to maintain a clear conscience about its taste" (51). In his novel, Ellison moves Adorno's argument from periphery to center and explores the history of jazz as a securing

and expanding of the parameters of the limited space for the quality (jazz or hibernation) that Adorno allows for marketing purposes.

Instead of merely dismissing Adorno as a cultural elitist, it is
far more fruitful to address the evolution of his own terms—in
other words, to consider whether the encroachment of technology
and the culture industry is a process which halts once uniformity
is supposedly reached. Florindo Volpacchio has argued that technical advances in market machinery were in direct response to the
need to accommodate an increasingly diverse and fragmented
consumer public. For its own survival the entertainment industry
has had to accommodate heterogeneity (Volpacchio 120). Given
Adorno's own pessimistic concerns regarding the momentum behind the culture industry, it is difficult to imagine how it would
come to a standstill or avoid diversification in its own interest.
There is an inkling of this awareness in a peripheral reference to
jazz late in *Aesthetic Theory,* but whether the covert spaces of jazz
would have attained visibility in the final version of Adorno's un-
finished manuscript is a matter of speculation.

Notes

1. The reasons for this neglect derive in part from the fact that until 1991 there
had been no adequate critical examination of the socio-historical and ideological
dimensions of jazz criticisms. This lack led Gary Carner, in the introduction to
the special issue on jazz that *Black American Literature Forum* (25.3) published in
1991, to argue that after seventy years of jazz literature, it is finally time for some
serious attempt to examine it (443). As an illustration of the state of scholarship
on the question of Adorno and jazz, it is worth noting that in the same year *Telos*
published a special issue on Adorno, jazz, and popular music (87.1). While
Adorno receives only a passing swipe in *Black American Literature Forum, Telos* examines Adorno's views without a single reference to the array of scholarship *Black
American Literature Forum* was exploring at the same time.
2. The importance of African American music to this novel has often been
cited, most notably by Houston Baker, Jr., Kimberly Benston, and Berndt Ostendorf. Their work will be discussed later in this essay.
3. The foundations for these arguments were first provided in Andreas Huyssen's "Adorno in Reverse: From Hollywood to Richard Wagner," which was first
published in *New German Critique* 29.2–3 (1983): 3–38, and then later included in
After the Great Divide. For Huyssen's entire argument, see *After the Great Divide* 16–
43. It is important, however, to note that while, with regard to the effects of the
culture industry, there are similarities between Adorno's critique of Wagner and
of jazz, Adorno's association of Wagner with the beginning of the culture industry

is in large part a rhetorical counter to Wagner's anti-Semitism. By locating the beginning of the culture industry with Wagner, Adorno subtly rebuts Wagner's claim that Jewish financial interests are corrupting German culture. Thus a simple association of the two critiques is highly problematic. Unlike his discussion of the culture industry and jazz, Adorno's discussion of the culture industry and Wagner is inseparable from his critique of Wagner's anti-Semitism. I examine the problematic nature of this comparison in the chapter of the book manuscript to which this article belongs.

4. Despite these general statements by Adorno, which challenge high-low cultural dichotomies, his fixation on European music demonstrates that he only made cultural concessions on a theoretical level and was unable to finally turn his recognition that high-low distinctions were "obsolete" into a serious consideration of the critical dimensions of "light" music. In his discussion of what he calls the "incestuous choice" of the German intellectual exiles who fled from Nazi Germany to Los Angeles, Mike Davis has implicitly provided a partial explanation for this tendency in Adorno's writings. Davis notes that "segregated from native Angelenos, the exiles composed a miniature society in a self-imposed ghetto, clinging to their old-world prejudices like cultural life-preservers" (*City of Quartz* 47). While Davis' metaphor of the "life-preserver" highlights the personal investment in Adorno's, Horkheimer's, Schönberg's, and Mann's German cultural predilections, they also saw themselves as contributing to the preservation of the culture that the Nazis were destroying.

5. Adorno began to develop this critique of jazz as far back as 1936 in his essay "On Jazz," in which he claimed that use value of jazz intensifies rather than supersedes alienation because its innovations are produced "in terms none other than its marketability" (48). He repeats the same argument in "Fetish Character of Music and the Regression of Hearing" and again in 1941 in his review of Sargeant and Wilder: jazz "cheats the masses as soon as it holds them in its grip" ("Review" 170).

6. See, in particular, John Gennari, "Jazz Criticism: Its Development and Ideologies" 496–504.

Works Cited

Adorno, Theodor W. "Abschied vom Jazz." 1933. *Gesammelte Schriften*. Vol. 18. Frankfurt am Main: Suhrkamp, 1984. 795–99.

———. *Aesthetic Theory.* 1970. Trans. C. Lenhardt. New York: Routledge, 1984.

———. *Dissonanzen.* Göttingen: Vandenhoeck und Ruprecht, 1962.

———. "On the Fetish-Character in Music and the Regression of Listening." 1938. *The Essential Frankfurt School Reader.* Ed. Andrew Arato and Erike Gebhardt. New York: Urizen, 1978. 270–99.

———. *Introduction to the Sociology of Music.* 1962. Trans. E. B. Ashton. New York: Continuum, 1989.

———. "Jazz." *Encyclopedia of the Arts.* Ed. Dagobert D. Runes and Harry G. Schrickel. New York: Philosophical Library, 1946. 511–13.

———. "On Jazz." 1936. Trans. Jamie Owen Daniel. *Discourse* 12.1 (1989–90): 45–69.

———. "Perennial Fashion—Jazz." 1953. *Prisms.* Trans. Samuel Weber and Shierry Weber. Cambridge: MIT P, 1981. 119–32.

------. *The Philosophy of Modern Music*. 1949. New York: Continuum, 1985.

------. Review of *American Jazz Music* by Wilder Hobson and of *Jazz: Hot and Hybrid* by Winthrop Sargeant. *Studies in Philosophy and Social Science* 7.9 (1941): 167–78.

------. *In Search of Wagner*. 1952. Trans. Rodney Livingstone. New York: Verso, 1981.

Adorno, Theodor W., and Joachim-Ernst Berendt. "Für und Wider Jazz." *Merkur: Deutsche Zeitschrift für Europäisches Denken* 7.9 (1953): 887–93.

Adorno, Theodor W., Else Frenkel-Brunswik, Daniel J. Levison, and R. Nevitt Sanford. *The Authoritarian Personality*. New York: Harper, 1950.

Adorno, Theodor W., and Max Horkheimer. *Dialectic of Enlightenment*. 1944. Trans. John Cumming. New York: Continuum, 1991.

Arato, Andrew, and Erike Gebhardt. *The Essential Frankfurt School Reader*. New York: Urizen, 1978.

Baker, Houston A., Jr. *Afro-American Poets*. Madison: U of Wisconsin P, 1988.

------. *Blues, Ideology, and Afro-American Literature: A Vernacular Theory*. Chicago: U of Chicago P, 1984.

Baraka, Imamu Amiri. [LeRoi Jones.] *Black Music*. 1967. Westport: Greenwood P, 1980.

------. *Blues People*. New York: William Morrow, 1963.

------. *Daggers and Javelins*. New York: William Morrow, 1984.

Baugh, Bruce. "Left-Wing Elitism: Adorno on Popular Culture." *Philosophy and Literature* 14.1 (1990): 65–78.

Benjamin, Walter. "The Work of Art in the Age of Mechanical Reproduction." *Illuminations*. Trans. Harry Zohn. New York: Schocken, 1968. 217–51.

Benston, Kimberly W. "Controlling the Dialectical Deacon: The Critique of Historicism in *Invisible Man*." *Delta* 18 (1984): 89–103.

------. "Performing Blackness: Re/Placing Afro-American Poetry." *Afro-American Literary Study in the 1990's*. Ed. Houston A. Baker, Jr. and Patricia Redmond. Chicago: U of Chicago P, 1989. 164–85.

Berman, Russell A., and Robert D'Amico. "Introduction: Popular Music from Adorno to Zappa." *Telos* 87.1: 71–77.

Berry, Mary Frances, and John W. Blassingame. *Long Memory: The Black Experience in America*. New York: Oxford UP, 1982.

Brown, Lee B. "The Theory of Jazz Music: 'It Don't Mean a Thing.'" *Journal of Aesthetics and Art Criticism* 49.2 (1991): 115–27.

Carner, Gary. "Introduction [to Special Volume on Jazz]." *Black American Literature Forum* 25.3 (1991): 441–48.

Collier, James Lincoln. "The Faking of Jazz." *New Republic* 18 Nov. 1985: 33–40.

------. *The Making of Jazz*. Boston: Houghton Mifflin, 1978.

------. *The Reception of Jazz in America*. New York: Institute for Studies in American Music, 1988.

Cowley, Julian. "The Art of Improvisers: Jazz and Fiction in Post-Bebop America." *New Comparison* 6 (1988): 194–204.

Craig, Gordon. *Germany 1866–1945*. New York: Oxford UP, 1978.

Daniel, Jamie Owen. "Introduction to Adorno's 'On Jazz.'" *Discourse* 12.1 (1989–90): 39–44.

Davis, Mike. *City of Quartz: Excavating the Future in Los Angeles*. New York: Vintage, 1992.

Deleuze, Gilles, and Félix Guattari. *Kafka: Toward a Minor Literature*. Trans. Dana Polan. Minneapolis: U of Minnesota P, 1986.

DeVeaux, Scott. "Constructing the Jazz Tradition: Jazz Historiography." *Black Literature Forum* 25.3 (1991): 525–60.

Ellison, Ralph. *Invisible Man.* 1952. New York: Vintage, 1972.

———. *Shadow and Act.* New York: Random House, 1964.

Gennari, John. "Jazz Criticism: Its Development and Ideologies." *Black American Literature Forum* 25.3 (1991): 449–523.

Heble, Ajay. "The Poetics of Jazz: From Symbolic to Semiotic." *Textual Practice* 2.1 (1988): 51–68.

Hobson, Wilder. *American Jazz Music.* New York: Norton, 1938.

Hodeir, André. *Jazz: Its Evolution and Essence.* Trans. David Noakes. New York: Grove P, 1956.

Hohendahl, Peter. *Reappraisals: The Shifting Alignments in Postwar Critical Theory.* Ithaca: Cornell UP, 1991.

Hullot-Kentor, Robert. "The Impossibility of Music: Adorno, Popular and Other Music." *Telos* 87.1 (1991): 97–117.

Huyssen, Andreas. "Adorno in Reverse: From Hollywood to Richard Wagner." *New German Critique.* 29.3–4 (1983): 8–38.

———. *After the Great Divide.* Bloomington: Indiana UP, 1986.

Jameson, Fredric. *Late Marxism: Adorno, or, the Persistence of the Dialectic.* New York: Verso, 1990.

Jay, Martin. *Adorno.* Cambridge: Harvard UP, 1984.

———. "Adorno in America." *Permanent Exiles.* New York: Columbia UP, 1985. 120–37.

———. *Dialectical Imagination.* Boston: Little, Brown, 1973.

Kofsky, Frank. "Afro-American Innovation and the Folk Tradition in Jazz: Their Historical Significance." *Journal of Ethnic Studies* 7.1 (1979): 1–12.

———. "Black Nationalism in Jazz: The Forerunners Resist Establishment Repression, 1958–1963." *Journal of Ethnic Studies* 10.2 (1982): 1–27.

———. *Black Nationalism and the Revolution in Music.* New York: Pathfinder P, 1970.

Koval, Howard. "Homogenization of Culture in Capitalist Society." *Popular Music and Society* 12.4 (1988): 1–16.

Leonard, Neil. "The Jazzman's Verbal Usage." *Black American Literature Forum* 20.1–2 (1986): 150–60.

Levin, Thomas. "For the Record: Adorno on Music in the Age of Its Technological Reproducibility." *October* 55.4 (1990): 23–47.

Lott, Eric. "Love and Theft: The Racial Unconscious of Blackface Minstrelsy." *Representations* 39.2 (1992): 23–50.

Lyne, William. "The Signifying Modernist: Ralph Ellison and the Limits of the Double Consciousness." *PMLA* 107.2 (1992): 319–30.

Naison, Mark. "Communism and Harlem Intellectuals in the Popular Front: Anti-Fascism and the Politics of Black Culture." *Journal of Ethnic Studies* 9.1 (1981): 1–25.

Neal, Larry. "Ellison's Zoot Suit." *Ralph Ellison: A Collection of Critical Essays.* Ed. John Hersey. Englewood Cliffs: Prentice Hall, 1974. 58–79.

Nye, William P. "Theodor Adorno on Jazz: A Critique of Critical Theory." *Popular Music and Society* 12.4 (1988): 69–73.

Ostendorf, Berndt. "Anthropology, Modernism, and Jazz." *Ralph Ellison.* Ed. Harold Bloom. New York: Chelsea House, 1986. 145–72.

de Romanet, Jerome. "Musical Elements in *Invisible Man* with Special Reference to the Blues." *Delta* 18 (1984): 105–18.

Sales, Grover. *Jazz: America's Classical Music.* New York: De Capo, 1992.

Sargeant, Winthrop. *Jazz: A History.* New York: McGraw-Hill, 1964. Rpt. of *Jazz: Hot and Hybrid.* 1938.

Savery, Pancho. "Ellison's Existential Blues." *Approaches to Teaching Ellison's Invisible Man.* New York: MLA, 1989. 65–74.

Schönherr, Ulrich. "Adorno and Jazz: Reflections on a Failed Encounter." *Telos* 87.1: 85–96.

Schuller, Gunther. *Early Jazz: Its Roots and Musical Development.* New York: Oxford UP, 1968.

Starr, S. Frederick. *Red and Hot: The Fate of Jazz in the Soviet Union.* New York: Oxford UP, 1983.

Stepto, Robert B. *From Behind the Veil: A Study of Afro-American Narrative.* Urbana: U of Illinois P, 1979.

Strout, Cushing. "'An American Negro Idiom': *Invisible Man* and the Politics of Culture." *Approaches to Teaching Ellison's Invisible Man.* New York: MLA, 1989. 79–85.

Tanner, Tony. "The Music of Invisibility." *Ralph Ellison.* Ed. Harold Bloom. New York: Chelsea House, 1986. 37–50.

Thomas, Lorenzo. "'Communicating by Horns': Jazz and Redemption in the Poetry of the Beats and the Black Arts Movement." *African American Review* 26.2 (1992): 291–98.

Townsend, Peter. "Adorno on Jazz: Vienna versus the Vernacular." *Prose Studies: History, Theory, Criticism* 11.1 (1988): 69–88.

Volpacchio, Florindo. "The Unhappy Marriage of Music and Emancipation." *Telos* 87.1 (1991): 118–23.

Weiner, Marc A. "*Urwaldmusik* and the Borders of German Identity: Jazz in Literature of the Weimar Republic." *German Quarterly* 64.4 (1991): 475–87.

Williams, Martin. *The Jazz Tradition.* Rev. ed. New York: Oxford UP, 1983.

Zuidervaart, Lambert. *Adorno's Aesthetic Theory.* Cambridge: MIT P, 1991.

The Signifying Corpse: Re-Reading Kristeva on Marguerite Duras

Karen Piper

> Wherever I go, I see signs of society's death everywhere. It's like hallucinating.
>
> —Marguerite Duras[1]

Politics, in the postmodern arena, has been driven underground.[2] Althusser's "overdetermination," Baudrillard's "simulation," Foucault's "death of man"—each of these figures speaks out of the same political impotence. The postmodern subject finds himself irrevocably welded into the structures that contain him— the postmodern subject finds himself a *body without organs*.[3] I say "him," however, precisely because I propose that the overdetermined subject is also a gendered subject, and that "body without organs" is a figure not for some revolutionary androgeny but precisely the impotence of the overdetermined subject. In contrast to this neutered figure (man *minus*), I intend to examine the textual reproduction of intact female bodies as allegorical signifiers for political revivification in the work of Marguerite Duras. Situating Freudian "lack" back where it belongs (upon the male desire for

© 1995 by *Cultural Critique*. Fall 1995. 0882-4371/95/$5.00.

his missing phallus), I will return the female *parts* (roles) to their political significance.

Kristeva's recent study *Black Sun* situates the novels of Marguerite Duras within that tenuous psychological space called depression, or what she terms "*la maladie du grièf.*" This psychological status acts upon the text, producing the language of Duras as "distorted speech" or "the discourse of dulled pain" (226). This reading of Duras' language may lead to positioning her characters within a space of psychological subjectivity (abstracted from the absolute subjectivity of Duras herself);[4] while no one could deny Duras' melancholia, one may easily question what (Duras'?) melancholia may produce. Duras, as product of melancholy, writes. I will ask not, "who is Duras?" but, "what is this writing and how does it relate to the politics of production?" Walter Benjamin has suggested that writing produces knowledge as *stored* (dead) object, that all writing is allegorical in the sense that it produces death. What contributes to the production of allegory, according to Benjamin, is precisely *melancholy:* "If the object becomes allegorical under the gaze of melancholy, if melancholy causes life to flow out of it and it remains behind dead, but eternally secure, then it is exposed to the allegorist . . ." (184). We come full circle to Kristeva, but with a drastic revision: Duras' *grief* becomes not an "individual psychic unease" leading to "independent, unified subjects" but a method and result of social production. Melancholy (which is non-locatable) produces allegory, which is dead and so dissolves melancholy.[5] As Kristeva suggested, Duras confronts a "nothing" (and much has been written on this "white space"/silence); however, this "void" is her own construction and so cannot absent itself (258). Benjamin writes, "these allegories fill out and deny the void in which they are represented, just as ultimately, the intention does not faithfully rest in the contemplation of bones but faithlessly leaps forward to the idea of resurrection" (233). I propose to read Duras' characters as positions taken within the order of structure/knowledge/power inside(out) her texts. If one concurs with Jameson that politics is the "Unconscious" undercurrent animating (post)modern textual production, what becomes important in any hermeneutic model is de-centering the subject/character in order to subvert the reified symbols of imagination. If politics indeed is "underground," then interpretation becomes not an assignation of possible meanings, but an archaeology of dead objects: interpretation becomes exhumation.

The desire of Duras (through her characters) to eliminate herself/(themselves) as object is far from an impotent suicidal response to depression, but a restructuring of how these knowledge-objects ("man," characters, corpses, governments) themselves are organized and controlled. Duras destroys the illusion of self-determination,[6] and in so doing, reorganizes subjectivity around a different order. As Foucault has suggested in *The Order of Things*, "[m]an is an invention of recent date. And one perhaps nearing its end" (386). "Man" as object is eliminated, but only under the melancholic gaze of a woman. The *character* can no longer signify—only the *corpse*. The character cannot signify precisely because the "character" as representation of a monadic subject is merely a production of recent history. Duras demolishes the character for the sake of the corpse—Benjamin likewise suggested of the characters of *Trauerspiel*, "[i]t is not for the sake of immortality that they meet their end, but for the sake of the corpse. . . . Seen from the point of view of death, the product of the corpse is life" (217).

The "corpse," according to Benjamin, is the gateway to the "homeland of allegory" (216). If the *symbol* is the appropriation of the eternal essence of things, *allegory* is the acknowledgment that these essences are *dead;* the object can always and only be a corpse. "Allegories are, in the realm of thoughts, what ruins are in the realm of things," Benjamin explains (178). The *character* is killed, but the *corpse* is cracked open for signification. "Even the singular, the individual character, is multiplied in the allegorical," Benjamin writes (193)—and the character is multiplied precisely through his/her *decay*, through the fecundity of decomposition.

How is the "allegorical" related to "overdetermination"? Benjamin would claim that allegory reveals history "as petrified, primordial landscape," a space in which "man's subjection to nature is most obvious" (166). All of history's sorrows, in effect, become "expressed in a face—or rather in a death's head" (166). While "overdetermination" has as its object a specific individual/character, the "allegorical" reveals *subjection* with the mock faciality of "death's head." Allegory puts history back together as a *face;* politics acquires a mouthpiece, but only dialectically. If the overdetermined male bemoans his (specific) loss in the face of (his) structures of power, the overdetermined female *dies* (the only true loss of agency). What happens, however, when a woman enacts (or writes) this death as allegory? It is dialectically reclaimed; the corpse speaks.

Reading the corpse in this fashion postulates not only a new formation for this particular text, but also a methodology for the reading of the postmodern—the corpse acts as both subject and method of critique. The corpse designates distance, stoppage, and abjection; but in order to understand this reading of the corpse, we must first redirect our notion of *symbolic* representation to that of *allegorical* representation. Paul de Man has laid out this distinction carefully in "The Rhetoric of Temporality," where he writes:

> The subjectivity of experience is preserved when it is trans-
> lated into language; the world is then no longer seen as a con-
> figuration of entities that designate a plurality of distinct and
> isolated meanings, but as a configuration of symbols ultimately
> leading to a total, single, and universal meaning. (*Blindness*
> 188)

What is significant in de Man's formulation of the *symbol* is that it is not a totalizing signifier in its own right, but that it tends to an absolute reading of *subjectivity*. de Man explains:

> Whereas the symbol postulates the possibility of an identity
> or identification, allegory designates primarily a distance in
> relation to its own origin. . . . In so doing, it prevents the self
> from an illusory identification with the non-self, which is now
> fully, though painfully, recognized as non-self. (207)

The (mimetic) symbol in this sense pronounces nostalgia, origin, and "the illusion of self-determination." The mimetic reading of texts postulates its own identity-theory; allegory renounces the de-sire to identify. The corpse, therefore, can only be *dead* in a mimetic sense—allegorically, the corpse is *alive*.

What de Man describes at the level of the symbolic order, Georg Lukács recognizes as the production of the bourgeoisie:

Man finds himself confronted by purely natural relations or
social forms mystified into natural relations. They appear to
be fixed, complete and immutable entities which can be ma-
nipulated and even comprehended, but never overthrown.
But also this situation creates the possibility of praxis in the
individual consciousness. Praxis becomes the form of action
appropriate to the isolated individual, it becomes his ethics.
(19)

Individual praxis is, in this sense, made *possible* only by (symbolic)
reification. What in de Man's figuration appears to be a strictly
literary hermeneutic becomes for Lukács a product of material relations. Capitalism provides the structural framework for individu-
ally acting agents/characters. Just as structural overdetermination
requires that the subject speak, so narrative overdetermination pre-
scribes that only a hermeneutical breach can offer a resuscitation.
To let *destruction* be spoken out (of the symbolic/class order), not
through itself, but through a series of veils that would disclose its
meaning—this, I propose, is the subject of *Moderato cantabile*.

Rather than situating anarchy in an abstract ideology, Duras
embodies and refigures it into bodily processes within her texts—
the corpse becomes a site representing both destruction and political liberation. Duras defines *"destruction capitale"* during an interview: "The destruction of someone as a person . . . The destruction
of all police . . . The destruction of memory . . . The destruction of
judgment . . . I am in favor of closing schools and universities, of
ignorance . . ." (108). This destruction recognizes human beings as
objects of capital, commodities to be moved and controlled, who
find liberation only in their refusal to exist. Walter Benjamin has
described this type of character in *Illuminations:* "The destructive
character knows only one activity: clearing away . . . because everything cleared away means to the destroyer a complete reduction,
indeed eradication, of his own condition" (300). This is an anarchy
of self-immolation, in which textual beings as objects are extir-
pated, symbolically tearing down the structural certainty of their
surroundings (the text, the city, the commodities of capital).[7] The
corpse becomes the imploding center in *Moderato cantabile*, drawing the characters into itself while at the same time annihilating

the anesthetizing distance between reader/narrative structure. The abstract power of any *structure,* which is maintained through an implied impotence before it, becomes at once disrupted and grounded in the power of the body.

If, then, the corpse is alive, what might we say it signifies? While I would not suggest that the corpse is important for any *one thing* other than a method of reading, it does offer a site in which the political *may be allowed to* emerge, regardless of authorial intent. Duras' novel *Moderato cantabile* allows for the destruction of the subject as a site for containing knowledge, the scream of rebellion, the sight of the abject—all configured in the dismembered body of the heroine, the corpse. The corpse is the body/non-body Kristeva describes in *Powers of Horror:*

> The corpse (or cadaver: *cadere,* to fall) . . . is cesspool and death. Without makeup or masks, refuse and corpses show me what I permanently thrust aside in order to live. Such wastes drop so that I might live, until, from loss to loss, nothing remains in me and my entire body falls beyond the limit-cadaver. If dung signifies the other side of the border, the place where I am not and which permits me to be, the corpse, the most sickening of wastes, is a border that has encroached upon everything. It is no longer I who expel, "I" is expelled. (4)

The subversive nature of the heroine/corpse exists precisely in these borders—encroaching upon everything, yet remaining indefinable. The corpse is the refuse that cannot be washed away, for it is the refuse that constitutes identity itself. *Moderato cantabile* represents the refuse of the author, which will remain forever a part of her identity—her corpse—into which her readers delve and emerge.

Moderato cantabile, far from the sweet and melodious story the title suggests, is centered around the sound of a scream. Anne is a character drawn toward a scream coming from a bar; she enters into this world in order to discover its absent source, the corpse. She tells Chauvin, the man in the bar who saw the murder, "I think I must have screamed something like that once, yes, when I had the child" (79). Anne describes the state of child-bearing as the nearest comparison she can make to the scream of abjection, but the child became a carrier of cultural models and piano lessons, losing that connection with the animalistic scream that produced him. Maturation for the child becomes a process of acquiring signification, which does not correspond to the passion of his production. Language, in the same way, is a barrier that hides the scream—having an abstract significance that Duras serves to exploit, reverse, and eliminate by demonstrating its ironies and misnomers. Duras' movement beyond paradigmatic borders/limitations creates first and foremost a site of narrative possibility.

Duras depicts other screams in *Moderato cantabile*, the screams of trees outside Anne's house. These are screams that Anne fears, saying, "People ought to live in a town where there are no trees trees scream when there's a wind . . . you hear them screaming on the beach like someone murdered" (89). Chauvin replies, "[y]ou have never screamed. Never" (90). This statement seems to contradict Anne's earlier claim to have screamed during childbirth. Is Chauvin denying the scream of child-bearing or is he contrasting her repressed status to the release of sound from the trees? Connecting this statement with the one which precedes it further complicates the meaning. Chauvin claims, "[y]ou go to the railings, then you go away and walk around the house, then you come back again to the railings. . . . You have never screamed. Never" (90). Why would Chauvin connect a walk outside with screaming? Possibly Chauvin has anticipated, even hopefully awaited, a scream as Anne has walked out by the railings, with him watching. In this sense, the child-birth scream is a long-forgotten and repressed emblem of what Chauvin has been waiting to hear. He is waiting for Anne to break, to find what makes the trees scream, to bring herself to an orgasmic scream that will destroy her husband's power (as shadow of domesticity) over her.

Anne finds herself on the verge of madness as she enters further into the story of the heroine/corpse. She forfeits her boundaries of self-definition through class (upper) and status (married) to enter into the realm of an elusive storyteller. When the ability to define selfhood is forfeited, what then remains? Duras answers this question during an interview: "It's a hope that I'm expressing. I hope that there will be more and more madmen: I make this statement with pleasure, with satisfaction" (121). She earlier defines *le fous:* "A madman is a person whose essential prejudice has been destroyed: the limits of the self" (109). Capital destruction is the vaporization of the self—as soon as the self disintegrates, there are multitudes. The loss of the self as definitive site becomes the death of the infrastructure of civilization; as Foucault explains, "[m]adness invokes and makes necessary the world's end" (120). This statement is only apocalyptic in the sense that the complete destruction of *sense* is predicted . . . and without contemporary formulations and organization of reality, it is impossible to say what would follow.

In order for there to be an "I," there must be something against which the "I" is defined. This other is what Kristeva calls the "abject," that which revolts me, which makes me flee into my own skin, which sets my boundaries. The abject, however, is also that which is hidden within the very refuse of the self, as Kristeva explains:

> If it be true that the abject simultaneously beseeches and pulverizes the subject, one can understand that it is experienced . . . when that subject, weary of fruitless attempts to identify with something on the outside, finds the impossible within; when it finds that the impossible constitutes its very being, that it is none other than abject. (5)

To recognize that this body which sustains life is also refuse and corpse is to accept the rejection which is the abject. When the other that is expelled is recognized as myself, I lose my boundaries. Duras writes, "I would like to destroy it (knowledge) in order to replace it with a void. The complete absence of man" (114). This absence is the beginning and end of madness, the space where other voices emerge from the silence—the voice of the oppressed, excluded, corpse (whether this be earth, woman, feces, dead races, or political prisoners).

Anne's identity proceeds to lose the boundaries created through social ritual and culturally prescribed morality; as this occurs, the narration itself changes form. Punctuation becomes arbitrary; the conversation between Anne and Chauvin becomes dissolving language. Chauvin describes, or fabricates, the story of a relationship that led a man to shoot a woman at her request, while the responses of Anne begin more and more to resemble those of the murdered woman. By overlapping these two narratives to the point of synthesis and imbuing her characters with a shadowy but all-knowing presence, Duras usurps and over-turns the believability (implying distance) of her narrative stance. The novel becomes the site of the corpse itself, with the corpse taking preeminence over the boundaries of the possible in a realistic narrative.

Anne and Chauvin do not talk *to each other;* they talk *away from themselves.* This may be seen as the same conversation between reader and author, described by de Man as the opposite of a self-clarifying dialogue:

> It would be more accurate to say that the two subjectivities involved, that of author and that of the reader, co-operate in making each other forget their distinctive identity and destroy each other as subjects. Both move beyond their respective particularity toward a common ground that contains both of them, united by the impulse that makes them turn away from their particular selves . . . it brings the reader back, for a moment, to what he might have been before he shaped himself into a particular self. (64)

This is where we may return to the concept of "overdetermination" as a masculine project, for I propose that the coming out of the overdetermined self is a coming into a bodily ground—that the "he" of de Man's quotation should really be a "she," for this project has always been explicitly feminist.

Anne, at the sound of a scream, embarks on a journey toward her own annihilation. She tries to break through the rules of her class in society by becoming fascinated with a realm with no rules— the realm of revulsion, alcoholism, vomiting, and death. Hers is the story of a seduction, but a seduction that is intentionally sought out. Anne is sexually seduced by the idea of death, and Chauvin is the narrative vehicle: he brings death to her with his story. Only he knows the secret of the murder in the bar, which she must draw out of him in order to account for the scream. She beckons Chauvin into revealing the story of death just as the woman who was murdered seduced her lover into creating death itself. Anne embarks along the same path, following the parallel leads. Anne says of that other couple, "[t]hey talked for a long time, a very long time, before it happened" (81). And so they talk for a long time, a very long time.

Chauvin is trying to break Anne of a habit, the habit of life. He says, "[y]ou get into the habit of living. But it's only a habit" (103). He is there to free her from dinner parties where "the salmon passes from guest to guest, following a ritual that nothing can disturb . . ." (106). His power over Anne is sexuality itself, in which the scream of orgasm may be released. His power is the power of perversion. Kristeva writes:

> The abject is related to perversion . . . abject is perverse be-
> cause it neither gives up nor assumes a prohibition, a rule,
> or a law; but turns them aside, misleads, corrupts; uses them,
> takes advantage of them, the better to deny them. It kills in
> the name of life—a progressive despot; it lives at the behest of
> death . . . (15)

Anne begins to live only "at the behest of death." Chauvin pos-sesses a secret death-narrative with which he draws her to the threshold. He lives only in the obsessively desirous state of her presence.

Finally, Anne deserts her husband and leaves her child at home to go and meet Chauvin. Even after this decisive act, after she has been publicly condemned as a drunken adulteress, Anne does not remain with Chauvin. There is a premonition of death as they first kiss: "They lingered in a long embrace, their lips cold and trembling, so that it should be accomplished, performing the same mortuary ritual as their hands . . ." (117). Anne, however, rejects. Kristeva describes this rejection of that which attracts:

> There looms, within abjection, one of those violent, dark re-
> volts of being, directed against a threat that seems to emanate
> from an exorbitant outside or inside, ejected beyond the scope
> of the possible, the tolerable, the thinkable. It lies there, quite
> close, but it cannot be assimilated. It beseeches, worries,
> and fascinates desire, which, nevertheless, does not let itself
> be seduced. Apprehensive, desire turns aside; sickened, it
> rejects. (1)

The death of the woman attracts Anne and leads her to Chauvin, who has been waiting for her a long time. She is fascinated, but not seduced. She turns back in the end to her familiar life, confronting, instead, a *different* form of death: a life of habit that is no longer

life. "I wish you were dead," Chauvin says after his rejection. Anne
responds, "I am" (118). It is difficult to say, however, that this death
will be final. Anne says she might not be able to leave things as they
are, and we never know if the affair continues on the next day, just
as before. Duras implies a compulsion toward life, even among the
dead, that cannot be ignored. When Anne says that the murdered
woman will never speak again, Chauvin responds:

> Of course she will. Suddenly one day, one beautiful morning,
> she'll meet someone she knows and won't be able to avoid say-
> ing good morning. Or she'll hear a child singing, it will be a
> lovely day and she'll remark how lovely it is. It will begin. (116)

This statement enacts not only a sudden leap from realistic narrative, but also a premonition of the death/life dialectic, which the
narrative textually intertwines.

Several critics have described Anne and Chauvin's kiss as a
symbolic recreation of the murder of the woman in the bar, infer-
ring a certain sadism in Chauvin's desire.[8] This reading repeats
precisely the error of using symbol to return to psychological unit-
ies. While tenable if the characters are seen as possessing separate
and individualistic psychological spaces, this reading disregards
the main credo of Duras—destruction. What may be witnessed as
sadism becomes liberation under this light. The question then becomes not, "[d]id Chauvin succeed in killing Anne?" but "[d]id destruction take place?" The destruction that was occurring was not
only the (apocalyptic) abolition of class distinctions, but the destruction of society itself.

Just as the title of this novel suggests a misleading opposite to
the tone of the novel, so the sign "Chauvin" may be read as a severed representation (or ironic reversal) of the character it introduces. Duras releases her characters from the bounds of fixed
meaning in language by drawing contradictions between work and
happening to an extreme—they act both as destroyers of the social
order of capitalist class distinctions and of the linguistic order of
fixed meaning. Class barriers are eclipsed through the sexual attraction between dock-worker and aristocrat, and linguistic order
is eclipsed by the disruption of the readers' association between
sign/signifier. Chauvin, in the position of destroyer in this novel, is

also rendered completely helpless outside of the presence of this woman. For the reader, then, interpretation becomes not so much a game of de-coding as a game which disrupts the codification process entirely. Death, in *Moderato cantabile,* is at once death and absolutely non-death. Duras' figuration of death becomes an allegorical signifier of political liberation. She enters into the perversity of reasoning backwards, toward death instead of life, in order to subvert the bourgeois order of oppression (or, in psychosexual terms, the order of repression) in which Anne resides.

The corpse becomes the amorphous site of possibility, which does not resist or react. This is a form of extreme pacifism, which Duras saw as being best exemplified by the May '68 protests in Paris, and which Blanchot describes: "It is that absence of reaction which permitted the manifestation to develop . . . Everything was accepted. The impossibility of recognizing an enemy . . . all that was vivifying" (31). For three weeks in May 1968, the life of the city of Paris stopped—because so many students and workers simply refused to continue producing, whether knowledge or goods. They placed themselves outside of everything, outside of the means of production or any sort of definition. They represented a force that could not be easily quelled, because it lacked any direction or cohesiveness. Duras wrote of the corresponding 60's protests in the United States: "They're creating a vacuum, but we can't yet see what is going to replace what was destroyed in them . . ." (115). The presence of the people in their refusal to submit to existing definitions of themselves creates a site for absolute possibilities for definition.

The immediate aims of the '68 protests were both silenced and quelled; however, the disruption and refiguration of the life of Paris had occurred. The city, as process, was arrested—the (inert)ia of the city, whose movements were internalized within its dwellers as paradigm for cognition, (dis)rupted; non-moving bodies replaced the reified motion of the city.[9] This stoppage, according to Marx, could have revolutionary affects in its own right. Marx (reading Feuerbach) claims:

> So much is this activity, this unceasing sensuous labor and creation, this production, the foundation of the whole sensuous world as it now exists that, were it interrupted only for a year,

Feuerbach would not only find an enormous change in the natural world, he would very soon find that the whole world of men and his own perceptive faculty, nay his own existence, were missing. (*German* 46)

Such is the way in which modes of production become means of perception so that one cannot cease without the other. *To find one-self missing:* this is precisely the attraction of the signifying corpse.

Jean Baudrillard in *The Ecstasy of Communication* describes the way in which what was once spectacle (e.g., television, car, radio) has become present within the spectator, to the extent that the distance from the spectacle is annihilated (confirming its absolute authority through its absorption into the subject).[10] Baudrillard writes: "Our private sphere has ceased to be the stage where the drama of the subject at odds with his objects . . . is played out: we no longer exist as playwrights or actors but as terminals of multiple networks" (16). Car, war plane, television are in this way made active participants within the life of the subject—there is no more room for private deliberation or decision, only for reception and push-button control.[11] Liberation from this invasive totalitarian spectacle can be achieved only through active non-participation in the life of the spectacle-subject. No longer is the annihilation of the offending object (war plane, pollutants, city) as *other* sufficient or even possible—the self that has subsumed these telematic powers must participate in their death, in order to re-vivify the bodily powers of its origin.[12]

Abjection, in this communal presence, signifies the corpse-like anarchy of doing nothing. "If all the young people in the world start doing nothing . . . the world is in danger. So much the better. So much the better" (116), Duras claims. It is in this way that May of '68 becomes the most successful failure. Instead of the overthrow of one government by another through revolution, Duras believes in the destruction of the previous order, and then a waiting period. "It is very hard to pass from one state to another. Abruptly. . . . It is necessary to wait . . . You don't do something unless you *undo* what's gone before" (120). Duras' solution (to capitalism-war oppressions) is essentially an ironic non-solution: decentralization of social life through popular (non)co-operation—the creation of a community that can only be defined negatively. Duras writes of Woodstock: "It was simply an experience of life in common. Completely negative."[13]

Destruction is, for Duras, a non-doing that is an *un*doing—an act of discourse defined by the impossibility of definition—language folding in upon itself. As we read in Elaine Scarry's *The Body in Pain,* "physical pain does not simply resist language but actively destroys it, bringing about an immediate reversion to a state anterior to language" (4). Just as physical pain disrupts language, so representations of destruction/pain for Duras become a practice of interpretation—the interruption of social and linguistic order provides a means of entering the text and disengaging from it. Duras places herself in the margins of the text, waiting for apocalypse and genesis.

"Take me. Deform me, make me ugly," the heroine of *Hiroshima mon amour* invokes her lover; "[y]ou destroy me. You're so good for me" (25). Duras describes this relationship in her notes: "To give oneself, body and soul, that's it. That is the equivalent not only of amorous possession, but of a *marriage*" (112). The "marriage" of *la Française* and *le Japonais* represents (and is always framed within) a language of opposites, juxtapositions. Even when *le Japonais* first meets *la Française,* he describes his attraction in opposites: "You're a beautiful woman, do you know that? . . . A trifle ugly . . . That's what I noticed last night in that café. The way you're ugly . . ." (32). Even the characters themselves are interchangeable and not-themselves. *La Française* is anonymous, unnameable *"elle"*—which is also Nevers. *Le Japonais* is Hiroshima, but also the corpse which *la Française* had once caressed.

As in *Moderato cantabile, Hiroshima mon amour* contains a secret death-narrative, the story of the corpse, which must be drawn out (or bodily re-possessed) in order to unite ("marry") the two lovers. As in *Moderato cantabile,* the man is continually encouraging the woman to drink—to compulsively drown in the language, the death, the alcohol. As in *Moderato cantabile, le Japonais* knows a story he could not possibly have known, drawing out secret details of the woman's life. *La Française* tells: "One day, I'm twenty years old. It's in the cellar. My mother comes and tells me I'm twenty. My mother's crying" (58). *Lui* asks, "[y]ou spit in your mother's face?" and *Elle* responds, "[y]es" (58). Duras adds the note of explanation, "[a]s if they were aware of these things together" (59). *Le Japonais* has consumed and become the story of *la Française*'s madness in Nevers, as he has made himself corpse in his act of love for Riva.

Recognition of the self as corpse is a process through which Riva has always already gone in her love for the German. She states, "I can say that I couldn't feel the slightest difference between this dead body and mine" (65). In her sharing of the death narrative, she has shared of the corpse—which *is le Japonais*, which is Hiroshima itself, a city that ironically "never stops," for fear of suffocating, finding itself a corpse. When *le Japonais* discovers that he is the only one to have shared this narrative, he is overwhelmed with joy and love. This is now their shared immolation, their bodies "aflame with his memory" (78), the memory of themselves on fire.

Riva's interior monologue reveals the desire for destruction in the love of *le Japonais:*

> This city was made to the size of love. You were made to the size of my body. . . . I always expected that one day you would descend on me. . . . Take me. Deform me to your likeness so that no one, after you, can understand the reason for so much desire. . . . A time will come. When we'll no more know what thing it is that binds us. (77)

The name that unites them is the name of their deaths—Hiroshima, Nevers—made into one death, one body, one word. Riva, however, rejects—seeing in the loss of memory an impending separation. Chauvin, in *Moderato cantabile,* says after Anne's rejection, "I wish you were dead" (118); *le Japonais* repeats this cycle in *Hiroshima mon amour* with, "I would have preferred that you had died at Nevers," and Riva responding, "[s]o would I" (84). Riva chooses to forget, due to the fear of forgetting, what had been discovered in the body of the corpse with *le Japonais.* She keeps the lights in the city running, for fear of suffocating in the silence.

Moderato cantabile and *Hiroshima mon amour* follow each other's parallel leads, demonstrating the inter-changeability of characters within each text, but also *between* each text. Opposites are fused, then forgotten—but remain present in the lapse of time that is a text. Duras has noted at the end of *Hiroshima mon amour:* "Certain spectators of the film believed that she 'ended up' by staying at

Hiroshima. It's possible. I have no opinion" (13). In the same way, the question about whether the affair will go on between Chauvin and Anne is a mute point. What is crucial is the disruption of boundaries between yes/no, life/death, text/non-text. The "limit of her refusal" (*Hiroshima* 13) to which Duras takes Riva could just as easily be called a realization of affirmation—what is important is the threshold or crossing-over point, beyond which no opinion is necessary.

Recognizing themselves corpse while dwelling within the limits of refuse—or refus(e)al, Duras' characters act out their rebellion. What Kristeva has called "grief" could also be called "grievance"—both imply a malady of sorts, but with different loci. Duras has said during an interview that there is only one true democracy: "The true democracy is to feel every day the loss of the world" (my translation).[14] This type of democracy would preclude investment, accumulation, and competition—the very things that define "democracy" in most parts of the world. Duras explains in the same interview: "living together with the world, this very poverty, that I call the loss of the world" (my translation).[15] Thinking the disaster may in this respect bring about not depression, but community.[16] Admittedly, Duras may be said to be often looking back to Hiroshima, the Holocaust, and other disasters of the past. We must not, however, delimit our reading of Duras to a language founded upon these facts, thereby precluding the language of resistance (the French Resistance, the community of lovers, madness, May of '68) that shapes her texts.

Detouring around Kristeva's reading of Duras' "dulled discourse" for these reasons, we find nevertheless that Kristeva's notion of the abject permeates the works of Duras. Baudrillard recognized the submersion of the subject in the spectacle, Marx recognized the submersion of the subject in the commodity (both processes leading to control and submission of the subject)—Kristeva, on the other hand, recognized the *equation* of subject and abject (a bodily subversion to both of the former processes).

Moderato cantabile presents a communion of lovers that cuts through the barriers of social and linguistic stratification. Blanchot, in response to Duras, has commented: "The community of lovers—no matter if the lovers want it or not, enjoy it or not, be they linked by chance, by the passion of death—has as its ultimate goal the destruction of society" (48). Within this realm called love or anarchy, the corpse is a figure of liberty, of satiated sexuality, of the "waiting period" after the scream, in the space of the unspeakable dismemberment of society.

Fredric Jameson claims that "politics" has gone underground; indeed all that remains may be the allegorical corpse, waiting to signify.

Notes

1. I am constructing Duras in a specific historical moment (late 1960's to early 1970's), prior to the neo-conservatism of her later years.

2. Fredric Jameson makes this claim in *The Political Unconscious.*

3. "Body without organs" is Deleuze and Guattari's equivocal term from *Anti-Oedipus:* "The body without organs is the unproductive, the sterile, the unengendered. . . . The death instinct: that is its name" (8). While I would not claim that the *body without organs is*—solely and essentially—the object of *overdetermination* (or *simulation*), there are definite linguistic overlaps. "Machines attach themselves to the body without organs as so many points of disjunction, between which an entire network of new syntheses is now woven, marking the surface off into co-ordinates, like a grid," Deleuze and Guatarri describe (8). Compare this to Baudrillard: "we no longer exist as playwrights or actors but as terminals of multiple networks" (16) or "[f]rom the moment that the actors and their phantasies have ceased to haunt this stage, as soon as behavior is focused on certain operational screens or terminals, the rest appears as some vast useless body, which has been abandoned and condemned . . . the human body, our body, seems superfluous in its proper expanse" (19). I would propose that Baudrillard's "abandoned body" is similar to the "body without organs"—while this body is not necessarily located upon the individual subject, it does include (t)his body (the de-sexed) as an object of definition. Deleuze and Guattari have asked, What happens when anti-production (the body without organs) is injected into production? I intend to ask, What happens when gender is injected into the "unengendered?"

4. I am aware that Kristeva may object to this view of a unified subject. Nonetheless, Kristeva's analysis suggests that Duras' work presents us with an impotent psychosexual melancholia, impotent in the subject's inability to either consume or name herself. She writes, "[e]ven the soundest among us know just the same that a firm identity remains a fiction. Suffering, in Duras' work, in a mannered way and with empty words evokes that impossible mourning, which, if its process had been completed, would have removed our morbid lining and set us up as independent, unified subjects" (258). I propose that the realization of "independent, unified subjects" through the completion of suffering is far from the impossible teleological end/goal of Duras. Instead, active and bodily disruption of structural domination is Duras' credo.

5. Benjamin calls this process "the essense of melancholy immersion" (232), a method by which objects producing melancholy are turned into allegories rather than being "secured" symbolically.

6. Duras has stated in a collection of interviews, *Woman to Woman*, that her work is an attempt to destroy "the illusion that man determines himself" (105).

7. Marx describes clearly the absorption of the self into the object of labor, which is also a distancing from the object: "The worker puts his life into the object and this means that it no longer belongs to him but to the object. So the greater the activity, the more the worker is without an object. What the product of the labor is, that he is not" (79). The distance of the worker from the *objectives* of production relegates him/her to the status of object itself. The relationship of worker to object becomes absorption of the worker and domination of the object.

8. Trista Selous writes: "The reader is strongly encouraged to assume that the dog-like behavior and final death of the woman correspond in some sense to Anne's desires, even if she and Chauvin stop at a kind of symbolic resolution . . . the masochism of her position is evident" (207). Carol Murphy concurs: "We are prepared for Chauvin's verbal murder of Anne by the crushing of the magnolia on her dress . . ." (78).

9. Herbert Marcuse describes the lifeless movement of "the machine" in *One Dimensional Man:* "Underneath its obvious dynamics, this society is a thoroughly static system of life: self-propelling in its oppressive productivity and in its beneficial coordination" (17).

10. As the distance from the spectacle is annihilated, Baudrillard claims that the distance from *origin* is inversely heightened: "Private telematics: each individual sees himself promoted to the controls of a hypothetical machine, isolated in a position of perfect sovereignty, at an infinity distance from his original universe; that is to say, in the same position as an astronaut in his bubble, existing in a state of complete weightlessness which compels the individual to remain in perpetual orbital flight and to maintain sufficient speed in zero gravity to avoid crashing into his planet of origin" (15).

11. Baudrillard describes the car as "something (or some*one*, since at this stage there is no more difference) to which you are *wired*, the communication with the car becoming the fundamental stake, a perpetual test of the presence of the subject" (13).

12. According to Baudrillard, within the "operational definition of being" the body "seems superfluous in its proper expanse" (18). For the same reasons, the landscape, "the immense geographical landscape seems a vast, barren body whose very expanse is unnecessary . . . from the moment that all events are concentrated in the cities" (19).

13. "C'était simplement une expérience de vie en commun. Complètement négative" (*Cahiers* 54). This part was edited from the translation—translation mine.

14. "La veritable democratie—c'est de vivre chaque jours cette perte du monde." From an unpublished interview, recorded by *les disques du crépuscule* and copyrighted by Duras ("interview").

15. ". . . à vivre en commun avec le monde, cette pauvreté là, que j'appelle la perte du monde."

16. Maurice Blanchot in *The Writing of the Disaster* describes the possible thought patterns that may result from living as-if-in impending apocalypse. He writes, "The thought of disaster, if it does not extinguish thought, makes us insouciant with regard to the results this thought itself can have in our life; it dismisses all ideas of failure and success; it replaces ordinary silence—where speech lacks— with a separate silence, set apart, where it is the other who, keeping still, announces himself" (12–13).

Works Cited

Baudrillard, Jean. *The Ecstasy of Communication*. Trans. Bernard and Caroline Schutze. New York: Semiotext(e), 1988.

Benjamin, Walter. *The Origin of German Tragic Drama*. Trans. John Osborne. London: NLB, 1977.

Blanchot, Maurice. *The Unavowable Community*. Trans. Pierre Joris. Barrytown: Station Hill P, 1988.

———. *The Writing of the Disaster.* Trans. Ann Smock. Lincoln: U of Nebraska P, 1986.

Deleuze, Gilles, and Félix Guattari. *Anti-Oedipus*. Trans. Robert Hurley, Mark Seem, and Helen R. Lane. Minneapolis: U of Minnesota P, 1986.

de Man, Paul. *Blindness and Insight: Essays in the Rhetoric of Contemporary Criticism*. Minneapolis: U of Minnesota P, 1986.

Duras, Marguerite. "la destruction la parole." *Cahiers du Cinéma* 160 (1969): 45–60.

———. "interview." *The Fruits of the Original Sin*. Paris: Les Disques du Crépuscule, 1981.

———. *Hiroshima mon amour.* Paris: Gallimard, 1960.

———. *Moderato cantabile.* Paris: Les Editions de Minuit, 1958.

Duras, Marguerite, and Xavière Gauthier. *Woman to Woman*. Trans. Katherine Jensen. Lincoln: U of Nebraska P, 1987.

Foucault, Michel. *The Order of Things*. New York: Vintage, 1973.

Jameson, Fredric. *The Political Unconscious*. Ithaca: Cornell UP, 1981.

Kristeva, Julia. *Black Sun: Depression and Melancholia*. Trans. Leon S. Roudiez. New York: Columbia, UP, 1989.

———. *Powers of Horror.* Trans. Leon Roudiez. New York: Columbia UP, 1982.

Lukács, Georg. *Theory of the Novel*. Trans. Anna Bostock. Cambridge: MIT P, 1987.

Marcuse, Herbert. *One Dimensional Man*. Boston: Beacon, 1972.

Marx, Karl, and Friedrich Engels. *The German Ideology*. Moscow: Progress, 1976.

———. *The Marx-Engels Reader.* New York: Norton, 1978.

Murphy, Carol. *Alienation and Absence in the Novels of Marguerite Duras*. Lexington: French Forum, 1982.

Scarry, Elaine. *The Body in Pain*. Oxford: Oxford UP, 1985.

Selous, Trista. *The Other Woman: Feminism and Femininity in the Work of Marguerite Duras*. New Haven: Yale UP, 1988.

Empowerment through Information:
A Discursive Critique

Marie-Christine Leps

An always imperative *need to know* is widely registered in contemporary discourse, in the mass media, in government policies regarding the nation's role in the information age, in businesses engaged in a globalizing economy, and, of course, in academic institutions, where what we do is always of vital interest. The need to know activates social, economic, and political relations; it usually precedes and invariably succeeds normal practice, ensuring its continuance: reports by the American media and military, for example, most often concluded that a primary lesson of the war in Iraq was the need for better access to more information; what was lacking, apparently, was not military power but intelligence—true, but not necessarily in that sense. An integral part of everyday apprehension and praxis, the need to know is a major factor in what Pierre Bourdieu would call the *habitus* of Western industrialized societies, those "historical schemes of perception and appreciation which are the product of the objective division of social classes" and which, because they are "shared by the majority of social agents," render possible "the production of a common

© 1995 by *Cultural Critique*. Fall 1995. 0882-4371/95/$5.00.

and sensible world, the world of common sense" (546; my translation). The habitus is what allows the results of past relations of
domination and resistance to appear natural rather than social. My
aim in this paper is to begin to historicize the contemporary need
to know, or at least to outline the domains of knowledge and relations of power which would have to be investigated in order to
ascertain their effects on subjectivity and agency in social discourse.[1] My focus will be current developments in telematics and
their articulation in the micro-politics of the "new social movements"; I will briefly show how government and business strategic
plans for telematics construct a model of power-knowledge relations which is also advanced by social criticism emanating from the
left: in spite of conflicting notions of subjectivity and diametrically
opposed social objectives, these discourses agree to promulgate the
possibility, indeed the necessity, of large-scale empowerment
through information. I will then turn to the novel *White Noise* by
Don DeLillo, which registers some of the difficulties of agency associated with the Information Age while inscribing the possibility of
resistance and alteration.

It would first be necessary to trace, however briefly, the genealogy of the need to know in the radical redistribution of knowledge and power relations effected in the Age of Education in Western industrialized countries. At the beginning of the nineteenth
century, working-class, government, religious, and business
groups were united in their belief that knowledge is power, and
therefore, because of their different political agendas, forcefully
opposed on the question of access. Landowners saw no reason for
teaching heads to reason rather than hands to work; working-class
associations (such as moral-force Chartists) identified knowledge
as essential to political emancipation; religious authorities strug-
gled with each other (as in England) or against the government (as
in France) in order to impart their doctrine to the largest possible
numbers. Arduous and usually conflictive economic, legal, political, and social developments eventually made possible the production of forms of knowledge appropriate for mass consumption:
during the last quarter of the century, free, national systems of
education and a cheap, mass-produced press were established.
However, the subjects, objects, and purpose of knowledge had
been transformed in the process: these discursive practices offi-

cially addressed the people of the nation rather than specific classes, and instituted knowledge as an all-purpose agent of progress and enlightenment rather than as a specific instrument of power.[2] It remained for intellectuals to continue promulgating knowledge as the main road to emancipation, as well as their role of formulating the needs of a somehow mute proletariat.

This remapping of the relations between knowledge and power was made possible in large part by the rise of "objective information," a new product first developed by the penny dailies in answer to political and economic imperatives. In order to avoid political persecution or taxation, and in an effort to attract the largest possible readership, newspapers overtly moved away from their previous product, political opinion, to offer news and objective information. In its first issue (February 26, 1884), *Le Matin*, which had the motto "*Le Matin* sees all, knows all, says all," expressed its program as follows: "*Le Matin* will be a newspaper which will not have any political opinions, which will not be enfeoffed [sic] to any bank, which will not sell its patronage to any business; it will be a newspaper giving news information, telegraphic, universal and true." Officially relinquishing political subsidization, the penny dailies depended on advertising and circulation for their economic survival. Readers became part of the production process: in order to attract advertisers, newspapers had to produce readers—or more specifically, it was the potential consumer in every reader which was targeted and marketed. From the beginning, mass consumerism and "objective information" were in it together. As competition was fierce, newspapers striving to increase circulation had to angle their presentation of potentially controversial economic, political, social, or religious issues in such a way as to offend the fewest possible readers and thereby produce a mass readership cutting across class barriers. From this precarious position came many of the characteristics of new journalism (still active today): the insistence on the human interest story, the personal interview, the many columns of miscellany, more sports, and less politics. Thus economic and political determinants drew the limits of the sayable of the press, usually identified with "public opinion."

This form of knowledge would be adopted in various discursive practices, and especially in politics and education, since it was particularly appropriate for generating a passive consumption of hegemonic truths rather than an active participation in their determination or contestation. Indeed, "world-wide coverage" of "all the latest news" normally implies that the developments leading to the day's events are either neglected or summarily reported. The reader of mass journalism is thus deluged with enormous quantities of information about places and events over which he or she has little or no control, and about as much understanding. The spatialized world of up-to-the-minute information therefore tends to devaluate events by making them appear either as unforeseeable happenings or as inescapable proof of the truth of ideological constructs. Strikes are typically described as unfortunate outbreaks of irrational or violent behavior, rather than as strategies of resistance in conflicts developing over time. Faced with such reports, simply turning to the next story is not an unusual reaction—nor is it an unwelcome one. Similarly, nineteenth-century national systems of elementary education, which transmitted hegemonic truths (of patriotism, militarism, and acceptance of "social station," i.e., class position) almost as effectively as illiteracy itself, served to subjectivize individuals rather than empower them, if one understands empowerment to mean the multiplication of possibilities for social transformations. The rise of objective information was therefore an essential correlative to the development of relations of mass production and consumption, in their articulation to "the public" as subject in the political arena.

After the Second World War, power and knowledge relations were again redistributed in social organizations now identified as late capitalist or postindustrial, and were usually characterized by three main developments: first, by automation and the displacement of the labor force to the service industries (roughly forty-five percent of North American employees are identified as "information workers"); second, by the globalization of the economy with the rise of multinational corporations and the international division of labor; third, by ever-expanding state apparatuses for public administration. All of these developments are contingent upon the expansion of information technology (IT), which first gained real prominence with weapons research and development during the Second World War, and has continued to receive major funding from the military ever since.[3] Information has now become all at once a consumer good (with nations being characterized as information rich or poor), a booming and diversified industry (complete with professional associations and international congresses), a field of scholarly inquiry (with the rise of information science), and the constant preoccupation of states, whose primary raw material is information.[4] These changes have also transformed the subjects of knowledge: information is most often predicated not to a particular class, nor to the people of the nation, but rather to specific groups identified by common pursuits and practices, such as feminist, lesbian and gay, and anti-racist groups, ethnic, student, or professional groups, environmental or green groups, consumer or special interest groups. A somewhat startling consensus exists between government agents, marketing executives, and social critics who claim that information must be made relevant to these "new social movements" and that the local production and wide circulation of such tailored information will serve to *empower* them (there is much talk of *enabling* limits in the humanities and *enabling* technologies in business). The micropolitics of new social groups are at once the hope of the left (as in Ernesto Laclau and Chantal Mouffe's *Hegemony and Socialist Strategy*) and the primary targets of strategic planning by both government and business. Telematics— the interconnection of computers and telecommunications also known as videotex—can serve as a case in point.

In a 1978 report commissioned by former President Valery Giscard d'Estaing, entitled *L'Informatisation de la société*, Simon Nora and Alain Minc (then inspector general and inspector of finance) identified the role of information technology as crucial to the balancing of "the increasingly powerful assertion of the prerogative of the state" with the "growing exuberance of civil society." More specifically, they noted that in a polymorphous information society, social conflicts would no longer be centered on relations of production (thus rendering both the liberal and Marxist grids ineffective); that in a hyper-productive environment work would be devalued and that history would be driven by cultural conflicts between groups engaged in diverse projects and propelled by new desires (114–15; my translation). Telematics could then play an important role in the distribution of power, allowing a convergence between "the strategy of the center [i.e., the state] and the desires of the periphery" (123). The report proposed a three-fold strategy for the exercise of state power: when faced with foreign competitors, the state should unhesitatingly use its powers of decree; when dealing with internal forces of unequal strength, it should regulate them in order to favor the weaker parties; however, most often state powers should encourage the autonomy and responsibility of forces which, in attempting to assert themselves, meet with obstacles, chief among them the state itself—in such cases, state powers should erase themselves and *"stimulate those which contest them"* (14; my emphasis). When the French government launched the national Minitel service, ease of access was a founding principle: anyone can publish on Minitel, and over 6000 services presently exist. This means that groups can publish and circulate information relatively cheaply to each other's homes and offices as well as to the wider audience of Minitel users. In the United States, legislation and public policy concerning telematics are still a matter of contention, but the corporate-owned commercial services that do exist (Compuserve, Prodigy), while maintaining control of publication, equally welcome wide-ranging access, for it is in their best (economic and strategic) interest to do so. However, access to all of these services comes at a price, the price of the trace: the production and circulation of information through telematics can be registered and used to produce added information on consumer habits and preferences, on medical, political, and sexual concerns (since sexual chat services are among the most popular)—all of which constitute invaluable information for state and business administration.

Indeed, the concentration of economic enterprises into huge multinational conglomerates and the concurrent segmentation of markets require the production of information about world trends as well as the identification of the needs of specific, local target markets. The introduction of telematics in the home and in business environments allows the generation of precisely this kind of information: the user of information becomes the object of more information through usage. The necessity of universal access, promulgated by Jean-François Lyotard in *La condition postmoderne* (a report commissioned by the Council of Universities and the Government of Québec), gives "the public free access to the memories and data banks" and helps promote the universal saturation that is precisely required by business to generate information about target markets (107–08; my translation). Discussing this very paradox, Kevin Wilson in his *Technologies of Control* underlines the fact that legislative measures concerning privacy and access in North America have served to normalize existing procedures: noting that the privacy laws give individuals "some measure of control primarily through access rights to [their] personal files," Wilson asserts that "on a societal level, however, legislation does not jeopardize a fundamental category of corporate control administered through forms of public surveillance" (78).

The informatization of the workplace, in both manufacturing and service industries (from pulp and paper mills to insurance companies and the telecommunications industry), systematically reproduces this paradox. When everyone's performance (or lack thereof) is registered in a general electronic text, the question of access is inevitably contentious; however, with "flatter" organizations, that is, with organizations cutting back on middle management and relying more on IT, the trend is to give universal, or almost universal, access. In her book entitled *In the Age of the Smart Machine: The Future of Work and Power,* Shoshana Zuboff discusses these issues at length and documents the reaction of one pulp and paper mill to this new experience:

> As long as operators get more information, too, why should they care that I have the data? They should expect we will question them for purposes of improvement. It is not my data. It is our data, all of it. It is OK for you in the pulping unit to question someone in woodyard. We want to build in a healthy contesting nature. If it is a legitimate business question in an area that you have some control over, you have to respond to questions, no matter who puts it to you. . . . Leadership should be functional, not hierarchical. (346)

There is indeed much elaboration on this move away from hierarchical authority to the horizontal networking of more equally empowered participants in informatized processes of production. Examples are given of workers "taking charge of the line," usually through team work, rather than answering to supervisors, or again of employees given the freedom to imagine and develop new products based on their knowledge of the company and of consumer needs or desires. Individuals are thus allowed to participate actively in their work environment, to take control of immediate organization and planning rather than simply submit to managerial decisions handed from above. An article entitled "The Knowledge Creating Company" in the *Harvard Business Review* (November–December 1991) began by stating that "In an economy where the only certainty is uncertainty, the one sure source of lasting competitive advantage is knowledge." The author is not referring to universities or research institutes as knowledge-creating companies but rather to car manufacturers, office equipment and household appliance manufacturers, who could only survive by empowering their employees to create new knowledge. Amazingly, this process is described in terms of self-production and resistance to subjectivization: "to create new knowledge means quite literally to re-create the company and everyone in it in a nonstop process of personal and organizational self-renewal." An article by Stephen Covey, entitled "People Power," in the December 1991 issue of *Executive Excellence* starts by describing empowerment as "high on the list of needs to survive and succeed in the 1990s." Arguing that empowered employees tend to co-operate better, to define co-missions better aligned with company goals, Covey, chair of the Covey Leadership Center, states that "We all need the power to do and to be, because when we lose our agency, we abdicate our power to act and become things to be acted upon" (Shelton 7–8). Presumably, equal access to the organization's electronic text will enlist employees into a shared culture, a consensual view of the company mission: the Chief Executive Officer of Federal Express perhaps best summarizes this situation when he expresses his belief that empowerment meant that employees do not just work for Federal Express—they are Federal Express (Shelton 7–8).

This identification of workers and organizations can also be read as the effect of the implementation of surveillance and normalization procedures leading to what less sanguine executives refer to as "exception management," described as follows by one plant manager:

> From my desk I can look at any plant. They all know what I am looking at. They can see it, too, and how they stack up. They will compare themselves internally, and this creates a certain level of competition. It can extend all the way down to

the individual. The hourly worker will know that if this exception goes up the line, it will come right back to him. Once he learns that he is going to be questioned on it, he will manage his own responses more effectively. A worker under these conditions does not need to be controlled—you simply expect him to respond to the information the same way you do. (Zuboff 351)

In this view, electronic texts install a superpanopticon where total visibility leads to anticipatory conformity to rules. Horizontal surveillance works to exacerbate pressures to fit into a process whose determination is out of everyone's hands since it is set by global economic trends. At this stage of development, Zuboff argues, "the electronic text becomes the symbolic surrogate for the organization's vital activities," to which the supervised and supervising community of workers must submit (356).

This negative map never for a moment discredits the process, however. Just as the development of modern penitentiaries (where panoptic mechanisms are perhaps most blatantly deployed) has always been accompanied by a counterdiscourse of reform, the development of Information Technology generally, and electronic surveillance in particular, has been criticized ever since its beginning: *1984,* one must remember, was written in 1948. In both cases, critiques of surveillance systems invariably call for the establishment of more surveillance systems: bad prisons should be replaced by better prisons where real reform, real discipline, real education would take place (Foucault, *Discipline and Punish* 234–35). Similarly, critiques of business or government superpanopticons usually end in calls for more surveillance: we need laws to watch the watchers; access to information about the information gatherers will empower those who are watched to watch—there seems to be no way out of the game.

The model whereby a group is empowered by using information to further its interests in praxis admits the traditional humanist subject (integral, rational, and largely in control) as well as the postmodern subject (decentered and engaged in multiple discursive positions), along with the legitimating narrative of the first (the progressive emancipation of humanity) and the play of paralogism of the other (where local projects can, "through a chain of equivalences," render effective resistance and transformations in power relations). Agency thus rests, problematically, in informed group praxis, and access to the production and dissemination of information in discourse is the key. The "need to know" is perhaps the most accepted truth of our time, or, better stated, the most generalized experience of our time, in Foucault's sense of experience as "the correlation, in a culture, between domains of knowledge, types of normativity, and forms of subjectivity" (Foucault, *L'Usage des plaisirs* 10; my translation).

Don DeLillo's *White Noise* effectively draws the map of these correlations and registers how the experience thus generated affects agency, and in the novel access is the problem. Its characters' lives are completely saturated by normalization procedures which articulate their thoughts, actions, desires, and fears in terms of the logic of mass commodification and which render agency—the active transformation of relations of power and knowledge—virtually unthinkable (but not necessarily for the narrator, and, by extension, its reader, as I will argue later on). Jack Gladney's narrative of his life as Chair of the Department of Hitler Studies at the College-on-the-Hill and as father and step-father to several children by multiple marriages gives a dystopic representation of group agency based on information in both professional and family environments. At first blush, however, everything seems to be running smoothly: by inventing Hitler studies in North America, Jack has provided himself and his institution with a higher profile and a greater authority in the academic world; at home, he and his wife "tell each other everything" and thereby create a shared space of "irony, sympathy and fond amusement" (11, 35). Jack operates in two distinct spheres of action, one on the hill, in "an ever serene edge of the townscape, semidetached, more or less scenic, suspended in political calm," and the other at "the end of a quiet street" (85, 4); in both areas, knowledge and praxis are meshed for the promotion of the well-being of the group: agency at its best. However, from the start normalization procedures are shown to interconnect these purportedly different spheres and subordinate them to the exigencies of the process of mass commodification and the government of individuals.

This is clear from the opening scene: university life is not presented by a library or classroom scene, but rather by the arrival of the students in a long parade of parent-driven station wagons, overladen with commodities articulating subjectivity to consumption (music, junk food), to "lifestyles" (fashion, fitness, sports), to sexuality (and its contraceptive devices). The description is worth quoting at length:

> The station wagons arrived at noon, a long shining line that coursed through the west campus. In single file they eased around the orange I-beam sculpture and moved toward the dormitories. The roofs of the station wagons were loaded down with carefully secured suitcases full of light and heavy clothing; with boxes of blankets, boots and shoes, stationery and books, sheets, pillows, quilts; with rolled-up rugs and sleeping bags; with bicycles, skis, rucksacks, English and Western saddles, inflated rafts. As cars slowed to a crawl and stopped, students sprang out and raced to the rear doors to begin removing the objects inside; the stereo sets, radios, personal computers; small refrigerators and table ranges; the cartons of phonograph records and cassettes; the hairdryers and styling irons; the tennis rackets, soccer balls, hockey and lacrosse sticks, bows and arrows; the controlled substances, the birth control pills and devices; the junk food still in shopping bags—onion-and-garlic chips, nacho thins, peanut creme patties, Waffelos and Kabooms, fruit chews and toffee popcorn; the DumDum pops, the Mystic mints.
>
> I have witnessed this spectacle every September for twenty-one years. It is a brilliant event, invariably. (3)

The students are not just consumers but also commodities dropped off by their parents: the narrator tells us that "this assembly of station wagons, as much as anything they might do in the course of the year, more than formal liturgies or laws, tells the parents they are a collection of the like-minded and the spiritually akin, a people, a nation" (3–4). Like the readers of mass journalism, the students, as subjects of knowledge, are defined as both consumers and commodities of the knowledge production process.

The value of Hitler as an object of knowledge equally rests in its crowd appeal and its continued circulation in the mass media; this is revealed when an admiring colleague enlists Jack's help to establish his own department of Elvis studies. Jack enters Murray's seminar on Elvis, and both professors begin parallel monologues converging to demonstrate how Hitler and Elvis were "the same," mama's boys who rushed to their deaths according to the typical life contract imposed on famous personages. With the help of careful staging, academic credibility is successfully transferred to Elvis, and colleagues and students form a crowd sharing Jack's professional aura. Objects of knowledge are completely interchangeable: a fascist dictator who is always on television or a rock star who never dies equally work to maintain the process of mass commodification, the normalization of domains of knowledge and forms of subjectivity. There is a scene early in the novel where Jack brings his friend Murray to the local tourist attraction, a red barn whose only claim to fame is fame itself: as the signs say, it is "THE MOST PHOTOGRAPHED BARN IN AMERICA." Murray sees the crowds assembled at the barn site as involved in religious submission to a simulacrum; he is "immensely pleased" to know that they can no longer see the barn but only take pictures of taking pictures: "We can't get outside the aura. We're part of the aura. We're here, we're now" (13). In this space-time arrangement, however, the only agency possible is the organized mass consumption recorded by the narrator (with road signs, tour buses, forty parked cars, a souvenir booth with pictures and postcards, and elaborate photography equipment). Knowledge, pleasure, leisure, imagination, and desire are inscribed in economic exchange, and the group stands as a node in a wider process determining its position as commodity-consumer. Similarly, Jack's position as inventor of a whole new academic field, Hitler studies, assigns him a strictly limited range of action, articulated by marketing needs. His identification as Hitler expert rests entirely on his assumption of a persona and the maintenance of academic rituals. The university chancellor informs him that to acquire credibility he must "grow into Hitler": he must gain weight, change his clothing and accessories, and alter his name to J. A. K. Gladney, becoming, in Jack's words, "the false character that follows the name around" (17).

The Gladney family also serves as an extremely efficient relay station for the circulation of commodities and information. Jack describes their purchases in terms of masses and crowds which fill their souls with security and contentment (20). Babette serves up the same kind of wellness by teaching a continuing education class on "how to stand, sit and walk," where any scrap of knowledge— on "yoga, kendo, trance-walking," on Sufi dervishes or Sherpa mountaineers—reassures the aged in their attempts "to ward of death by following rules of good grooming" (27). The older children enact various disciplinary functions, ranging from Heinrich's "critical-observer" position to Denise's constant surveillance of her mother, while Steffie plays the compliant subject, answering computer-generated telephone marketing surveys testing "current levels of consumer desire" as well as acting out the part of the victim for a group called SIMUVAC, which specializes in simulating emergency evacuations (48, 205). All the family members apprehend events and individuals through film and advertisement scenarios or broadcast news formats. Driving his son to school, Jack describes the following scene: "A woman in a yellow slicker held up traffic to let some children cross. I pictured her in a soup commercial taking off her oilskin hat as she entered the cheerful kitchen where her husband stood over a pot of smoky lobster bisque, a smallish man with six weeks to live" (22; see also 44–45, 146, 155, 159, 160). Constantly searching for meaning, asking each other questions, sharing disinformation, they inevitably face useless knowledge. When Jack is exposed to toxic chemicals he is informed that they may form a "nebulous mass" in his body which may or may not kill him in the next thirty years. This conclusion is arrived at after computer searches and extensive testing in special laboratories, leading to an interview where both the attendant and the patient are most anxious to keep the process running smoothly and according to the norm:

> "What about appetite?' he said.
> "I could go either way on that."
> "That's more or less how I could go, based on the printout."
> "In other words you're saying sometimes I have appetitive reinforcement, sometimes I don't."
> "Are you telling me or asking me?"
> "It depends on what the numbers say."
> "Then we agree."
> "Good"
> "Good." (277–78)

The incipient forms of this "bio-power," which invade both bodies and souls, lead to a constant, crippling fear of death. Jack rightly feels death everywhere around him, in the sounds of the freezer or the traffic, in the things accumulating in the house, in technology, on television, and in tabloids, for death is the limit of relations of power-knowledge exercised in the meticulous production of everyday life.[5] The novel thus shows how local centers of power-knowledge (university departments, suburban families, health or emergency centers, media and advertising agencies, shopping malls) are inextricably interconnected: environmental disasters such as toxic waste clouds are also present as "nebulous masses" of illness and fear in individuals, and as data in computer banks monitoring the health of the population. The narrative development itself interrelates economic, political, professional, personal, familial, religious, and police relations of knowledge and power and shows how their interlocking results in the production of hegemonic truths and everyday lives which work to maintain the process of production and circulation of commodities and information and of information as a commodity.

The novel ends with two scenes of crowds uselessly searching for meaning in the sweeping narrative of a beautiful sunset (whose beauty may or may not derive from the presence of toxins), and in the confused jumble of grocery shelves. In both cases, they don't know what to think or feel: "some people are scared by the sunsets, some determined to be elated, but most of us don't know how to feel, are ready to go either way" (324). It hardly seems to matter, for the result is the same: the crowds wait patiently every night to see the sunset and every day at the cash register, where confusion never reaches the terminals "equipped with holographic scanners, which decode the binary secret of every item, infallibly. This is the language of waves and radiation," the narrator tells us, "or how the dead speak to the living" (326).

This inevitable continuance of the process and the impossibility of agency are, however, also denied by the novel, because of the laughter that runs through it at every level: the characters constantly make each other (and the reader) laugh about their fears and behavior; the narrator tells wonderfully funny stories of panic in airplanes or lunch-time conversations among savvy New York émigrés to the provinces; and the text tells the incredibly bad joke of Hitler Studies being institutionalized as mass "edutainment" in 1968, the year emblematizing the energy and struggles of new social movements around the world. *White Noise* thus forcefully inflicts the experience of information overload and its negative effects on agency, while all the time retreating from it, in the counterexperience of incisive wit and liberating laughter, drawing out the possibility of irreducible difference. Both narrator and reader are distanced from the information-commodity circuit and are equipped with a different kind of knowledge, one which discerns the limits of the "empowerment through information" argument.

The correlation between discursive practices (in universities and night schools, on television and in newspapers, in advertising and telemarketing, in mass production and consumption, in government and family politics) achieved by DeLillo's fiction is reiterated in the kind of work I have been doing here, usually labeled discursive criticism, that is, the historical study of systems of knowledge and technologies of power as they are articulated in discourse. In this particular case, the process of discursive criticism is at first disconcerting as it renders visible the close articulation—at times the verbatim reproduction—of the strategies of the left and those of business and government planners. Of course, this finding confirms the functional value of the main working hypothesis in discursive criticism, i.e., that interconnected discursive practices produce normal statements as well as their critique as they position both the subjects and objects of knowledge, and defines the process of knowledge production.[6] Rather than ruling out the possibility of transformation, the correlations discerned by discursive criticism work to map out the grounds for intervention in many ways, of which I will note two:

—first, they prevent the reiteration of a process to be apprehended as its radical critique: it is at least useful to know that leaders in business see the need to empower their employees to break down traditional barriers, destroy the bureaucracy, renew their selves, and respect the value of otherness as the best way to achieve reasonable rates of ROI (return on investment), for it is important to know that governments recognize the need to encourage social groups which oppose them as the most profitable way of exercising power—useful, if only to differentiate critical discourse from its target;

—second, by positioning discursive criticism itself in the current organization of knowledge and drawing its implication in the exercise of power, the diagram of these correlations can trace not only the possibility but the necessity of strategic alliances and interventions.

I do not mean to imply that in the end we all share a common language and therefore need only to adjust our sights and synchronize our watches to reach the same target. Rather I suggest the opposite; I would think that the wide circulation of an unanswerable "need to know," the constant discursive reaffirmation that knowledge is power, or better yet, in the up-to-date version, that knowledge is empowerment, serve only to naturalize, reinforce, and maintain established relations of power.

Information is the site of multiple contradictions: it is hailed as the most efficient tool for empowerment and feared as the most powerful means of enslavement; it is said to allow individuals to remake their selves and to subjectivize them as nodes in production processes. As noted by Derrida, "coherence in contradiction expresses the force of a desire" (248), and I would argue that information is becoming the ultimate object of desire in late-capitalist societies. It is at this juncture that discursive criticism can intervene: to reinscribe "Information" in the establishment of power-knowledge relations, to draw its crucial role in what Foucault terms the government of individuals, and thus to problematize the given of information into a question—to map the conditions of possibility of an imperative need to know and thus chart its possible transformation, in and through the actualization of other desires, in altered practices. This process would necessarily comprise a critical ontology of ourselves, and involve, in Foucault's words, "a historico-practical test of the limits that we may go beyond, and thus [stand] as work carried out by ourselves upon ourselves as free beings" ("What is Enlightenment?" 47).

Notes

An earlier and much shorter version of this paper, with a different title, was presented at the XIIIth Congress of the International Comparative Literature Association, Tokyo, August 1991.

1. This paper is part of a book-length study tentatively entitled *Needing to Know: On Power-Knowledge Relations in the Information Age.*

2. A longer discussion of these developments and of the rise of "objective in-

formation" in the mass-produced press can be found in my *Apprehending the Criminal: The Production of Deviance in Nineteenth-Century Discourse*, chapters 4 and 6.

3. See Noble, *Forces of Production: A Social History of Industrial Automation;* Braun and MacDonald, *Revolution in Miniature*.

4. Nora and Minc, in their *L'informatisation de la société*, state that with the exception of the atom, no other area has received as much government attention since 1945 (63).

5. Foucault discusses modern relations of power as exercised in the production of life in both *The History of Sexuality*, Volume I, *An Introduction*, Part Five, "Right of Death and Power over Life," and in his lecture entitled "Omnes et Singulatim: Towards a Criticism of 'Political Reason.'"

6. As argued by Foucault in *Discipline and Punish:* "the subject who knows, the objects to be known and the modalities of knowledge must be regarded as so many effects of these fundamental implications of power-knowledge and their historical transformations" (27–28).

Works Cited

Bourdieu, Pierre. *La distinction: Critique sociale du jugement.* Paris: Editions de Minuit, 1979.

Braun, Ernest, and Stuart MacDonald. *Revolution in Miniature: The History and Impact of Semiconductor Electronics.* Cambridge: Cambridge UP, 1978.

DeLillo, Don. *White Noise.* New York: Viking, 1985.

Derrida, Jacques. "Structure, Sign and Play in the Discourse of the Human Sciences." *The Structuralist Controversy: The Languages of Criticism and the Sciences of Man.* Ed. Richard Macksey and Eugenio Donato. Baltimore: Johns Hopkins UP, 1972. 247–65.

Foucault, Michel. *Discipline and Punish: The Birth of the Prison.* Trans. Alan Sheridan. New York: Vintage, 1979.

———. *The History of Sexuality,* Volume 1: *An Introduction.* Trans. Robert Hurley. New York: Random, 1978.

———. "Omnes et Singulatim: Towards a Criticism of 'Political Reason.'" *The Tanner Lectures on Human Values.* Ed. S. M. McMurrin. Salt Lake City: U of Utah P, 1980–81. 2: 223–54.

———. *L'Usage des plaisirs.* Paris: Editions Gallimard, 1984.

———. "What is Enlightenment?" *The Foucault Reader.* Ed. Paul Rabinow. New York: Pantheon, 1984. 32–50.

Laclau, Ernesto, and Chantal Mouffe. *Hegemony and Socialist Strategy: Towards a Radical Democratic Politics.* London: Verso, 1985.

Leps, Marie-Christine. *Apprehending the Criminal: The Production of Deviance in Nineteenth-Century Discourse.* Post-Contemporary Interventions Series. Ed. Stanley Fish and Fredric Jameson. Durham: Duke UP, 1992.

Lyotard, Jean-François. *La condition postmoderne: rapport sur le savoir.* Paris: Editions de Minuit, 1979.

Noble, David F. *Forces of Production: A Social History of Industrial Automation.* New York: Knopf, 1984.

Nora, Simon, and Alain Minc. *L'informatisation de la société: rapport à M. le Président de la République.* Paris: La documentation française, 1978.

Shelton, Ken. "People Power." *Executive Excellence* 8.12 (December 1991): 7–8.
Wilson, Kevin G. *Technologies of Control: The New Interactive Media for the Home.*
    Studies in Communication and Society. Madison: U of Wisconsin P, 1988.
Zuboff, Shoshana. *In the Age of the Smart Machine: The Future of Work and Power.* New
    York: Basic, 1988.

BOOKS RECEIVED

Abu-Lughod, Janet L. *From Urban Village to East Village: The Battle for New York's Lower East Side.* Cambridge: Blackwell, 1994.

Adorno, Theodor W. *Adorno: The Stars Down to Earth and Other Essays on the Irrational in Culture.* Ed. Stephen Crook. New York: Routledge, 1994.

Barnouw, Dagmar. *Critical Realism: History, Photography, and the Work of Siegfried Kracauer.* Baltimore: Johns Hopkins UP, 1994.

Barry, Jonathan, and Christopher Brooks, eds. *The Middling Sort of People: Culture, Society and Politics in England, 1550–1800.* New York: St. Martin's, 1994.

Bartra, Roger. *Wild Men in the Looking Glass: The Mythic Origins of European Otherness.* Trans. Carl T. Berrisford. Ann Arbor: U of Michigan P, 1994.

Bernheimer, Charles, ed. *Comparative Literature in the Age of Multiculturalism.* Baltimore: Johns Hopkins UP, 1995.

Bjornson, Richard. *The African Quest for Freedom and Identity: Cameroonian Writing and the National Experience.* Bloomington: Indiana UP, 1991.

Boym, Svetiana. *Common Places: Mythologies of Everyday Life in Russia.* Cambridge: Harvard UP, 1995.

Bratton, Jacky, Jim Cook, and Christine Gledhill, eds. *Melodrama: Stage, Picture, Screen.* London: British Film Institute, 1994.

Bremond, Claude, Joshua Landy, and Thomas Pavel, eds. *Thematics: New Approaches.* Albany: State U of New York P, 1995.

Buell, Frederick. *National Culture and the New Global System.* Baltimore: Johns Hopkins UP, 1994.

Cacciari, Massimo. *The Necessary Angel.* Trans. Miguel E. Vatter. Albany: State U of New York P, 1994.

Calvet, Louis-Jean. *Roland Barthes: A Biography.* Trans. Sarah Wykes. Bloomington: Indiana UP, 1994.

Cohen, Anthony P. *Self Consciousness: An Alternative Anthropology of Identity.* New York: Routledge, 1994.

Collings, David. *Wordsworthian Errancies: The Poetics of Cultural Dismemberment.* Baltimore: Johns Hopkins UP, 1994.

Cooley, John, ed. *Earthly Words: Essays on Contemporary American Nature and Environmental Writers.* Ann Arbor: U of Michigan P, 1994.

Copjec, Joan, ed. *Supposing the Subject.* New York: Verso, 1994.

Danielsen, Dan, and Karen Engle, eds. *After Identity: A Reader in Law and Culture*. New York: Routledge, 1995.

Doyle, Laura. *Bordering on the Body: The Racial Matrix of Modern Fiction and Culture*. New York: Oxford UP, 1994.

Eliot, George. *Impressions of Theophrastus Such*. Ed. Nancy Henry. Iowa City: U of Iowa P, 1995.

Elliott, Bridget, and Jo-Ann Wallace. *Women Artists and Writers: Modernist (im)positionings*. New York: Routledge, 1994.

Fraad, Harriet, Stephen Resnick, and Richard Wolff. *Bringing it All Back Home: Class, Gender and Power in the Modern Household*. Boulder: Westview P, 1994.

Freedman, Sarah Warshauer. *Exchanging Writing, Exchanging Cultures*. Cambridge: Harvard UP, 1994.

Fussell, Paul. *The Anti-Egotist: Kingsley Amis, Man of Letters*. New York: Oxford UP, 1994.

Gammel, Irene. *Sexualizing Power in Naturalism: Theodore Dreiser and Frederick Philip Grove*. Calgary: U of Calgary P, 1994.

Guérin, Daniel. *The Brown Plague: Travels in Late Weimar and Early Nazi Germany*. Trans. Robert Schwartzwald. Durham: Duke UP, 1994.

Hedges, Elaine, and Shelley Fisher Fishkin, eds. *Listening to Silences: New Essays in Feminist Criticism*. New York: Oxford UP, 1994.

Jameson, Fredric. *The Seeds of Time*. New York: Columbia UP, 1994.

Kang, Liu, and Xiaobing Tang, eds. *Politics, Ideology, and Literary Discourse in Modern China: Theoretical Interventions and Cultural Critique*. Durham: Duke UP, 1994.

Keenan, John P. *How Master Mou Removes Our Doubts*. Albany: State U of New York P, 1994.

Kincaid, James R. *Child Loving: The Erotic Child and Victorian Culture*. New York: Routledge, 1992.

Ko, Dorothy. *Teachers of the Inner Chambers: Women and Culture in Seventeenth-Century China*. Stanford: Stanford UP, 1994.

Kramer, Jane. *Whose Art Is It?* Durham: Duke UP, 1994.

Laguerre, Michel S. *The Informal City*. New York: St. Martin's, 1994.

Landlow, George P., ed. *Hyper/Text/Theory*. Baltimore: Johns Hopkins UP, 1994.

Langum, David J. *Crossing Over the Line: Legislating Morality and the Mann Act*. Chicago: U of Chicago P, 1994.

Lawler, Justus George. *Celestial Pantomime*. New York: Continuum, 1995.

Loshitzky, Yosefa. *The Radical Faces of Godard and Bertolucci*. Detroit: Wayne State UP, 1995.

MacCannell, Juliet Flower, and Laura Zakarin, eds. *Thinking Bodies*. Stanford: Stanford UP, 1994.

Magnus, Bernd, and Stephen Cullenberg, eds. *Whither Marxism?: Global Crises in International Perspective*. New York: Routledge, 1995.

Meyer, Moe, ed. *The Politics and Poetics of Camp*. New York: Routledge, 1994.

Mitchell, William C., and Randy T. Simmons. *Beyond Politics: Markets, Welfare, and the Failure of Bureaucracy*. Oakland: Westview P, 1994.

Moore, Henrietta L. *A Passion for Difference: Essays in Anthropology and Gender*. Bloomington: Indiana UP, 1994.

Natoli, Joseph. *Hauntings: Popular Film and American Culture 1990–1992*. Albany: State U of New York P, 1994.

Pease, Donald, ed. *National Identities and Post-Americanist Narratives*. Durham: Duke UP, 1994.

Pease, Donald E., ed. *Revisionary Interventions into the Americanist Canon*. Durham: Duke UP, 1994.

Pilkington, Hilary. *Russia's Youth and Its Culture*. New York: Routledge, 1994.

Rabinowitz, Paula. *They Must Be Represented: The Politics of Documentary*. New York: Verso, 1995.

Rodriguez, Ileana. *House/Garden/Nation: Space, Gender, Ethnicity in Post-Colonial Latin American Literature by Women*. Trans. Robert Carr. Durham: Duke UP, 1994.

Roth, Michael S., ed. *Rediscovering History: Culture, Politics, and the Psyche*. Stanford: Stanford UP, 1994.

Salecl, Renata. *The Spoils of Freedom: Psychoanalysis and Feminism After the Fall of Socialism*. New York: Routledge, 1994.

Schor, Naomi, and Elizabeth Weed, eds. *The Essential Difference*. Bloomington: Indiana UP, 1994.

Sedgwick, Eve Kosofsky. *Fat Art, Thin Art*. Durham: Duke UP, 1994.

Sinfield, Alan. *Cultural Politics: Queer Readings*. Philadelphia: U of Pennsylvania P, 1994.

Stabile, Carol A. *Feminism and the Technological Fix*. Manchester: Manchester UP, 1994.

Stull, Bradford T. *Religious Dialectics of Pain and Imagination*. New York: State U of New York P, 1994.

Tester, Keith, ed. *The Flaneur*. New York: Routledge, 1994.

Tiffin, Chris, and Alan Lawson, eds. *De-Scribing Empire: Post-Colonialism and Textuality*. New York: Routledge, 1994.

Willinsky, John. *Empire of Words: The Reign of the OED*. Princeton: Princeton UP, 1994.

Wolfreys, Julian. *Being English: Narratives, Idioms and Performances of National Identity from Coleridge to Trollope*. New York: State U of New York P, 1994.

CONTRIBUTORS

James Harding is an assistant professor in English at Eastern Michigan University, where he teaches modern drama and literary theory. He has published in *Diacritics, Journal of Aesthetics and Art Criticism, Theatre Journal, Eighteenth Century Life,* and *Clio.* His article is a chapter from a forthcoming book titled *Adorno and "A Writing of the Ruins": Essays on Modern Aesthetics, Literature and Culture.*

N. Katherine Hayles is a professor of English at UCLA. In *The Cosmic Web* and *Chaos Bound,* Hayles has written on the interweavings of contemporary literature, literary theory, and science. She is currently working on a book on the history of cybernetics.

Eva Knodt, assistant professor of Germanic Studies at Indiana University, has just completed a two-year Mellon Fellowship at Stanford University. She is the author of *"Negative Philosophie" und dialogische Kritik: Zur Struktur poetischer Theorie bei Lessing und Herder* and the co-editor of a special issue of *New German Critique* on Niklas Luhmann. She has published articles on Herder, Nietzsche, and Habermas, and wrote the foreword to the English translation of Niklas Luhmann's *Social Systems* (forthcoming from Stanford University Press).

Marie-Christine Leps is associate professor of English and graduate social and political thought at York University. She is the author of *Apprehending the Criminal: The Production of Deviance in Nineteenth-Century Discourse,* and is currently working on issues relating to subjectivity, agency, and transnational literacy in the so-called "Information Age."

Marjorie Levinson is professor of English at the University of Michigan and is a leading critic of British Romanticism and theorist of literary history. She has edited *Rethinking Historicism: Critical Readings in Romantic History* and has written *Keats' Life of Allegory: The Origins of a Style* and *Wordsworth's Great Period Poems.*

Niklas Luhmann is the leading exponent of a general theory of functionally differentiated, self-reproducing social systems. English translations of his writings include *Social Systems* (forthcoming), *Essays on Self-Reference, Ecological Communication, Political Theory of the Welfare State, Love as Passion,* and *The Differentiation of Society.* He is professor emeritus of sociology at the University of Bielefeld, Germany.

Timothy W. Luke is professor of political science at Virginia Polytechnic Institute. In his recent work, he has written on ideology, resistance, ecology, and the social representation of disasters. He is the author of *Social Theory and Modernity, Screens of Power: Ideology, Domination, and Resistance in Informational Society,* and *Shows of Force: Power, Politics, and Ideology in Art Exhibitions.*

Brian Massumi is professor of comparative literature at the Humanities Research Centre of Australian National University in Canberra. He is widely known as a translator of the work of Deleuze and Guattari and others, is author of *A User's Guide to Capitalism and Schizophrenia: Deviations from Deleuze and Guattari,* and has recently edited *The Politics of Everyday Fear.*

Karen Piper is a doctoral candidate in comparative literature at the University of Oregon. She is currently working on colonial and post-colonial geographies in the novel and on the relation between postmodernism and post-colonialism.

William Rasch is an assistant professor of Germanic Studies at Indiana University. He has written on theories of complexity and self-reference in Luhmann, Lyotard, and Habermas, is the co-editor of a special issue of *New German Critique* (Winter 1994) on Luhmann, and is currently working on a book on the status of observation in information theory, cybernetics, and systems theory.

Cary Wolfe is an assistant professor of English at Indiana University. He works on American literature, culture, and critical theory, and has published essays on Sartre, Kenneth Burke, Luhmann, Cavell, and others. His study *The Limits of American Literary Ideology in Pound and Emerson* was published in 1993. He is currently completing a book-length project to be called *Critical Environments: Theory Thinks the "Outside."*

THE SAVAGE FREUD AND OTHER ESSAYS ON POSSIBLE AND RETRIEVABLE SELVES
Ashis Nandy

One of India's leading public intellectuals, Ashis Nandy is a highly influential critic of modernity, science, nationalism, and secularism. In this, his most important collection of essays so far, he seeks to locate cultural forms and languages of being and thinking that defy the logic and hegemony of the modern West.

The core of the volume consists of two ambitious, deeply probing essays, one on the early success of psychoanalysis in India, the other on the justice meted out by the Tokyo War Crimes Tribunal to the defeated Japanese. Both issues are viewed in the context of the psychology of dominance over a subservient or defeated culture.

This theme is explored further in essays on mass culture and the media, political terrorism, the hold of modern medicine, and, notably, the conflict or split between the creative work of writers like Kipling, Rushdie, and H. G. Wells, and the political and social values they publicly and rationally present. Also included is a controversial essay by Nandy on the issue of sati, or widow's suicide.

"With his characteristic brilliance, Nandy offers provocative and insightful readings of the cultural politics of colonial and postcolonial India."—Gyan Prakash, Princeton University

Princeton Studies in Culture/Power/History: Sherry B. Ortner, Nicholas B. Dirks, and Geoff Eley, Editors
Paper: $15.95 ISBN 0-691-04410-4   Cloth: $49.50 ISBN 0-691-04411-2
Available from Princeton only in the U.S., Canada, and Australia

PRINCETON UNIVERSITY PRESS

AVAILABLE AT FINE BOOKSTORES OR DIRECTLY FROM THE PUBLISHER: 800-777-4726
WORLD WIDE WEB SITE: HTTP: //AAUP.PUPRESS.PRINCETON.EDU/PUPRESS

d i f f e r e n c e *s*

A Journal of Feminist Cultural Studies

differences, edited by Naomi Schor and Elizabeth Weed, focuses on how concepts and categories of difference—notably but not exclusively gender—operate within culture. Situated at the point of intersection of cultural studies and feminism, the two most exciting fields of critical inquiry to have opened up in recent years, **differences** is affiliated with the Pembroke Center for the Teaching and Research on Women at Brown University.

Issues of Special Interest

More Gender Trouble: Feminism Meets Queer Theory, edited by Naomi Schor and Elizabeth Weed, Volume 6, Numbers 2–3, $16.70

The City, edited by Naomi Schor and Elizabeth Weed, Volume 5, Number 3, ~~$11.75~~ $8.75

On Addiction, edited by Naomi Schor and Elizabeth Weed, Volume 5, Number 1, ~~$11.75~~ $8.75

The Phallus Issue, edited by Naomi Schor and Elizabeth Weed, Volume 4, Number 1, ~~$14.70~~ $8.75

Notes from the Beehive: Feminism and the Institutution, edited by Naomi Schor and Elizabeth Weed, Volume 2, Number 3, ~~$11.75~~ $8.75

Queer Theory: Lesbian and Gay Sexualities, edited by Teresa de Lauretis, Volume 3, Number 2, $14.70

PRICE REDUCED

Subscription (3 issues); $32.00 individual; $60.00 institution; foreign surface postage add $10.00; foreign air mail postage add $20.00 Send orders to: Journals Division, Indiana University Press, 601 N. Morton, Bloomington, IN 47404. Phone: (812)855-9449. FAX: (812)855-8507. Email: Journals@Indiana.Edu

FOUND

Paul Gilroy

Etienne Balibar

Rosi Braidotti

Alice Jardine

Stanley Aronowitz

Nancy Miller

Ammiel Alcaly

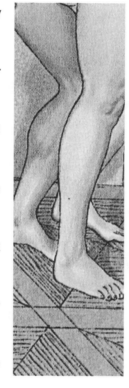

6

OBJECT

Subscriptions $7 per issue/ $16 for 3 issues
Send check to: The Center for Cultural Studies CUNY Grad Center, 33 West 42 Street, Room BM08, NY, NY 10036

Where

you can

still

hear

people

thinking

for

them-

selves

Personal Voices on Cultural Issues

David Bromwich, "Free Speech"

Catharine Stimpson and Ross Posnock,
"Two Views of Multiculturalism, Identity Politics"

Clifford Geertz, "Disciplines"

Edward W. Said, "Orientalism, an Afterword"

Tim Dean, "On the Eve of a Queer Future"

Marina Warner, "The Body in Photography"

Adam Phillips, "The Future of Fear"

Arts • Literature • Philosophy • Politics

RARITAN

Edited by Richard Poirier

$16/one year $26/two years
Make check payable to RARITAN, 31 Mine St., New Brunswick NJ 08903